Cambridge Monographs in African Archaeology
73
Series Editors: John Alexander, Laurence Smith and Timothy Insoll

Archaeological Investigations of Iron Age Sites in the Mema Region, Mali (West Africa)

Tereba Togola

BAR International Series 1736
2008

Published in 2016 by
BAR Publishing, Oxford

BAR International Series 1736

Cambridge Monographs in African Archaeology 73
Series Editors: John Alexander, Laurence Smith and Timothy Insoll

Archaeological Investigations of Iron Age Sites in the Mema Region, Mali (West Africa)

ISBN 978 1 4073 0178 5

© The estate of T Togola and the Publisher 2008

The author's moral rights under the 1988 UK Copyright,
Designs and Patents Act are hereby expressly asserted.

All rights reserved. No part of this work may be copied, reproduced, stored,
sold, distributed, scanned, saved in any form of digital format or transmitted
in any form digitally, without the written permission of the Publisher.

BAR Publishing is the trading name of British Archaeological Reports (Oxford) Ltd.
British Archaeological Reports was first incorporated in 1974 to publish the BAR
Series, International and British. In 1992 Hadrian Books Ltd became part of the BAR
group. This volume was originally published by Archaeopress in conjunction with
British Archaeological Reports (Oxford) Ltd / Hadrian Books Ltd, the Series principal
publisher, in 2008. This present volume is published by BAR Publishing, 2016.

Printed in England

BAR titles are available from:

        BAR Publishing
        122 Banbury Rd, Oxford, OX2 7BP, UK
EMAIL   info@barpublishing.com
PHONE +44 (0)1865 310431
FAX   +44 (0)1865 316916
        www.barpublishing.com

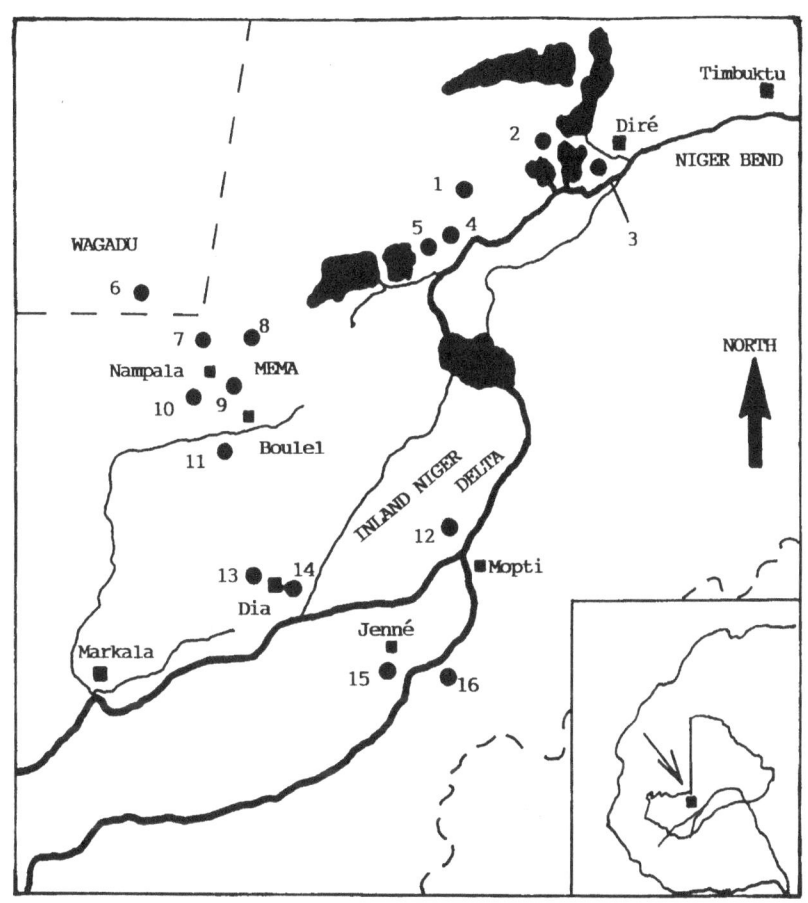

Frontispiece. The Méma. Its Location in the Middle Niger and in Mali

TABLE OF CONTENTS

In Memoriam: Dr. Téréba Togola vii
Preface xi
Acknowledgements xv
CHAPTER 1: Geomorphological, historical and archaeological background 1
    I: Geographical setting and geomorphology 1
    II: Historical background 3
    III: Prior archaeological research in the Méma and neighboring regions 4
CHAPTER 2: Reseach design and objectives 11
CHAPTER 3: The regional site survey. 13
    I: Survey methodologies 13
    II: The results of the survey 13
    III: Conclusions.. 21
CHAPTER 4: Excavations at Akumbu mound complex 23
    I: Site location and description 23
    II: Excavation methods 23
    III: Discussions of the excavation units and chronology. 25
    IV: Summary of occupation at Akumbu mound complex 33
CHAPTER 5: Excavated materials other than pottery 37
    I: Metallurgical remains 37
    II: Stone artifacts other than beads. 39
    III: Stone Beads 39
    IV: Spindle whorls 39
    V: Clay beads 39
    VI: Shell beads 40
    VII: Glass beads.. 40
    VIII: Cowrie shells... 40
    IX: Bone artifacts.. 40
    X: Botanical remains 40
    XI: Human skeletal remains 40
CHAPTER 6: Survey and excavation pottery 43
    I: Introduction. 43
    II: Methods of recovery and recording procedures. 43
    III: Definition of the recorded variables 44
    IV: Results of the analysis: survey pottery 50
    V: Results of the analysis: excavation pottery.. 55
    VI: Description of the diagnostic rim by assembalge. 55
    VII: Special pottery finds. 57
    VIII: Conclusions and discussions 57
CHAPTER 7: Conclusions 79
BIBLIOGRAPHY 85
APPENDIX 1: Preliminary Analysis of the Faunal remains 88
APPENDIX 2: Additional Human Remains from Akumbu (Mali) 98
APPENDIX 3: Survey Data for Sites in the Méma 99

List of Figures

Frontispiece:	The Méma. Its Location in the Middle Niger and in Mali	
Figure 1.1.	Geomorphological features of the Méma	2
Figure 1.2.	Map of the 'Tumuli' along the Middle Niger (Bedaux et al. 1978)	8
Figure 1.3.	Putative archaeological sites identified in the Méma from aerial photos by CIPEA (CIPEA 1980)	10
Figure 3.1.	Verified archaeological sites	14
Figure 3.2.	Méma site size distributions	15
Figure 3.3.	MAL. 75 IGN 872	17
Figure 3.4.	MAL. 75 IGN 1119	17
Figure 3.5.	MAL. 75 IGN 874	17
Figure 3.6.	Mal. 75 IGN 1121	17
Figure 3.7.	MAL. 75 IGN 998	17
Figure 4.1.	Map of Akumbu A and Akumbu B	24
Figure 4.2.	AK1. Natural strata	26
Figure 4.3.	AK1. Excavated levels	26
Figure 4.4.	AK1. Levels 6 and 7	27
Figure 4.5.	AK1. Levels 24, 29, and 34	27
Figure 4.6.	AK3. Natural strata	30
Figure 4.7.	AK3. Excavated levels	30
Figure 4.8.	AK3. Extended burial	31
Figure 4.9.	AK4. Natural strata	32
Figure 4.10.	AK4. Excavated levels	32
Figure 4.11.	AK4. Burnt clay structure	33
Figure 4.12.	Chronological relationship between excavation units AK1, AK3, and AK4	35
Figure 5.1.	Copper bracelet	37
Figure 5.2.	Copper analysis	37
Figure 5.3.	Stone beads	38
Figure 5.4.	Spindle whorls	38
Figure 5.5.	Clay beads	39
Figure 6.1.	Survey pottery data. Coded rims	45
Figure 6.2.	AK1 pottery data. Coded rims	46
Figure 6.3.	The Méma rim types	46
Figure 6.4.	Early Assemblage. Body sherd decoration by site	48
Figure 6.5.	Early Assemblage. Twine decorated body sherds by site	48
Figure 6.6.	Early Assemblage. Major rim forms	48
Figure 6.7.	Early Assemblage. Undecorated, slipped and twine decorated rims	49
Figure 6.8.	Early Assemblage. Multiple attribute rims	49
Figure 6.9.	Middle Assemblage. Body sherd decoration by site	49
Figure 6.10.	Middle Assemblage. Twine decorated body sherds by site	50

Figure 6.11.	Middle Assemblage. Major rim forms	50
Figure 6.12.	Middle Assemblage. Undecorated, slipped, and twine decorated rim sherds	51
Figure 6.13.	Middle Assemblage. Multiple attribute rims	51
Figure 6.14.	AK1 pottery. Body sherd decoration by level	52
Figure 6.15.	AK1 pottery. Twine decorated body sherds by level	53
Figure 6.16.	AK1 pottery. Major rim forms by level	53
Figure 6.17.	AK1 pottery. Undecorated, slipped and twine decorated rims	53
Figure 6.18.	AK1 pottery. Multiple attribute rims	54
Figure 6.19.	Early Assemblage. Examples of simple, carinated rims and pot lids (Fulani hats)	59
Figure 6.20.	Early Assemblage. Examples of everted rims	60
Figure 6.21.	Middle Assemblage and AK1 pottery collections. Examples of simples and carinated rims	61
Figure 6.22.	Middle Assemblage and AK1 pottery collections. Examples of pot lids	62
Figure 6.23.	Middle Assemblage and AK1 pottery collections. Examples of thickened out-turned rims	63
Figure 6.24a.	Middle Assemblage and AK1 pottery collections. Examples of everted rims	64
Figure 6.24b.	Middle Assemblage and AK1 pottery collections. Examples of everted rims	65
Figure 6.24c.	Middle Assemblage and AK1 pottery collections. Examples of everted rims	66
Figure 6.25.	Middle Assemblage and AK1 pottery collections. Examples of ledged and collared rims	67
Figure 6.26.	Middle Assemblage and AK1 pottery collections. Examples of bottle necks	68
Figure 6.27.	Late Assemblage. Examples of collared rims	69
Figure 6.28.	Late Assemblage. Examples of everted rims	70
Figure 6.29.	Complete vessels from AK1 and AK3	71
Figure 6.30.	Special pottery finds. Handles, bases, pottery cylinder, and bed rest	72
Figure 6.31.	Special pottery finds. Pottery mortar, pottery pestle, and human foot figurine	73
Figure 6.32.	Early Assemblage. Twine decorated rims	74
Figure 6.33.	Middle Assemblage. Channeled and twine decorated rims	75
Figure 6.34.	MiddleAssemblage. Channeled and twine decorated rims	76
Figure 6.35.	Middle Assemblage. Examples of channeled, twine decorated and painted body sherds	77
Figure 6.36.	Late Assemblage. Channeled and twine decorated rims	78

List of Tables

Table 3.1	Various Iron Age site clusters	16
Table 3.2	Site chronology within site clusters	18
Table 4.1	Reconstruction of depositional sequence in Unit AK1	28
Table 4.2	Reconstruction of depositional sequence in Unit AK3	31
Table 4.3	Reconstruction of depositional sequence in Unit AK4	33
Table 4.4	Radiocarbon dates obtained from the excavations at Akumbu	34
Table 5.1	Identifiable Iron objects	38
Table 5.2	Stone beads	38
Table 5.3	Spindle whorls	38
Table 6.1	Early Assemblage. Other decorative motifs on body sherds	43
Table 6.2	Middle Assemblage. Other decorative motifs on body sherds	44
Table 6.3	AK1 pottery collection. Other decorative motifs on body sherds	47
Table 6.4	Special pottery finds	50

In Memoriam

Dr. Téréba Togola
(1948 – 2005)

Our esteemed colleague and dear friend, Dr Téréba Togola, Directeur National du Patrimoine Culturel (Ministère de la Culture du Mali) died of kidney failure associated with typhoid on November 7, 2005. His health had been fragile since the summer, when colleagues who saw him at the Panafrican Congress of Prehistory in Botswana reported that he looked thin, drawn, and unwell. We will remember him always as a devoted champion of Mali's past, an outstanding field archaeologist and researcher, a kind and generous colleague and friend, and a devoted father and husband.

Téréba Togola was born in 1948 in the region of Sikasso (Bla, Cercle de Bougouni). After receiving his M.A. in history and geography at l'Ecole Normale Supérieure (ENSUP) in Bamako in 1980, he began his professional career in archaeology at l'Institut des Sciences Humaines (ISH). Working with Dr. Michel Raimbault, his former professor at ENSUP, he participated in several archaeological campaigns in the Middle Niger and Mema regions, where his own research would ultimately be focused. In early 1984, he worked with Professors Roderick and Susan McIntosh as ISH homologue in an archaeological survey around Timbucktu. Following that collaboration, he entered the graduate program in anthropology at Rice University in 1986, funded by a Fulbright Fellowship. With the McIntoshes, he undertook the first excavations and archaeological survey at Dia in January 1987. His pioneering doctoral research «Archaeological Investigations of Iron Age Sites in the Mema (Mali)» was funded by a prestigious National Science Foundation Dissertation Improvement Grant and supervised by R. and S. McIntosh. His investigations identified 108 Iron Age sites, including a number of iron production sites, and several occupation mounds measuring well in excess of 40 hectares in area. Excavations at the site of Akumbu resulted in the first ceramic Iron Age sequence for the Mema, spanning the 4th–14th centuries AD, and evidence for trade in tin bronze. He received the Ph.D. in 1993.

Upon returning home, Dr. Togola rejoined the ISH, where he was appointed Chef de section Archéologie à la Division Histoire – Archéologie. MANSA members will remember his hard work and successful organization of the biennial meetings held in Bamako in 1993. In 1995, he also helped organize the meetings in Bamako of the West African Archaeological Association. Between 1994–1997, he conducted numerous archaeological campaigns in the gold producing regions of Ségala, Tabakoto, Sadiola (région de Kayes), and Faboula (Kalana, Région de Sikasso), the Boucle de Baoulé, as well as collaborative research and excavation at Jenne-jeno.

In 1998, Dr. Togola was appointed as Directeur National des Arts et de la Culture. In this post, administrative responsibilities for all aspects of national Arts and Culture kept him on the move, traveling to many countries, attending meetings and seminars, all of which prevented him from spending much time doing the fieldwork he loved. He was an outstanding excavator, able to read the fine nuances of the soil and the clues it provided about events that unfolded long ago. In 2000 and 2001, he was able to undertake a research program in the Mema in collaboration with the University of Kyoto (Japan) and subsequently with the Ethnology Museum of Osaka. This is especially remarkable in view of the fact that he was very active during that period as Organizing Secretary of the Panafrican Congress of Prehistory, which was held in Bamako in 2001. That same year, he organized the Semaine Nationale des Arts et de la Culture (SNAC), an artistic and cultural forum bringing together artists from all regions of Mali. Dr. Togola put his fluency in both English and French to good use in interactions with a wide variety of researchers, collaborators, and funding agencies.

For his many services rendered to the nation, he was awarded the distinction of the honorary title «*Chevalier de l'Ordre National du Mali*» in September 2000.

With the restructuring of the Direction Nationale des Arts et de la Culture in 2001, Dr. Togola was appointed to lead the Direction Nationale du Patrimoine Culturel (DNPC). In this post, he emphasized the protection, management and promotion of Mali's cultural heritage. He participated in numerous conferences on the subject of the illicit antiquities trade and played an important role in assuring the extension in 2002 of of the bilateral agreement with the United States under the UNESCO Convention, protecting archaeological materials at risk of pillage in the Middle Niger region. A significant aspect of his tenure was the ongoing inventory of cultural heritage. In 2001, 63 sites and monuments were inventoried and registered, rising to 68 in 2004. The Komoguel Mosque (Région de Mopti) and the Kama bulon of Kangaba (Région de Koulikoro) were classified as national cultural heritage monuments in **2005**. One of Dr. Togola's most visionary and enduring projects was the «Cultural Map of Mali: Inventory of Cultural Heritage», a vast atlas bringing together the elements of cultural heritage in the eight regions of Mali and the District of Bamako. He worked feverishly on this ambitious project, successfully bringing it to publication in 2005 under the title: *Carte Culturelle du Mali, esquisse d'un inventaire du patrimoine culture.*

Dr. Togola was also successful in assuring the addition of the Tombeau des Askia (Région de Gao) to the UNESCO list of World Heritage sites in 2004, and the inscription of «Jaaral –Dégal» by UNESCO as a masterpiece of the intangible heritage of humanity. Significantly as well, under Dr. Togola's tenure, Timbucktu was withdrawn from the list of endangered world heritage sites.

Dr. Togola organized programs of archaeological research with Japanese collaboration in the Méma (2003) and at Gao (2002, 2004). At Gao, the research program, including regional site survey and rescue excavations in 2005 at the site of the Mosque of Kankou Moussa, was reinforced by SAREC (Swedish Agency for International Development).

Other projects inaugurated under Dr. Togola's aegis included the Culture Bank of Mali, initiated by the World Bank, which supports the creation of local, community museums and the promotion of activities generating revenue so that local populations can retain items of cultural heritage. In 2004, Dr. Togola initiated a project for the protection and promotion of the cultural heritage in the his natal village of Kalabancoro, financed by the «Karité Mali» Association, of which he was a founding member. In 2005, he directed another cultural heritage project in Koumantou (Région de Sikasso), establishing an artistic and cultural festival. He was a tireless promoter of Mali's cultural heritage at all levels. His passing is a huge loss for Mali's past and for those who have dedicated themselves to its study and preservation.

Publications and Reports

1982 *Inventaire analytique des sites archéologiques du Cercle de Bougouni*. Mémoire de fin d'études, Ecole Normale Supérieure de Bamako. Directeur de Mémoire : Michel Raimbault. Document non publié.

«Le pillage des sites archéologiques au Mali.» *Journal Jamana,* Bamako, Mali. N°42 En collaboration avec Michel Raimbault.

1989 (a) "Archaeology of the people without history", *Archaeology* 42 (1):75-80.

En collaboration avec R.J. McIntosh et S.K. McIntosh.

1989 (b) *The Méma, Mali : Overview and Research Prospects*. Mémoire de M.A. Département d'Anthropologie. Rice University. Houston. Document non publié.

1989(c) *The Bamana Secret Societies (Jow) : their relation with the Bamana social, political and belief systems and the meaning of their membership*. Mémoire de M.A. Département d'Anthropologie. Rice Universty. Houston. Document non publié.

1991 (a) «Les missions d'inventaire dans le Méma, Karéri et Farimaké (1984 et 1985)». En collaboration avec M. Raimbault. Dans *Recherches Archéologiques au Mali*. Editions Karthala. Ouvrage collectif dirigé par M. Raimbault et K. Sanogo, pp. 81 – 85

1991 (b) «Le mobilier céramique.» Dans *Recherches Archéologiques au Mali*. Editions Karthala. Ouvrage collectif dirigé par M. Raimbault et K. Sanogo, pp. 281 – 300.

1993 *Investigations of Iron Age sites in the Méma region (Mali)*. Thèse de Ph. D. Département d'Anthropologie. Rice University, Houston (USA).

1994 *Reconnaissance archéologique dans la zone du projet or, Sadiola (deuxième phase).* Rapport Final. En collaboration avec Famory Sissoko et Nafogo Coulibaly. Rapport ISH non publié.

1995 (b) "Memories, abstraction and conceptualisation of ecological crisis in the Mande World". Communication présentée à l'atelier *Global Change in Prehistory and History* organisé par *the Forest Service* (Etats-Unis) et *Rice University Center for the Study of Cultures*.

1995 (c) *Recherches archéologiques dans la zone de Faboula, Arrondissement de Kalana, Cercle de Yanfolila*. En Collaboration avec Famory Sissoko et Nafogo Coulibaly. Rapport ISH non publié.

1995 (d) "The good collector and the premise of mutual respect among Nations". *African Arts.* Autumn

1995. Volume XXVIII. N° 4. En Collaboration avec Roderick J. McIntosh et Susan K. McIntosh.

1995 (e) *Recherches archéologiques dans la Boucle du Baoulé, Mali. Rapport Final.* En collaboration avec Boua Traoré, Youssouf Kalapo, Josué Thiéro et Clément Traoré. Rapport ISH non publié.

1996 (a) "Iron Age occupation in the Méma region (Mali)". *African Archaeological Review* 13 (2): 91–110

1996 (b) *Reconnaissance archéologique dans la zone de Ségala, cercle de Keniéba.* En collaboration avec Youssouf Kalapo et Mahamadou Kaba. Rapport ISH, non publié.

1997 (a) "Mali's many shields of its past". *Nonrenewable Resources* 6 (2): 111–130. En collaboration avec R.J. McIntosh et B. Diaby.

1997(b) «A civilization under seige», *US/ICOMOS Newsletter* n°1 Janvier Février. En collaboration avec R.J. McIntosh, B. Diaby et S.K. McIntosh.

1997 (d) "Two millennia of human experience along the Middle Niger". Communication présentée au symposium intitulé *Four Rivers of Africa : historical archaeology and art in Africa.* Symposium organisé par *the National Museum of African Art (Smithsonian Institution)* Mai 1997.

1997 (e) "The Inland Delta and the Manding Mountains" dans *Museums and archaeology in West Africa*, ouvrage collectif dirigé par Claude Daniel Ardouin, pp. 59–67.

1997 (f) *Recherches archéologiques sur la concession minière Nevsun Resources LTD, Zone de Tabakoto, cercle de Keniéba.* En collaboration avec Mahamadou Kaba et Youssouf Kalapo. Rapport ISH, non publié.

1999 (a) *"Archaeology of the soul." Archaeology* 52 (3).

1999 (b) «La gestion du patrimoine culturel au Mali : bref aperçu historique». Actes sur Colloque International sur le Patrimoine Culturel Mauritanien, 29 novembre – 1er décembre 1999.

2000 (a) «Les peintures et gravures rupestres» dans *L'archéologie en Afrique de l'Ouest Sahara et Sahel.* Textes rassemblés par Robert Vernet, CRIAA, Nouakchott. Editions Spéciale France.

2000 (b) «Sites refuges et fortifications militaires» dans *L'archéologie en Afrique de l'Ouest Sahara et Sahel.* Textes rassemblés par Robert Vernet, CRIAA, Nouakchott. Editions Spéciale France.

2000 (c) "Memories, abstractions and conceptualisation of ecological crisis in the Mandé World" dans *The Way the Wind Blows: Climate, History, and Human Action*, ed. Roderick J. McIntosh, Joseph Tainter et Susan K. McIntosh. Columbia University Press: 181–192

2002 "The rape of Mali's only resource", dans *Illicit Antiquities: the theft of culture and the extinction of archaeology*, ed. Neil Brodie and K.W. Tubb. Routledge: 250-256.

2004 (a) "Reconnaissance Archéologique à Gao (Mali) et Environs – Rapport Préliminaire» dans *The African Archaeology Network : Report and a Review.* Editions Studies in the African Past-4, Dar Es Salaam University Press LTD. Textes rassemblés par Felix Chami, Gilbert Pwiti & Chantal Radimilahy. PP 1-26.

2004 (b) «Sauvegarde et valorisation du patrimoine au Mali : Bref aperçu historique». *Actes du XIème Congrès de l'Association Panafricaine de Préhistoire et Discipline Assimilée*, Bamako, 7 – 12 février 2001. Ed. Kléna Sanogo et Téréba Togola. Edition Soro Print Color, Bamako.

2004 (c) «Reconnaissance archeologique a Gao (Mali) et environs», *Nyame Akuma* 62: 50–61.

2005 *Carte Culturelle du Mali, esquisse d'un inventaire du patrimoine culturel national.* Ministère de la Culture. Impression IMPRIM COLOR, Bamako.

Prepared by Mamadou Cissé and Susan McIntosh

Togola at the excavations at the mosque of Kankou Moussa (Gao).

PREFACE

Susan Keech McIntosh and Roderick J. McIntosh

In 1989, when Tereba Togola undertook his dissertation research, no one had seriously studied Iron Age settlement mounds in the Méma during the preceding 30 years. It had been twenty years since R. Haaland did her pioneering work on iron-working sites on the Boulel Ridge. Subsequent to Dr. Togola's research, reported here and in a 1996 article in the *African Archaeological Review*, the pace of Iron Age research in the Mema has scarcely gained momentum, despite his promising results. For a number of years, the region was unsafe due to political unrest among and/or raiding by the Tuareg. In the late 1990's in particular, a series of hijackings of 4-wheel drive vehicles, accompanied by the murder of Europeans and Malians, took place between the Bend of the Niger and the Mauritanian border. It was not an auspicious period for Mema archaeology in general. Dr. Togola had always anticipated a return to his work in the Mema, just as he anticipated updating the manuscript for this volume. Both projects were delayed by the demands of his job. It was never remotely anticipated that this volume would be a posthumous publication. Tragically, Dr. Togola died of kidney failure associated with typhoid on November 7, 2005. Since 2001, he had been head of the Direction Nationale du Patrimoine Culturel (Ministère de la Culture du Mali).

In this forward, we try, briefly, to place Dr. Togola's research in the perspective of continuing archaeological investigations in the Méma, and to update the discussion of archaeological knowledge about the region. Dr. Togola took a long-term, diachronic perspective in his research, and conducted his initial field-work in 1989-90 with two other graduate students, Kevin MacDonald and Helen Haskell, whose focus was the Late Stone Age. This field research was supported by NSF doctoral dissertation grants to Togola (BNS-9001664) and Haskell (BNS-9001668) and a Watson Fellowship to MacDonald. The work of MacDonald and Raimbault et al. has been particularly important in understanding the LSA occupation of the Mema. Raimbault has focused on the extensive midden site of Kobadi, which was first recognized by Monod and Mauny in the 1950's for its rich aquatic fauna. On the slightly-raised beach of a paleolake, populations arriving from desiccating northern basins, such as the Azawad, fished (Nile perch and many species of catfish) and hunted crocodile, hippo, and lamantin (*Manatus senegalensis*) between 3400 and 2800 BP (Raimbault 1986; Raimbault & Dutour 1989 & 1990; Raimbault *et al.,* 1987). Significant numbers of grindstones suggest that processing vegetable material was important. There is no suggestion as yet that these may have included domesticated plants. The lithic assemblage indicates widespread connections and affinities throughout the Sahel, including the Hodh region to the northwest and the Ighazer basin to the east (Urbain 2001-2002). These "trans-sahelian" connections are postulated to have occurred in the context of a subsistence strategy of mixed herding, fishing, hunting, and collecting.

The issue of domestic cattle is of considerable interest. Bones of *Bos taurus* dominate the mammalian fauna in all excavation units (Jousse and Chenal-Velarde 2001-2002). Does this mean that herding was present throughout the occupation at Kobadi? MacDonald, whose research was concerned primarily with assessing the case for socio-economic diversity in the Méma during the LSA, suggests that it was not. He interprets Kobadi as having an earlier, fishing/hunting/collecting component associated with pottery of the Kobadi tradition,. He suggests that the cattle bones are associated with a later component with ceramic affinities relating to the Tichitt Tradition, marking the arrival of northern herders in the region. Sites with Tichitt-related pottery (the Ndondi Tossekel facies in the Mema) on the surface tend to have small "mini-middens" with bones of cattle and ovicaprids, and date to the period 1300–800 BC (MacDonald 1996). Additionally, at the settlement mound of Kolima-Sud, a site contemporary with Kobadi, faunal analysis has shown that cattle and ovicaprid remains do not appear until relatively late in the sequence (post 1400 cal BC) (MacDonald 1994). Further study will be necessary to confirm whether or not the subsistence strategy represented in the LSA of the Méma may have changed over time in its relative reliance on domestic livestock and wild resources. At Kobadi, in the units excavated thus far, natural strata could not be observed during excavations and all material from over a meter of deposits in each unit seems to have been consolidated for analysis (Jousse and Chenal-Velardé 2001-2002).

One objective of MacDonald's work in the Méma was evaluating the empirical evidence for the Pulse Model for cultural complexity (R. McIntosh 1993). The Pulse Model takes its starting point to be the demonstrable fact that the current Sahel zone has been subject to periodic climatic deterioration and amelioration over the last 4000 years, and during downturns, populations moved into the diverse and better-watered basins and floodplains, such as the Méma. The model then predicts that populations inhabiting closely-spaced micro-environments in these basins would in some cases begin to specialize in the extraction of certain subsistence resources, which they exchanged for other resources produced by other groups. The paradoxical pull of the greater extractive potential of specialization vs. the push of diversification in unpredictable environments via less risky generalizing strategies can be resolved by the emergence of relations of obligation, accommodation, and exchange among specialists. MacDonald (1994, MacDonald and van Neer 1994) provided a valuable initial dataset that demonstrated the different preferential locations of different types of LSA sites in the Mema and their apparent association with different types of ceramics and economies. Several radiocarbon determinations provide a preliminary chronological framework. As MacDonald rightly observed, further excavation work is required to refine and cross-check assemblage and temporal divisions, as well as to assess the subsistence data for sites of the different traditions and periods. The 1989-90 research has demonstrated quite eloquently that the Méma is a most suitable laboratory for the investigation of questions of subsistence specialization and the emergence of complexity.

The lack of archaeobotanical information from the Méma has been frustrating. In 2000, a research collaboration with the University of Osaka that focused on the domestication of African rice and other cereals prompted Dr. Togola to recommend further work at mounds around Kolima previously tested by MacDonald (1994, 1996). Mamadou Cissé worked with Shoichiro Takezawa (2004) in excavating sondages at Kolima Sud (second millenium BC) and Kolima Sud Est (first millennium BC). In both sites, African rice, long thought to have been initially domesticated in this zone of the Middle Niger, was absent. Sampling factors may be an issue here. At Kolima Sud Est in the early first millennium BC, however, domestic fonio is not only abundant and omnipresent, but is also found in clear ritual contexts (associated with purposeful cattle burials). Thus fonio domestication can be dated to at least the first half of the first millennium BC. (but its absence from the earlier levels of Kolima Sud cannot be taken as proof of non-domestication, for obvious sampling reasons).

Also in 2000, work on Iron Age mounds resumed, if only briefly. The Japanese expeditions excavated a sondage at the late first millennium AD Iron Age site of Kolima (Takezawa and Cissé 2004), where they failed to recover any domestic grains. Mamadou Cissé, Bart Makaske, Roderick McIntosh, Berté Sekou, and Joseph Tainter ranged throughout the region in January-February of that year, firming up the preliminary data needed to propose a larger program of excavation and survey. In addition to extensive "groundtruthing" to accompany interpretation of satellite and aerial images (for landform identification and initial hypotheses about subsidence and fluvial evolution), Tainter conducted pedestrian survey (to experiment with the most appropriate survey methodologies). At the same time, Cissé and McIntosh directed the excavation of a 2x2m unit (designated AK5) on Akumbu Mound B (one of several clustered *tells* in the immediate vicinity of Akumbu and previously tested by Dr. Togola). That unit was excavated only to a depth of 2.1m before the "mission" was aborted due to threat of banditry. The results of that short season are reported in de Vries et al. 2005.

June 2006,
Houston, Texas

de Vries, E., B. Makaske, J.A., Tainter, and R.J. McIntosh 2005. *Geomorphology and Human Palaeoecology of the Méma, Mali* (Wageningen: Alterra).

Jousse, H. and I. Chenal-Velarde. 2001-2002. Nouvelles données sur la faune mammalienne de Kobadi (Mali) au néolithique. Implications paléoéconomiques et paléoenvironnementales. *Préhistoire Anthropologie Méditerranéennes*. 10-11: 145-58.

MacDonald, K. C. 1994. *Socio-Economic Diversity and the Origin of Cultural Complexity Along the Middle Niger (2000 B.C. to A.D. 300)*. Ph.D. Dissertation. Faculty of Archaeology. University of Cambridge.

MacDonald, K. C. 1996. Tichitt-Walata and the Middle Niger: Evidence for cultural contact in the second millennium B.C.. In *Aspects of African Archaeology. Papers from the 10th Congress of the Panafrican Association for Prehistory and Related Studies*. eds. Gilbert Pwiti and Robert Soper. pp. 429-40. Harare: University of Zimbabwe Publications.

MacDonald, K.C. and W. van Neer 1994 Specialized fishing peoples in the later Holocene of the Méma region (Mali). *Annales du Musée Royal de l'Afrique centrale, Sciences Zoologiques*, no. 274:243-51.

McIntosh, R.J. 1993 The Pulse Theory: Genesis and accommodation of specialization in the Middle Niger", *Journal of African History* 34 (2): 181-220

Monod, T. and R. Mauny. 1957. Découverte de nouveaux instruments en os dans l'Ouest Africain. In *Proceedings of the 3rd Panafrican Congress on Prehistory, Livingstone 1955*. ed. J.D. Clark. pp. 242-47. London: Chatto & Windus.

Petit-Maire, N. and J. Riser (eds.). 1983. Sahara ou Sahel? (Marseille, Lamy).

Raimbault, M. 1986. Le gisement néolithique de Kobadi (Sahel Malien) et ses implications paléohydrologiques. *Changements Globaux en Afrique. Proceedings of the 1986 INQUA Symposium*. pp. 393-97. Dakar: INQUA.

Raimbault, M., C. Guerin, and M. Faure 1987 Les vertebras du gisement neeolithique de Kobadi (Mali). *Archaeozoologia* 12:219–38.
Raimbault, M. and O. Dutour. 1989. Les nouvelles données du site néolithique de Kobadi dans le Sahel Malien: La mission 1989. *Traveaux du Laboppratoire d'Anthropologie et de Préhistoire des Pays de la Méditerranée Occidentale* 1989: 175-83.

Raimbault, M. and O. Dutour. 1990.Découverte de populations mechtoïdes dans le Néolithique du Sahel malien (gisement lacustre de Kobadi); implications paléoclimatiques et paléoanthropologiques. *Comptes Rendues de l'Académie de Science de Paris. Séries III*. 310: 631-38.

Raimbault, M., C. Guérin, and M. Faure. 1987. Les vertébrés du gisement néolithique de Kobadi. *Archaeozoologia*. 1 (2): 219-38.

Takezawa, S. and M. Cissé. 2004. Domestication des céreales au Méma, Mali. In *Actes du XIéme Congrès de l'Association Panafricaine de Préhistoire et Disciplines Assimilées* (eds.)

Kléna Sanogo and Téréba Togola. (Bamako: Institut des Sciences Humaines), pp. 105-117.

Togola, T. 1993. *Archaeological Investigation of Iron Age Sites in the Méma* (Mali). Ph.D. dissertation. Department of Anthropology. Rice University.

Togola, T. 1996. Iron age occupation in the Méma region, Mali. *African Archaeological Review*. 13: 91-110.

Urbain, J-C. 2001-2002. L'Industrie lithique de Kobadi (Sahal Malien). Aspects techniques, socio-économiques et culturels. *Préhistoire Anthropologie Méditerranéennes*. 10-11: 135-44.

ACKNOWLEDGEMENTS

In the research in the Méma and the completion of this disseration, I have received great support from many individuals, organizations and institutions. For their assistance, sympathy, interest and generosity, I offer my most heartfelt thanks.

The Méma research project and this dissertation would never have been undertaken and completed without the advice, encouragement, patience, and material support of my advisors, Dr. Susan Keech McIntosh and Dr. Roderick J. McIntosh. I owe them a special debt of gratitude.

Special thanks are extended to Helen Haskell, the co-director of the Méma project, who made personal and financial sacrifices on behalf of the success of this project. I must also acknowledge her continuous encouragement, advice and support during the writing up of this dissertation.

Kevin MacDonald took part in all the expeditions in the Méma and kindly analysed the faunal remains from the excavations at Akumbu mound complex. I would particularly like to acknowledge his infinite effort, encouragement, and committment to the goals of this project.

Thanks are extended to Dr. Kléna Sanogo, Director of the Institut des Sciences Humaines du Mali, who granted official permission for the research and generously provided a Land Rover and a driver for the first expedition in the Méma.

My profound gratitude goes to Sandra Poznikoff and Karina Macovat (both Canadian students) who spent three weeks with us and helped with the excavations at Akumbu mound complex.

The assistance of Nafogo Coulibaly, Kechery Doumbia (who spent two weeks with us in the Méma), and Youssouf Kalapo (who helped with the pottery drawings) was instrumental to the success of this research program.

Additionally, thanks are extended to Mr. Bah (chef d'arrondissement de Nampala), and Sékou Sidibé (local informant and guide) for their assistance and support for the Méma project.

Funding for the Méma research program was generously provided by the National Science Foundation (Dissertation Improvement Grant 9001664). I am also grateful for the Fulbright award that made my graduate studies at Rice University possible, and the many kindnesses of Marilyn Hulbert and Linda Buggeln, Public Affairs Officers (1985-1991) for USIS at the American Embassy in Bamako.

CHAPTER 1
GEOMORPHOLOGICAL, HISTORICAL, AND ARCHAEOLOGICAL BACKGROUND

I: GEOGRAPHIC SETTING AND GEOMORPHOLOGY

The region traditionally known to Malians as the Méma is a plain of deep alluvial deposits that lies west of the current seasonally flooded Inland Delta of the Niger River and southwest of the of the Lakes Region (Frontispiece). As for most traditional regions in Mali, its geographical borders are loosely defined. Nampala, the biggest town of the area, is located at 15° 16' north and 5° 35' west. The Méma is also sometimes referred to in the literature as the "Dead Delta", a name that evokes the presence of a dense network of dry watercourses. This indicates that the Méma once formed a floodplain of pseudo-deltaic hydrology similar to that of the current active floodplain to the southeast.

Today, the Méma lies within the sahelian zone and is very dry. It receives only 150 to 400 mm of annual rainfall, all of which occurs during a short rainy season extending from July to September. This short rainy season alternates with an eight-month dry season and rising temperatures (Haaland, 1980; CIPEA 1980). Surface water is available only when the many depressions within the ancient floodplain are flooded by local rainfall. During the long dry season, water has to be drawn from wells dug 50 to 60m deep to reach the water table. These harsh climatic conditions are the major limiting factors for human population in the Méma. Current permanent occupation is restricted to scattered villages and hamlets. These are primarily inhabited by sedentary Rimaibé (former slaves of the Fulani), who practice *Pennisetum* millet cultivation and keep small herds of cattle, goats and sheep. During the rainy season (July through September), transhumant Fulani pastoralists move into the area with their herds to exploit the ephemeral lush flora of grass and the seasonally inundated ponds (Gallais 1967: 56-61).

The spotty distribution of modern permanent settlement in the Méma contrasts sharply with the situation during the last millennium. As discussed further in the chapter on the settlement pattern, our fieldwork has identified numerous Iron Age (IA) habitation mounds. This thriving human settlement, clearly associated with a period of climatic amelioration, extends back in time to the Late Stone Age (LSA).

Although various geomorphological investigations have been conducted on the Inland Niger Delta and its marginal zones by Furon (1929), Urvoy (1942), Tricart (1965) and Gallais (1967), no specific geomorphological studies of the Méma itself have ever been executed. Most of the studies listed above attempted to document the fluvial evolution of the Niger (particularly its southeastward trend) and the recently abandoned distributaries. Among these is the Fala de Molodo, a substantial relict distributary, leading north from Markala, and considered by many geomorphologists [e.g. Furon 1929, Urvoy 1942, Tricart 1965] to have carried the main flow of the Niger toward the basin of the Mauritanian Hodh during the long humid periods of the Pleistocene. The Méma floodplain forms the eastern part of the drainage system of the Fala de Molodo.

Based on the examination of aerial photographs of scale 1: 50,000, topographic maps, and on our own observations of the terrain during the survey, many geomorphological zones and landforms can tentatively be identified. These include:

(1) A longitudinal dune field extending in the northern and western fringes of the Méma (Figure 1.1). These longitudinal dunes, considered as part of the massive Pleistocene Erg of Ouagadou (Furon 1929; McIntosh 1983), are now superficially consolidated and covered with a flora of seasonal grasses and occasional acacia scrub.

(2) The Boulel Ridge, a low butte of ferrugeneous laterite, which crosses the southern part of the Méma. This lateritic formation, associated on either side with iron pan peneplain and covered with dense acacia or *brousse tigrée*, diminishes progressively from west to east and finally disappears in the eastern part of the Méma, right before the backswamp.

(3) The ancient floodplain with a mosaic of geomorphological features, including relict water corridors associated with systems of levees, the backswamp with dark clayey soil and multiple seasonally flooded pans, and a system of degraded dunes. The major water corridors and river channels were also identified by Furon (1929: 265-74) who made the first attempt to map the drainage system of the Fala de Molodo. From south to north, they comprise: a) the most eastern branch of the Fala itself (Furon's Bras Debo), which meanders south of the Boulel Ridge through a system of levees; b) the Niakene Maoudo running north of the Boulel Ridge; and c) the Bras de Nampala, running on the northwestern edge of the ancient floodplain. The latter branches off in the northern part of the Méma and curls west toward the basin of the Mauritanian Hodh. A fourth relict channel runs east-west within the backswamp and appears to connect the east branch of the Fala de Molodo and the Bras de Nampala to the west. These defunct water corridors, as well as the backswamp in the eastern sector of the Méma, are now occupied by seasonally flooded pans. Within the floodplain is a system of degraded dunes, reworked by fluvial activities.

All of these geomorphological features, except the Boulel ridge, were certainly modeled by the drainage system of the Fala de Molodo during the early Holocene. From 12500 to 5000 BP, humid conditions allowed a vigorous fluvial system to remodel the Pleistocene dune landscape (SK McIntosh & RJ McIntosh 1988: 89-133). The former

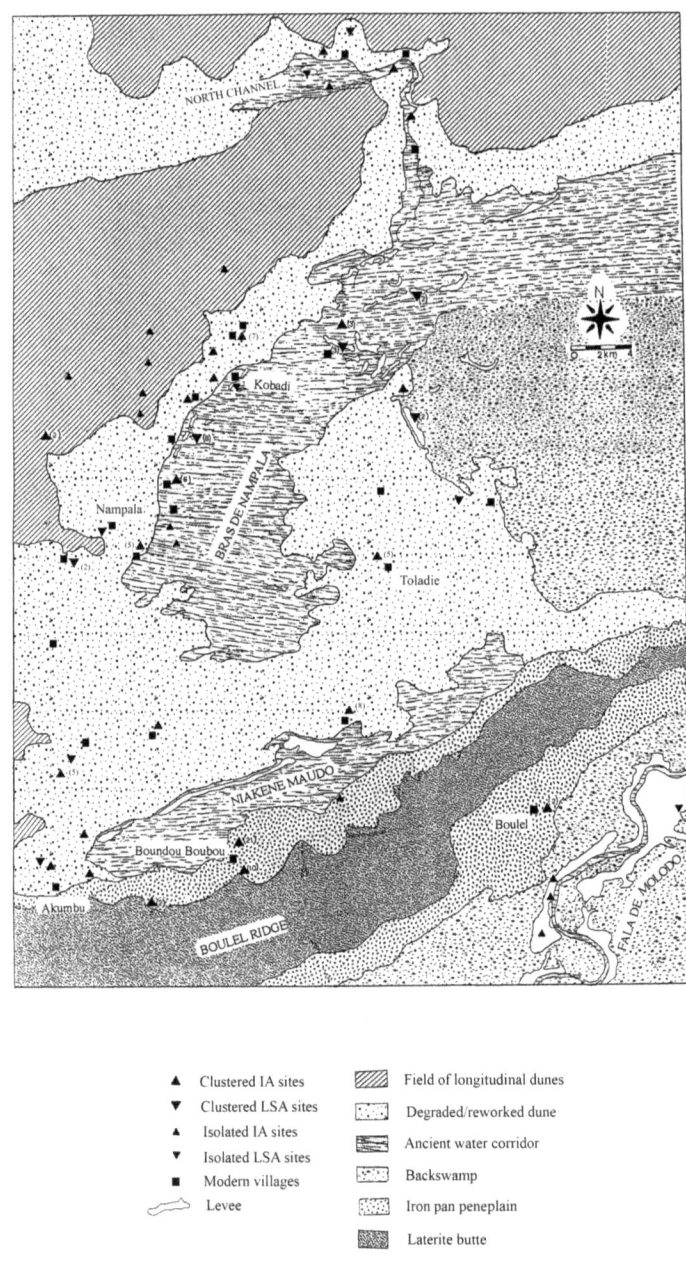

Figure 1.1. Geomorphological Features of the Méma

bed of the Fala de Molodo, the feeder of all these defunct watercourses, has partially been rejuvenated and utilised as an irrigation canal by the *Office du Niger* (ON), a large scale irrigation project initiated by the French to implement the agricultural expansion of the French Sudan.

Most of the modern villages in the Méma are located along the ancient water corridors. This preferential location is certainly related to water and farmland availability: the level of water along these relict watercourses is approximately 50m deep (compared to 65m within the longitudinal dunes) and the soil is sandy and dry enough during the rainy season to support millet cultivation.

Due to the fact that no detailed and expert geomorphological study is yet available for the Méma, these various geomorphological zones and landforms remain gross classifications. As a consequence, the causes and chronology of the desiccation of the Fala de Molodo, an important geomporphological event which undoubtedly affected prehistoric occupation in the Méma, are still speculative. It has been attributed to various subsidences of the eastern part of the Middle Niger Basin (Tricart 1965), the lowering of the base level of the Niger river relative to the Fala de Molodo (Gallais 1967), and the river's habit of abandoning its old channels and distributaries due to natural alluviation in a deltaic plain of low gradient (McIntosh 1983).

II: HISTORICAL BACKGROUND

Given the absence of substantive archaeological research, my reconstruction of the history of the Méma relies on oral traditions and on information provided by historical documents, such as medieval Arab sources and local chronicles written in Arabic.

The Arab medieval sources

The medieval Arab sources, written by travelers, geographers, and scholars from all parts of the Islamic world, including the Near East, Spain, and North Africa, constitute the most important written documents on the history of the Western Sudan for the period that extends roughly from the middle of the eighth century AD to the middle of the second millennium AD. However, these sources often pose problems in interpretation, particularly concerning the names of peoples and places they discuss. Neverless, they have attracted the attention of many modern historians, including Delafosse (1912), Monteil (1929), Mauny (1961), and Levtzion (1973), to cite only a few. Despite their importance, most of these sources are silent about the Méma. This omission of the Méma possibly reflects the selective character of these sources, all of which were mostly concerned with large independent polities such as Ghana, Mali, and Songhay. Only one Arab author, the renowned world traveler Ibn Battuta, actually visited the Méma, and mentions its name (Lewicki 1974; Cuoq 1975: 284-323; Levtzion & Hopkins1981: 279-304). He attests that a trade route through the Méma (the "Mima road") existed at the time of his travels (1352-3), and that an administrative hierarchy subject to the empire of Mali was operating during that period at "Mima", where he stayed six days (Lewicki 1974; Cuoq 1975: 284-323; Levtzion & Hopkins1981: 279-304). He also reported that Mansa Moussa, the Malian emperor in the first mid-14th century AD, went through Mima on his way for his legendary pilgrimage to Mecca in 1324 (Lewicki 1974; Cuoq 1975: 284-323; Levtzion & Hopkins1981: 279-304). Delafosse (1929, in Cuoq 1975: 312, note 1) identifies Ibn Batuta' s "Mima" as the current Méma, as does Monteil (1929: 63) who notes that "Mima" corresponds to the ancient Soninke kingdom founded in northern Macina after the extinction of the empire of Ghana.

The local chronicles

Following the external texts, the next documentary sources on the history of the Western Sudan are the indigenous chronicles. These, also written in Arabic, often rely intensively on oral or written accounts transmitted from one generation to another. Most of them are authored by indigenous scholars or writers from or attached to renowned Islamic learning centers like Timbuktu, Jenné, and Dia. Like the Arab sources, these local chronicles often pose problems of interpretation because of their clear tendency to shape the information they provide, to conform to the ideological climate of the moment, and to favor Islamic rulers and towns. Only two of these chronicles, incidentally the most elaborated and most renowned, the *Tarikh El Fetach* and the *Tarikh Es Sudan,* talk briefly about the Méma. The *Tarikh El Fetach*, written from 1519 to 1665 by three generations of the family of Mohamed Kati of Timbuktu, asserts that the Méma recovered its independence from Mali in 1433 at the same time as Timbuktu and Walata and remained a sovereign state until its conquest in the middle of the fifteenth century by the Songhay during the reign of Souleyman Dama (Kati 1964).

The *Tarikh Es Sudan*, written from 1627 to 1665 by Es Sa'di, the Imam of Jenné, notes that the Méma was conquered by the empire of Mali along with several other provinces when the expansion of this empire began under the reign of Sunjata (Es Sa' di 1900: 20).

The oral traditions

The Méma figures importantly in both Manden traditions and the Soninke legend of Wagadu, which is widely assumed to refer to the rise and fall of the empire of Ghana. The Wagadu legend retraces the movements of Dinga, the Soninké mythical ancestor comparable to a biblical patriarch, throughout the Western Sudan. Recently, a variant of the legend collected by a mission of the Malian *Division du Patrimoine Culturel du Mali* (DPC) (1985) attests that Dinga, before reaching the Wagadu, where one of his descendants founded the capital Kumbi Saleh, stayed in the Méma at a town called Akumbu. The remains of this town, where our excavations were conducted, were pointed out to the Malian DPC by local informants. Another variant of the legend, recorded by Monteil (1953), attributes the founding of the Soninké kingdom of Méma to a descendant of Biranin Tounkara, head of the Kusa clan, said to have accompanied Dinga in his early adventures. In this later variant, the emergence of the Méma kingdom and its capital city of the same name are placed after the dislocation of Wagadu and the subsequent dispersal of the Soninké. In this same version, Monteil (1929) also records the site of Gallu, a large habitation mound located between Nampala and Léré, as the remains of the ancient city of Méma. These various claims possibly allude to the Méma's political status, first as a vassal province of the Wagadu, and second as an independent state following the collapse of the Wagadu. This later event, attributed by the oral traditions to the killing of the snake Bida, the sacred guardian of the prosperity of the kingdom, led to the dispersal of the Soninké throughout West Africa, and to the formation of other smaller Soninké polities and towns including the Méma, the Diafunu, Dia, and the Kusta (Monteil 1953; Levtzion 1973; Bathily 1975). This type of political fragmentation is common in the history of the Western Sudan. Provinces always exploited the weakness of the centralized polities, such as Ghana, Mali, and Songhay, to become independent (Monteil 1929; Levtzion 1973). However, this independence was short lived, as generally they were again incorporated into the new emerging political authority. The independence of the Soninké kingdom of Méma, whose territorial extent is still unknown, probably lasted only a few decades. As discussed further below, it became a vassal province of Mali before its conquest by the Songhay around 1433 (Kati 1964).

The chronologies, if any, of the Soninké movements so prevalent and recurring in the oral traditions, are very uncertain. However, S.K. McIntosh (1981), considering the archaeological evidence from Jenné-jeno founded by proto-Soninké around 250 BC in the Inland Niger Delta, suggests that they may be a continuation of a trend that may have began as early as the first millennium BC in response to the increasing desiccation of the Sahara and possible difficulties with Saharan nomads pushing southward. The chronology and scope of the Soninké expansion into the Méma are critical to our understanding of the political evolution of the Méma, and also to the possible cultural affiliation and trade between the Méma and the Wagadu, widely assumed to correspond to the medieval empire of Ghana.

The epic of Sunjata, founder of the medieval empire of Mali, constitutes a pivot of the oral traditions of the Manden. The Manden, the cradle of the empire of Mali, is a traditional region located in the upper basin of the Niger River, and across the border of the modern states of Mali and Guinea. Many variants of the Sunjata epic (Monteil 1929, LyTall 1970, Niane 1971) recount the Méma as the place where Sunjata stayed during his exile prior to assuming the throne of Mali. However, Cissé (1988), in a version recounted by Wâ Kamissoko, a *griot* from the Manden, reports Nêma, a current locality in the Mauritanian Sahel, as Sunjata's exile place. Might this confusion be the result of difference in pronounciation by *griots*? In the Manden traditions, the interpretation of names of places involved in past events is difficult due to the fact that present-day places and more recent events are often projected into the prestigious past. In addition, the traditions themselves, especially the epic of Sunjata where the Méma is the most referred to, are recounted in dozens of versions. Apart from this confusion, most elements related to Sunjata's exile recorded by Cissé (1988), Niane (1971), Ly Tall (1970), and Monteil (1929) agree. Sunjata is said to have become a distinguished warrior at the court of Musa Tunkara, the ruler of Méma during his exile (Niane 1971). He left Méma with troops (including cavalry given to him by the king of Méma), to confront Sumaoro, the sorcerer and blacksmith king who had conquered the Manden during his absence. His victory against Sumaoro Kanté in 1240 (Niane 1971:123) marked the beginning of the expansion of the empire of Mali. Although the Méma was annexed to the empire of Mali, its ruler was allowed to retain his status as king because of his hospitality to Sunjata (Niane 1971:123).

A final tradition, also collected by the DPC (1985), reports that the Fulani Wuwarbé (from the Bakhunu), and their former retainers, the Rimaibé, entered the Méma only in the 19th century. Sekou Hamadou, the ruler of the Fulani of the Macina, allowed them to exploit the rich pastures of the area (DPC 1985).

These various sources give an incomplete picture of the Méma, focusing as they do on the shift in political authority in the area during the period of the Sudanese medieval empires of Ghana, Mali, and Sunghay. The earliest of these political authorities, the empire of Ghana, emerged only toward the middle of the first millennium AD. What happened in the area before this period still constitutes a gap in our knowledge which, unfortunately, has not been filled by the few erratic archaeological projects previously executed in the area and summarized below.

III: PRIOR ARCHAEOLOGICAL RESEARCH IN THE MÉMA AND NEIGHBORING REGIONS

This section outlines the archaeological data previously recovered and studied in the Méma and its neighboring regions which include the Wagadu (to the northwest), the Lakes regions, the Niger Bend (to the north), and the Inland Niger Delta (to the south). Until recently, the archaeological record in these regions encompassed mostly the second millennium AD, and, at best, the late first millennium AD. This situation, attributed to the long tradition in West African archaeology to substantiate the Arab documentary sources by focusing on historically known sites, has left large chunks of the prehistory of most of these regions unknown. However, stacks of evidence recently collected from the Upper Niger Delta (Jenné region) (SK McIntosh & RJ McIntosh 1980; SK McIntosh in press) and the Macina (Dia region) (Haskell et al. 1988) have demonstrated the precocity of important innovations, including the beginning of urbanism, regional trade, and the rise of complex societies. These innovations, dated at least to the mid- first millennium AD (SK McIntosh & RJ McIntosh 1980; SK McIntosh in press; (Haskell et al. 1988), were certainly not isolated phenomena, limited to the Jenné and Dia regions. They may have embraced all the regions which strategically extend along the production and distribution axis of the Middle Niger and early empire of Ghana.

The Wagadu
The Wagadu, located northwest of the Méma, extends in Soninké country and across the border between Mali and Mauretania (Frontispiece). Archaeological investigations in this region have been confined to the remains of the urban city of Koumbi Saleh, regarded by many scholars as the likely capital of the medieval empire of Ghana. The date of the founding of this empire is unknown. However, its existence at least by the ninth century is established by its brief mention by several Arab authors, such as al-Fazari writing at the end of the eighth century AD (Levtzion 1973: 3), and al-Ya' qubi writing in the ninth century AD (Lewicki 1974: 17-18; Cuoq 1975: 48-52; Levtzion and Hopkins 1981: 21). In the eleventh century AD, Al Bakri described Ghana as a city consisting of two towns, an Arab and Islamic district, and, seven kilometers away, the royal and indigenous town (Levtzion & Hopkins 1981: 80-81). The quest for the site of Kumbi Saleh began at the turn

of this century. In 1912, Delafosse drew attention to the extensive ruins of stone buildings called Koumbi Saleh in southern Mauretania (Mauny 1961: 73). Since then, a number of excavations, reported in Mauny (1961), were conducted on those ruins, and the adjacent cemeteries. In 1914, Bonnel de Mezières excavated several houses and tombs. Mauny (1961:73) reports that both the materials and plans resulting from these excavations may have been lost. In 1939 excavations at two houses by Lazartigues followed; but materials from these excavations may also have been lost (Mauny 1961: 73). In 1949 and 1950, Thomassey and Mauny (1951,1956) sunk several pits several other stone houses (clearly visible on the surface) and uncovered copper and iron objects. In 1951, Mauny and Szumowski (Mauny 1961) conducted excavations on several tombs and various architectural structures including public buildings such as part of the mosque. During more recent excavations, Sophie Berthier and Serge Robert (Berthier 1981) explored the lower occupation levels never reached by any of the previous investigations. These excavations yielded the presence of a pre-urban occupation dated to the sixth century AD. This pre-urban occupation was indicated by a 2m deposit with low density of occupation and an absence of stone architecture. Unfortunately, few other details are available on pre-urban deposits and the context of the site's founding which, to judge from the radiocarbon dates of the sixth century AD, seems to antedate North African influences. Also unfortunate is the fact that no investigations have been conducted on the African indigenous town described by al Bakri in the eleventh century AD (Levtzion & Hopkins 1981). As a result, any evidence is lacking for indigenous origins of the urban development of Kombi Saleh, and the context into which the later North African trade moved.

The Lakes Region
The Lakes Region, north and east of the Méma (Frontispiece), has been subjected to numerous archaeological investigations since the turn of this century. However, in spite of this early start and some extensive recent investigations, our knowledge of the archaeology and prehistory of this region is still limited due to poor research strategies. Most of the early archaeological investigations were confined to unsystematic excavations and the search for museum objects at highly visible funerary tumuli and megalithic monuments. In addition, some of these early works were never published at all. Fortunately, they have been synthesized by Mauny (1961) in his *Tableau Géographique de l' Ouest Africain*.

The earliest archaeological investigations to be undertaken in the Lake Region were surface collection and pot hunting by Bonnel de Mezières and Clozel in 1886. These were followed by uncontrolled and unpublished excavations by captain Florentin at a tumulus between Tindirma and Saia (Mauny 1961). Unlike these works is the relatively detailed report published by Desplagnes on his excavations at the tumuli of Killi or Koy Gourey (Desplagnes 1903: 155), near Goudam, and El-Oualaji, near Diré (Desplagnes 1907:54-66; 1951). Numerous burnt areas at the surface of these tumuli indicated that small fires had apparently been lit on their surface in an effort to harden their upper stratum. The tumulus of Koy Gourey contained the remains of two individuals, accompanied with rich grave offerings, and of 25-30 other people, presumably entombed at the same time (Desplagnes 1907: 54-66). Even more elaborate was the tumulus of El-Oualaji, in which Desplagnes uncovered a vaulted wooden burial chamber with a vertical shaft extending to the surface of the mound. This burial chamber contained two individuals laid out on a bed of branches and surrounded by weapons and jewelry (Desplagnes 1907: 54-66). Later investigations at the tumulus of Kouga in the same region by Mauny (Mauny 1961: 93) produced a single radiocarbon date of 1000 ± 150. At Killi and El-Oualaji, the outer layers of Kouga had been hardened by fires lit on the mound surface (Mauny 1961).

These tumuli clearly represent non-Islamic burial practices and indicate differences in social status and concentration of wealth. However, the duration of this practice of inhumation in large earthen tumuli remains unknown. Another important issue, not satisfactorily investigated, is the relationship between funerary tumuli and settlement mounds. The two kinds of sites, to judge from the various investigations, appear to exist side by side in the Lake Region. Both Szumowski and Mauny attempted to establish their morphological boundaries, but were only able to say that many of the tumuli, in fact, may be incorporated into habitation mounds (Szumowski 1957), or that the tumuli are higher, more rounded and the habitation sites lower and more extended (Mauny 1961: 92). Worthy of note, but adding to the confusion, is the fact that recent excavations at two habitation mounds, Mouyssam and Kawinza near Sumpi, have produced burials, though not as affluent as those at Killi and El-Oualaji.

The megalithic monuments found in the Niafunké area have also been subjected to early but restricted study. Among them, the megalithic concentration of Tondidarou, near Lake Takaji, is renowned not only for its size and the quality of its arrangement, but also because of its sad fate. Investigations by Desplagnes (Desplagnes1907), Maes (1924), and de Gironcourt (Mauny 1961: 129 - 134) indicated that there were at least 150 standing stone pillars, some of which were sculptured and engraved. In 1931, the site was a victim of uncontrolled excavations by Clérisse, a journalist from *l' Intransigeant* who dug trenches at the base of most of the megaliths, which subsequently fell. In Mauny's words (Mauny 1961: 129-131), the *triste odyssée* of the megalithic arrangement of Tondidarou had then begun. The best specimens were transported from the site to different locations, including the garden of the colonial administrator in nearby Niafunké, Bamako, Dakar and the *Musée de l' Homme* in Paris. The original disposition of this remarkable megalithic arrangement may never be known, since the maps compiled by Clérisse' s predecessors were too sketchy.

Recent investigations by Fontes and others (Fontes et al. 1980; 1991) have demonstrated that the megalith concentration of Tondidarou was actually associated with an earthern mound they interpreted as a tumulus, because of the presence at the surface of burnt clay features similar to ones signaled by both Desplagnes and Mauny at El Oualaji and Killi. This, however, is questionable given the presence of abundant domestic materials including pot sherds, grindstones, animal bones at the surface of that mound (Fontes et al. 1991: 41) and the fact that burnt clay features have been found at the surface of several habitation mounds of both the Lakes regions (Dembélé 1986, 1991; Raimbault 1991), the Upper Inland Niger Delta (SK McIntosh & RJ McIntosh 1980), and the Middle Sénégal Valley (SK McIntosh personnal communication). Charcoal collected from the uppermost strata of this mound associated with the megalith concentration of Tondidarou produced a seventh century AD radiocarbon date (Fontes et al. 1980: 38; 1991: 37-59).

During colonial times, the habitation sites of the Lake Region benefited from less attention and investigation, compared to the funerary tumuli and the megalithic monuments. Limited and non-stratigraphic excavations, which produced few artifacts, were executed in 1954/1955 by Mauny (Mauny 1961) at Jim-jim and Tondia, near Goudam. During the same campaign, a brief reconnaissance around those sites revealed that most prehistoric settlements, like present day villages, were preferentially located on high dunes near bodies of water (Mauny 1961).

More recent and intensive investigations in the Lake Region have focused largely on Iron Age mounds. Since the early 1980s, the *Projet Inventaire des Sites Archéologiques du Mali*, executed by the *Institut des Sciences Humaines du Mali* (ISH), has identified hundreds of mounds (all apparently habitation mounds) in an area stretching on the north western fringe of the Lake Region, and roughly from Léré to Diré (Dembélé 1986; Sidibé and Raimbault 1991; Raimbault & Sanogo 1991; Schmit 1986). Compared to the single site-oriented reconnaissance and excavation during colonial times, the adoption of such a regional perspective constituted a first step toward the description and understanding of settlement patterns in the Lakes Region during the prehistoric period. However, most of these sites were discovered in a more or less haphazard way by hired local informants (Dembélé 1986; Sidibé and Raimbault 1991; Schmit 1986), making their representativeness questionable. Most of these sites, like the *tells* of the Inland Niger Delta, occurred in clusters (Dembélé 1986; Sidibé and Raimbault 1991; Schmit 1986). Slag concentrations associated with furnace remains were found at the edge of many of the investigated mounds, especially the largest ones (Chieze 1991). The one consistent feature, occurring singly or in clusters at their surface, was deliberately burnt clay structures, similar to the ones reported from the tumuli of El Oualaji, Killi, and Kouga (Dembélé 1986; Sidibé and Raimbault 1991; Schmit 1986).

During the various campaigns of the ISH, the question of the function of the mounds of the Lake Region, especially their relationship with the tumuli, was raised again (Dembélé 1986; Sidibé and Raimbault 1991; Schmit 1986). In order to illuminate this question, excavations were conducted at three mounds, Kawinza (Sidibé & Raimbault 1991), Mouyssam (Dembélé 1986; Sanogo 1991; Raimbault, 1991) and Toubel (Raimbault 1991), all in the Sumpi area. In addition to abundant domestic debris (consisting essentially of ceramic fragments, bones, ash mixed with wood charcoal, and collapse of mud walls), all these excavations produced extended human burials (Sidibé & Raimbault 1991; Dembélé 1986; Sanogo 1991; Raimbault 1991). Various grave goods accompanying two of these burials consisted of polychrome painted ceramic bottles (at Kawinza) (Sidibé & Raimbault 1991: 273), an ovoid vessel and numerous shells beads (at Mouyssam) (Raimbault & Sanogo 1991: 301). However, unlike at Mouyssam and Kawinza, no grave offerings were found with the burial at Toubel (Raimbault 1991: 391). Radiocarbon dates obtained from the excavations at Mouyssam (dug to sterile soil) indicated that this mound was occupied between AD 240 - 540 (sample taken from 9.5 m depth) and AD 620 - 675 (charcoal sample from 0.7 m depth) (Raimbault & Sanogo 1991: 301,321). These dates indicate an overwhelmingly rapid accumulation of the deposits at Mouyssam (measuring nine meters depth at the site of the sondage) (Raimbault & Sanogo 1991: 301). A series of radiocarbon dates obtained from Toubel and ranging from AD 340 - 540 (4.4 m depth) to AD 1210 -1295 (0.5 m depth) (Raimbault 1991: 391) indicated substantially slower accumulation. Two radiocarbon dates, 1050 ± 40 BP and 1285 ± 70 BP, both from the uppermost strata, were obtained from the mound of Kawinza (Sidibé & Raimbault 1984; 1991: 273).

To date, the available data from the Lakes Region indicate only the presence of numerous Iron Age sites, comprising large habitation mounds, funerary tumuli and megalithic monuments. Given the fact that most researchers working in the Lakes Region have been inclined to focus on these highly visible types of sites, the presence of other ranges or types is still unknown. In addition, the chronological and functional relationships among sites have been poorly investigated.

The Niger Bend

Despite the presence of Timbuktu, an important commercial center during historical times, archaeological investigations in the Niger Bend (Frontispiece), at least until recently, have been a rarity. As suggested by SK and RJ McIntosh (1986), this failure of the Niger Bend to attract archaeologists may be attributed to the long practice in West African archaeology to substantiate and supplement Arab documentary sources by focusing on the earliest cities mentioned in those sources. The Niger Bend, with Timbuktu's relatively late founding in the twelfth century, would have been considered to have less archaeological potential compared to Gao, Ghana, Awdaghost, and even

Mali, which are all mentioned much earlier than Timbuktu (SK McIntosh & RJ McIntosh 1986).

Fortunately, intensive regional site surveys around Timbuktu and Gourma Rharous by the McIntoshes in 1984 (SK McIntosh & RJ McIntosh 1986) has remedied this early neglect of Niger Bend by archaeologists. This regional survey resulted in the identification of 43 archaeological sites and the discovery of important shifts in the settlement pattern and landform preferences through times. The tentative relative chronology (Early, Middle, and Recent) formulated for these sites was based on the characteristics of their surface materials, in particular the co-ocurrence of distinctive pottery forms and decorations (SK McIntosh & RJ McIntosh 1986). Early sites, dated approximately from 500 BC to 500 AD, were ephemeral in occupation and concentrated along seasonally flooded wadis. The ephemeral nature of occupation was probably due to the episodic nature of water availability. Middle sites (500 AD to 1500 AD) were large permanent settlements equally distributed along the wadis and in the dunefield, implying that increased water flow in those channels during that period permitted settlement to change from ephemeral to permanent. During the Recent period (1500 AD to 1900 AD) sites were small and exclusively distributed in the floodplain. This decrease in site size was attributed to depopulation, due to climatic deterioration, political instability, and /or population transfer to Timbuktu, the only urban settlement in area today (SK McIntosh & RJ McIntosh 1986). The results of this first systematic survey in the Niger Bend reinforce the evidence for extensive trade the first millennium and cultural connection along the Middle Niger, long advocated by the McIntoshes (1986; 1988). Not only is the Timbuktu Middle Assemblage pottery (tentatively dated between 500 AD and 1500 AD) similar to that of Jenné-jeno during the same period, but it also displayed close affinities to ceramics reported from other Middle Niger regions like the Lakes region (SK McIntosh & RJ McIntosh 1986).

The Inland Niger Delta

The Inland Niger Delta is located south and east of the Méma (Frontispiece). Like the Lakes Region, it is among the most favored regions for archaeological investigation in Mali. Archaeological work in this region began as early as the turn of the century, and went through two major phases: one prior and one subsequent to the 1970s. During the first phase, no site in the Inland Delta had been investigated extensively. Work was confined to limited and stray pits unsystematically sunk at the surface of the ancient cemeteries and settlement mounds that dot the landscape of the region so remarkably (Mauny 1961) (Figure 1.2). Throughout these long colonial decades and the early decades of Malian independence, archaeological reports emphasized stunning finds such as terra-cotta statuettes, imported objects, and beautiful pottery (Vieillard 1940; Sarr 1972). Those by Szumowski (1956; 1957) are by far the most detailed and contain sketchy stratigraphic information and show excellent drawings of intact and nicely decorated vessels. No archaeological report on the Inland Delta prior to the late 1970s provided qualitative and quantitative data. This, added to the lack of stratigraphic information, precluded assessment of important issues such as change through time. In summary, the various work before the late 1970's indicated that occupation in the Inland Delta appeared to have been exclusively Iron Age in date. No LSA deposits were mentioned in any of the reports. Most of the excavated sites appeared to be habitation mounds, or *tells*, which often displayed numerous burial features such as funerary urns at their surface.

During the second phase, the Inland Niger Delta was the subject of extensive archaeological investigations. Among these is the work of Bedaux and others at Toguéré Galia (near Sevaré), Toguéré Doupwil (on the Bani River) (Bedaux et al.1980), and the numerous campaigns of the McIntoshes around Jenné and Dia (SK McIntosh & RJ McIntosh 1980; Haskell et al. 1988; SK McIntosh in press).

The work of the Bedaux team, from the Institute of Anthropobiology of Utrecht, Holland, was conducted in a two-month period in 1975. It consisted essentially of cleaning sections of Toguéré Galia and Toguéré Doupwil already exposed by local quarrying for making mud for brick or by river erosion. Detailed stratigraphic information, anchored by a series of radiocarbon dates, indicated that both mounds were occupied sometime between the twelfth and sixteenth centuries AD (Bedaux et al. 1978: 189). A major credit to the Bedaux team was the collection of every bit of information available during the excavations. This resulted in the production of a complete site report, the first for the Inland Delta. Microbotanical and faunal samples collected and later analysed indicated the presence of domesticated cereals (African rice, sorghum, millet, and fonio) and domesticated animals (cattle, goat and sheep) at the two sites (Bedaux et al. 1978: 186). Analysis and seriation of artifacts were also undertaken. A total of 15 different pottery forms and 10 different decoration types were identified. These pottery forms and decoration types (including various twine patterns) apparently remained essentially unchanged throughout the occupation of the sites (Bedaux et al. 1978: 124-143).

The work of Bedaux and others was followed by the various research projects of the McIntoshes around Jenné in 1977 and 1981, and Dia in 1986/87. To date, these projects constitute the most extensive archaeological investigations ever undertaken in the Inland Delta (SK McIntosh & RJ McIntosh 1980; Haskell et al. 1988; SK McIntosh in press). The McIntoshes' original excavations in 1977 at Jenné-jeno, supplemented by further work at the same site and the nearby sites of Hambarketolo and Kaniana in 1981, have produced some outstanding results including detailed stratigraphic information supported by a series of reliable radiocarbon dates, and the establishment of successive ceramic sequences covering 1600 years. The series of radiocarbon determinations, the detailed

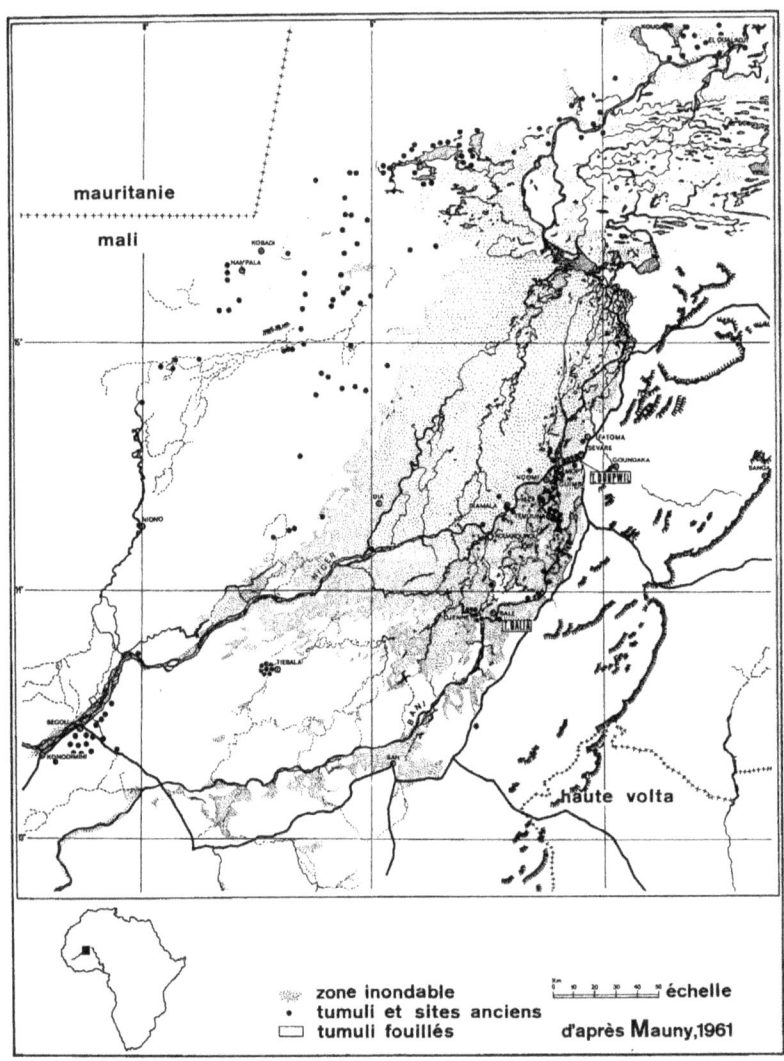

Figure 1.2. Map of the 'tumuli' along the Middle Niger (Bedaux et al. 1978).

stratigraphic information, and the pottery sequences, together allowed the McIntoshes to define four cultural phases at Jenné-jeno. Phase I/II (250 BC to 400 AD) covers the founding of the site by populations already acquainted with iron metallurgy and its rapid expansion to at least 25 ha. Phase III (AD 400 to AD 850), witnessed the maximum expansion of Jenné-jeno (which, along with neighboring Hambarketolo, extended over 40 ha), and several innovations, including the construction of a massive city wall, and the introduction of imported and status commodities such as copper and gold. Phase IV, (AD 850 to AD 1400) covers the decline of the site and its abandonment around 1400. This period of decline coincides with the appeerance of North African influences attested by the presence of rectangular mud building plans and artifacts such as spindle whorls and glass beads. The intensive surveys that accompanied the two seasons of excavations indicated that Jenné-jeno's growth (toward a complex urban settlement) and decline was reflected by the hinterland settlements which reached their greatest density between AD 700 and AD 1100. Most of these sites were abandoned by 1400 AD, due to climatic or cultural factors (SK McIntosh & RJ McIntosh 1980; SK McIntosh in press). Another important result of the surveys was the finding of simultaneously occupied sites within clusters, a notable aspect of site distribution and occupation dynamics in the Jenné area. Surface features and artifacts indicated that sites within clusters were functionally distinct, with small-sized ones less complex and the larger ones showing more functional complexity (SK McIntosh & RJ McIntosh 1980; RJ McIntosh 1991).

The second region of the Inland Delta investigated by the McIntoshes was the Dia region, located 100km northwest of Jenné. The 1986/87 research program in that region, similar in methodology to their previous work in the Jenné region, was intended to gather comparable data on the material culture (especially the pottery) and the evolution of settlement patterns to be compared with the information already available on the Jenné region (Haskell et al. 1988). This study also yielded several important results, including the finding from the excavations at Shoma and Mara (both in the vicinity of Dia) of pottery assemblages similar to those of Jenné-jeno's Phase I/II, Phase III, and Phase IV, and the widespread existence of site clustering (Haskell et al. 1988). This similarity in material culture, in particular the pottery, and model of occupation dynamics (i.e. site clustering) strongly suggest a cultural interaction and integration between the Jenné and Dia regions that began as early as the first millennium BC (Haskell et al. 1988).

In summary, because of the extensive archaeological programs executed during the last two decades, the Inland Niger Delta is now the best understood region in Mali. The detailed stratigraphic information, supported by a reliable series of radiocarbon dates, provided by both the Bedaux team (Bedaux et al. 1978) and the McIntoshes (SK McIntosh & RJ McIntosh 1980; Haskell et al. 1988; SK McIntosh in press) make available a continuous occupation and cultural sequence of nearly two millennia (250 BC to AD 1400) for that region. In addition, the Inland Niger Delta is now established as one of the prime regions in West Africa where important developments such as the beginning of urbanism, interregional trade networks, and the rise of complex societies are demonstrated to have been indigenous developments and not due to foreign roots or stimulus as once believed (SK McIntosh & RJ McIntosh 1984). This finding is mostly attributed to the adoption of new research strategies, such as investigating sites not mentioned in any historical documents in lieu of attempting merely to substantiate the Arab textual material, as was the rule during colonial times.

The Méma

Unlike the Inland Niger Delta and the Lakes Region, and probably because of the remoteness and harsh living conditions, archaeological exploration in the Méma has remained sporadic through the 1980s. The Méma first attracted the attention of modern researchers in the 1930s when Urvoy, head hydrologist of the *Office du Niger* irrigation project, compiled a map of the area between Sokolo and Niafunké on which he located 80 tumuli (included in Figure 1.2). These are actually settlement mounds, but he assumed them to be funerary tumuli because of their morphological resemblance to the northern tumuli of the Lakes Region (Mauny1961). Christoforoff, another hydrologist of the ON, excavated two of those 'tumuli'; Kolima and Péhé, respectively located 22km east of Namapla, and on the bank of the Fala de Molodo. Those excavations consisted of huge trenches of at least 10×10m, dug at several sectors of the sites (Mauny 1961: 97). The extreme bias in the collecting and reporting of artifacts is evident: only 300 and 160 objects respectively were reported from Kolima and Péhé. These artifacts included statuettes of horsemen, glass beads, spearheads, multi-legged vessels, enameled pot sherds (from Kolima), cowrie shells (from Péhé) bronze bracelets and rings and iron arrowheads (Mauny 1961: 97). Christoforoff, an opportunistic archaeologist, showed no interest in other artifacts such as common potsherds, faunal materials, or in the sites' natural stratigraphy.

The same criticism applies to Szumowski in his research programs at several IA mounds, including Kolima, Péhé (in the Méma), Surinda, Diura, Fétékolé, and Severa-Lodé (between the Méma and the Inland Niger Delta) (Szumowski 1957). Unsystematic excavations at some of these mounds including Péhé (already excavated by Christoforoff), produced strong evidence of iron production, and cremated human burials uncovered either inside or outside funerary urns (Szumowski 1957). Interesting, however, is Szumowski's suggestion of cultural connections between the Méma and the Inland Delta (Szumowski 1957), due to the presence of similar burial practices and ceramic attributes, specifically the decorative motif *barakalé* (the McIntoshes' braided twine 1), in both areas.

More recent investigations in the Méma have also been confined to IA mounds. In the mid 1970s, the *Centre International pour le Dévéloppemment de l' Elevage en Afrique* (CIPEA) identified 700 putative archaeological sites on aerial photographs covering an area of 46,000km^2, located between latitude13°55'-16°00' north and longitude 4°30'- 6°41' west (CIPEA 1981: 11). Most of these sites, according to the CIPEA report (1981), were located in Méma (Figure 1.3). However, no ground truth-test was ever conducted to verify the validity of this aerial photograph survey. Subsequent excavations by Randi Haaland (1980) (funded by the CIPEA) at sites B-E on the bank of the Fala de Molodo in the southern part of the Méma were intended to assess the anthropogenic factors contributing to the deterioration of the environment in the Méma during the last millennium. Haaland's investigations at these sites produced strong evidence of intensive iron production that included the presence of a huge slag heap measuring 600m x 50m, and the remains of a bowl-like furnace at the surface of site B (Haaland 1980). She postulated that the principal forces behind this industrial-scale iron production of the Méma may be found in the growth of the political authority of Ghana, (Haaland 1980) of which the Méma was once a vassal. However, this is more suggestive than definitive, given the fact that no studies of the cultural materials were conducted. She also provided some stratigraphic information and C14 dates, which indicated that the sites were occupied between the ninth and twelfth centuries AD (Haaland 1980).

A team of French archaeologists (Fontes, Saliège, and Person) briefly visited the IA mound of Kolima in 1980 and collected wood charcoal samples for radiocarbon dating from the uppermost strata of that mound (Fontes et al. 1980; 1991). This produced a C14 date of 1280 AD -1310 AD (Fontes et al. 1980: 38; 1991: 35). However, there was no stratigraphic information for this site. A similarly uncorroborated fifth century date, obtained from wood charcoal samples collected from the lower levels of a deep ravine undercutting the deposits, was also available for the large habitation mound of Toladié (Raimbault 1986). However, as for Kolima, no stratigraphic information was available for this mound.

Geomorphological, Historical, and Archaeological Background

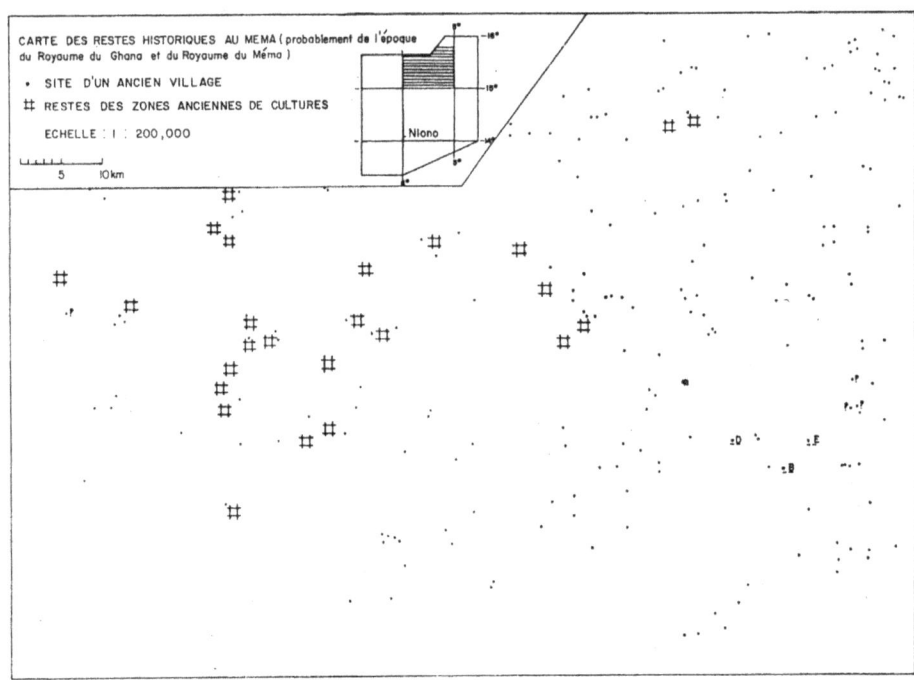

Figure 1.3. Putative archaeological sites identified in the Méma from aerial photographs by CIPEA (CIPEA 1980)

In 1984, the *Division du Patrimoine Culturel du Mali* (DPC) inventoried and published the list of 102 archeological sites (all apparently IA habitation mounds) in the Méma, and several hundred more in the Karery and Farimaké, respectively south and south-east of the Méma. As for the sites inventoried in the Lakes Region by the ISH, most of these sites were indicated by hired local informants (Raimbault & Togola 1991), which does not insure that these sites represent all sites or even all kinds of sites present in the Mema.

As for the IA, little was known about LSA occupation in the Méma. This period was represented by only two verified sites, Kobadi, a 360m long elongated midden located on levee slope on the bank of the ancient channel Bras de Nampala (Monod & Mauny 1957; Mauny 1961), and Tiabel Goudiodié, a low shell midden mound located on the bank of the Fala de Molodo (Guitat 1972). This site was again briefly visited by the DPC in 1984 (DPC 1985). A third possible LSA site, Kolima Sud, near the IA mound of Kolima excavated earlier in this century by Christoforoff, was mentioned in passing by Raimbault and Sidibé (1984). However no other details or description were available for this site. Of these LSA sites, only Kobadi had been the object of some preliminary archaeological investigations, including surface collection in 1955 by Monod and Mauny (Monod & Mauny 1957) and shallow test pits at several locations of both the levee and the midden in 1986, 1987, and 1989 by Raimbault (Raimbault et al. 1987; 1990). These preliminary investigations revealed the presence of nearly one hundred burials (all in the midden), and yielded abundant remains of fish, large aquatic fauna, and a few bones of domestic cattle, as well as bone harpoons, ground stones and ceramics with strong affinities to those of the Saharan LSA (Monod & Mauny 1957; Raimbault et al. 1987). Anthropological analysis on numerous skeletons from Kobadi showed close affinities to African *cromagnoid* populations present in the Sahara around 7000 BP (Raimbault et al. 1991: 631-32). This, together with the radiocarbon dates, the faunal remains, and the artifacts, strongly suggests that Kobadi illustrates the southerly movements and adaptations of LSA pastoralist/hunting/ gathering populations documented at other sites like Karkarichinkat (Smith 1979), and Dhar Tichitt (Munson 1976; Holl 1985).

This overview of the various archaeological projects undertaken in and around the Méma shows how little archaeological research has contributed to the history of the area. Only a limited number of Iron Age sites have been the object of excavations. The sparse information available from these various programs illustrates their highly selective character. Thus, the range of archaeological sites present in the area, and how they vary with regard to size, surface features and artifacts, and location on different landforms was unknown. No information on chronological and functional differences among the IA sites was available. Unlike the Inland Niger Delta, where we now possess a continuous stratigraphic and cultural sequences of nearly two millennia, there was no sequence of artifacts for any IA sites of the Méma at the time the research discussed here was begun.

CHAPTER 2
RESEARCH DESIGN AND OBJECTIVES

Due to the dearth of information on both the history and archaeology of Méma, the Méma archaeological research program was designed as an exploratory inquiry. The primary objective of the archaeological research program executed from December 1989 to June 1990 was to collect basic data that will permit a preliminary analysis of settlement pattern and radiocarbon and ceramic chronology as well as a careful description of the material culture of the Méma during the Iron Age (IA). Research comprised two components: a) a regional site survey and b) the excavations at the IA site complex of Akumbu. These two components were intended to complement each other. They also had the broad common goal to collect basic information from which future research questions and research strategies could be derived.

The specific survey and excavation methodologies were developed to begin the process of answering the unresolved questions of Méma prehistory and early history. Of fundamental importance was the question of the kinds of archaeological sites present in the Méma, their chronology and distribution within the landscape. To answer this question, we needed to develop a survey of regional scope that would gather basic data on the nature, location, and distribution of archaeological sites (of all periods) in relation to the different geomorphological zones of the Méma. The chronology of iron technology and the nature of the LSA/IA transition were also of prime concern. To answer this question, we needed sites at the very end of the LSA and very beginning of the IA (and, with luck, sites with the transition in undisturbed stratigraphic position), in order to see changes in relation to landforms, water resources, or other critical resources (such as ore or fuel for the smelt). Hence, we needed to establish a preliminary chronology for the surveyed sites by correlating their surface assemblages with archaeological material from the excavation and to document the nature and patterns of occupation in the Méma at various stages of its history. What was the way of life (economy, environmental preferences) of the early IA populations and how did this change through time? What were their occupations, industries and trade connections? These are questions of ecological adaptation and economy that require excavation at deeply stratified sites, as well as inferential data derived from changes in settlement pattern over time. What were the reasons for population density decline, at least in the early historic period? To answer this, one needs to document changing landform preferences and basic fluvial geomorphology as evidence of changing climatic and environmental conditions. Finally, is there evidence for increasing social complexity, towns and state formation? Here we must be attentive in survey to changes in distribution of site sizes, types of materials found on their surface and the nature of relations between sites.

The first component of the research program is the regional site survey. As argued in the preceding chapter, previous archaeological surveys conducted in the area have concentrated on the inventory of sites identified by local informants, without evaluating the extent to which these sites represent the full range of sites present in the Méma. Consequently, no description of the settlement patterns in the Méma and their evolution through time with reference to landforms is yet available.

The presence of 80 mounds (interpreted as funeral tumuli) between Sokolo and Niafunké, was signaled in the 1930s by the hydrologists of the Office du Niger (ON) (Mauny 1961: 97). As demonstrated by Cristoforoff's later excavations at Kolima and Péhé, the rationale behind the effort of the hydrologists of the ON was to find sites thought to contain museum objects. A more recent effort at site discovery in the area was based on an aerial photo survey by the CIPEA (1981), but was not accompanied by a ground reconnaissance. Raimbault and Togola (1991) relied on information provided by local informants. Such research strategies concentrate on the most visible sites and fail to discover the small sites, generally not noticed by local populations. It is thus not surprising that by the time this research program began, the LSA in the Méma (generally characterized by small and shallow stratified sites) was represented by only Kobadi and Tiabel Goudiodié briefly visited by the DPC (1985) and Raimbault (1986). In neighboring regions, only the surveys executed by the McIntoshes in the Upper Niger Delta (SK McIntosh & RJ McIntosh 1980; Haskell et al. 1988) and in the Niger Bend (SK McIntosh and RJ McIntosh 1986) had been conducted at both a regional scale and according to rigorous sampling schemes.

The ideal survey of settlement is one conducted without bias (that is, nothing in the research design prevents sites of a particular type from being recorded) and with a view to ensuring representativeness. The survey strategy that insures the most accurate discovery of site population within a region is a 100% prospection, or a meter by meter search of an entire region (Binford 1964; Fish and Kowalewski 1990). However, rarely are funds and manpower available for such an undertaking. Fortunately, partial prospections that use sophisticated sampling schemes based on mathematical theories of probability at all levels of data collection allow one to obtain adequate and representative data useful in the study of cultural process (Binford 1964; Mueller 1975). One suggested approach is to stratify the survey region on the basis of ecological criteria (e.i., soil types or geomorphological landforms) (Binford 1964). Within each ecological zone, the location of sample units to be searched for cultural remains are then selected by a randomization procedure (usually, the use of a random number table). However, it should be noted that there is no widespread agreement among archaeologists about what sampling strategy is the most efficient. Indeed, Redman (1974) stresses that the sampling strategy should be chosen in accordance with the archaeologist's goals, and the type of terrain to be investigated. Because of the limited prior information about types and location of sites in the Méma, we adopted a survey methology that was not randomized, but which gave maximum information given the logistical problems of doing research in the Méma. I primarily wanted to conduct the survey at a regional scale, sampling all major geomorphological zones and landforms present in the region, and recording all types of sites encountered.

The sample units, which cross-cut the various geomorphological zones, were judgmentally selected and ran from known villages. They were one kilometer wide and of variable length (from 10 to 40 kilometers). Undeniably, this judgmental strategy is less preferable than a statistically random strategy. However, we hoped that partitioning the study area with numerous long (though narrow) transects across the various environmental zones would be productive for site discovery. We also believed that important shifts in the settlement pattern and landform preferences through time certainly occurred in the Méma. Therefore, we hoped that the sample units, given their distribution across the various geomorphological zones, would allow us to obtain reliable samples of most of the site types present in the Méma. The principal logistical reason for using long narrow transects was that those maximized the use of the field vehicle, which we had use of for a limited period and for which fuel was very expensive. Other reasons for using judgement sample units rather than a statistically random strategy included the limited number of personnel (we had a survey crew of only two), and the difficulty of orienting ourselves in the flat landscape of the Méma Sahelian zone (which lacks any landmarks).

The procedures and results of the regional survey are reported in Chapter 3. During survey we also selected a cluster of sites for excavation. The excavations at this mound complex, locally known as Akumbu, was the second component of the research program. This mound complex, with deeply stratified deposits, promised to yield a long sequence of human occupation (spanning possibly the LSA to the middle IA). It was selected for excavation for several reasons: **1**: Its size (it was, after Toladié, in the east of the study area, the second largest mound complex encountered during the survey; **2**: Its importance to the oral traditions that links it, as mentioned above, to the creation and development of the Soninké medieval Empire of Ghana (DPC 1985); **3**: The presence of concentrations of LSA materials (especially pottery) found on the flanks of the degraded dune that runs beneath Akumbu B, suggested that the Akumbu mound complex might yield evidence of continuous occupation extending back in time to the LSA; and **4**: The relative proximity of the site to the excavation team's home base of Nampala.

Understanding a site of Akumbu's size in a very limited time (only two months were devoted to the excavation component of the research program) was clearly difficult. Therefore, our primary objectives in the excavations were the recovery of artifact sequences (particularly pottery) anchored by absolute radiocarbon dates. These artifact sequences could be used to verify and expand upon the information in the dating of the sites surface-collected in the course of the regional survey. We also hoped that the collection of paleobotanical and faunal data from a stratigraphic context might shed some light on climatological and environmental changes (in particular the desiccation of Fala of Molodo) and their impact on human occupation in the Méma during the IA. Also, the retrieval of chronologically-grounded data illuminating trade or other contacts between the Méma and other regions of the Middle Niger or elsewhere was an important goal of the excavations.

Because of the preliminary nature of the research program and the pressure of time as well as the restricted number of qualified personnel (only three unit supervisors were available), we opted for small test units, controllable in the limited period devoted to the excavation phase. In total, four limited excavation units were opened. These four test pits, one 1m x 1m, two 2m x 2m and one 2m x 3m, were judgmentally placed on various parts of Akumbu A, and B and on the area with scatters of LSA artifacts. Thus, only 15 square meters of the Akumbu mound complex surface were penetrated by excavations during this first and exploratory mission. The results of these excavations are reported in Chapter 4.

CHAPTER 3
THE REGIONAL SITE SURVEY

I: SURVEY METHODOLOGIES

The regional survey, executed in December 1989 and February 1990 by myself and K. MacDonald (a Cambridge graduate student), was conducted on the western fringe of the Méma floodplain, and over a block of 25km east-west by 50km north-south (Figure 3.1). This survey block contained two major known IA mounds: Akumbu (whose founding is linked by the Soninké traditions to the rise of the medieval empire of Wagadu), and Kolima (excavated by Christoforoff in the 1930s), and the known LSA site of Kobadi. Kobadi has been subjected to surface collection by Monod and Mauny in the 1950s (Monod & Mauny 1957) and shallow test pits by Raimbault (1986; 1987; 1991). The survey block was covered by topographic a map *(Feuille de Nampala* - ND 30 XIX) of scale 1: 200, 000, and a series aerial photographs of scale 1:50,000 *(*Series MAL1975). These were obtained from the agency of the *Institut Géographique National* in Bamako. The survey within this block was conducted on explicit, but not randomized sample basis. The sample units were one kilometer wide transects placed approximately four kilometers apart. As noted above, orienting ourselves, thus plotting accurately the sites, turned out to be a major problem in the flat landscape of the Méma Sahelian zone (which lacks any landmarks). We decided to run the transects north-south from present-day villages indicated on the topographic map. These transects crosscut all the major geomorphological zones of the area. These landforms, tentatively identified from examination of aerial photographs, topographic maps and observations of terrain during the survey, have been already discussed in the section devoted to the geomorphology (Figure 1.2). Among these various geomorphological features, only the backswamp occupying the easternmost sector of the Méma floodplain could not be investigated due to time limitations.

The sample area constitutes approximately 20% of the main survey block. We also surveyed 100% of the area within a five kilometer radius around Akumbu, where excavations were conducted. This intensive survey around Akumbu was intended to elucidate the nature and evolution of human occupation in the hinterland of this expanded mound complex. Two additional surveys were conducted on a narrow and ancient river channel leading toward the Mauritanian Hodh from the Méma's ancient floodplain and on the southern edge of the Boulel Ridge and the banks of Fala de Molodo, where Haaland (1980) excavated intensive iron smelting sites in 1978. Our primary interest in this second separate survey block was to examine the known slag accumulation (associated with remains of smelting furnaces) outside the village of Boulel, the IA mound of Péhé, and the and the vicinities of these sites. Site specific survey was also conducted at the known LSA site of Tiabel Goudiodié (on the Fala de Molodo), and the LSA sites of Nampala and Diaguina, all discovered by chance.

Due the size of the area to be covered, the limited time available and the limited number of personel, the survey was conducted by four-wheel-drive vehicle. Except along the Boulel ridge, which is covered by dense acacia scrub (and where foot survey was necessary), both cross-country driving conditions and visibility were superb in the Méma. In the dry season, the soil is consolidated and there is almost no ground cover to hide archaeological remains. Within the transects, all terrain within a distance of approximately 500m on either side of the vehicle was examined to detect archaeological sites. Significant scatters of artifacts and clustered features, such as remains of smelting furnaces, could be detected within this distance due to the good visibility and the fact that the soil was clear of vegetation. This was particularly true for levees, where these types of sites were more likely to be found. All archaeological sites discovered were thoroughly walked and recorded in terms of their location, size, surface features, and the type of landform on which they were situated. For each site, the presence of surface artifacts, such as ground stones, iron slag, iron objects, and other miscellaneous artifacts was noted. At all the LSA sites and at more than 75% of IA sites identified we conducted intensive surface pottery collection. This involved collecting all ceramics from one or a series (depending of the size of the sites), of 2m x 2m squares judgmentally placed at different parts of the sites. Additionally, preferential general surface collection was made at each site surface collected. For sites at which pottery collection was not executed, the characteristics of the pottery were noted. The pottery collected at the site surfaces were later recorded in terms of various ceramic attributes, which were compared with those of the radiocarbon dated pottery from the excavations at Akumbu mound complex. This process, supplemented by noting the absence or presence of *fossile directeurs* or time marker artifacts, such as tobacco pipe fragments, was intended to establish a gross relative chronology for the sites identified during the survey.

II: RESULTS OF THE SURVEY

In total, 137 archaeological sites were identified and recorded within the study area. These included 28 LSA sites, characterized by the presence of stone artifacts, concentrations of animal bones, ceramics, and the lack of any metallurgical evidence. These LSA sites are being analyzed by H. Haskell in her project on the LSA occupation and transition between LSA and IA in the Méma. The far more numerous IA sites, comprised 109 sites, including 94 habitation mounds, 15 iron slag concentrations associated with remains of smelting furnaces and tuyeres, and two urn fields (see Appendix 2). The overwhelming first impression of the habitation mounds was of their morphological resemblance to the *tells* of the deeper basins of the Middle

The Regional Site Survey

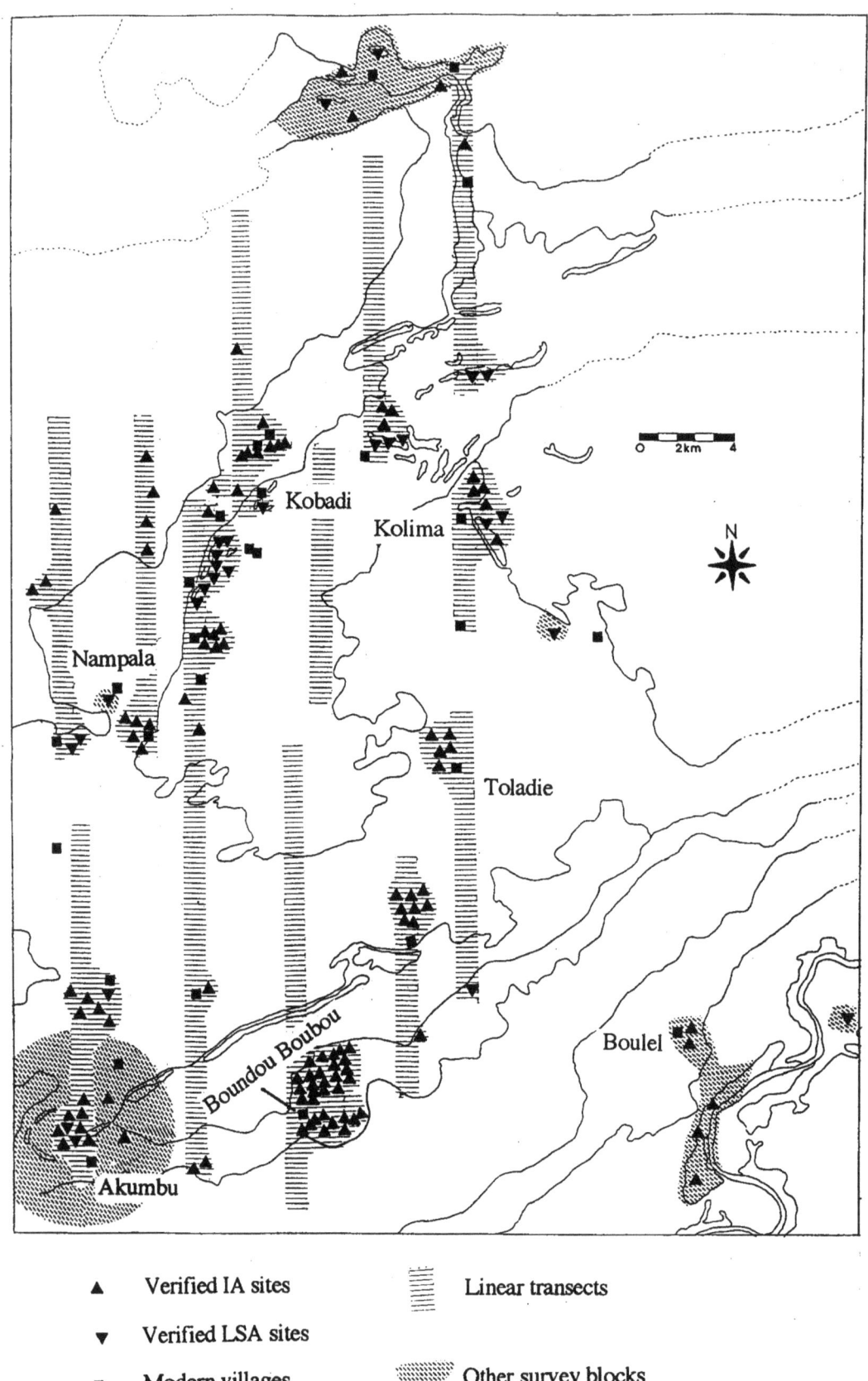

Figure 3.1: Verified archaeological sites

Niger, with dense scatters of fragments of ceramic and other artifacts such as iron slag covering their surface.

Site chronology

As already noted, an approximate and relative chronology for the sites uncovered during the survey was provided by comparison of their surface pottery with pottery from the excavations, and by the presence of a time marker artifact, i.e., tobacco pipe fragments. These crude processes remain for the moment the only means of dating the sites within the survey area and limit the precision of any phase chronology. More than 90% of the IA sites recorded whose pottery characteristics were noted during the survey could be assigned to one the three pottery assemblages (Early, Middle, and Late) described in the chapter on the pottery.

A total of 49, or more than 50% of the IA habitation sites, displayed Early Assemblage pottery on their surface. This suggests that the final occupation at these sites occurred in the mid-first millennium AD. As already noted, a fifth century radiocarbon date obtained at AK3 was associated with a deposit containing numerous elements of Early Assemblage. Since no site with Early Assemblage ceramics on the surface was excavated, the duration of occupation at these sites has yet to be determined. However, a hint that their occupation may extend back in time several more centuries, and possibly to LSA deposits, is given by their thick cultural deposits of up to 5m.

Sites with Middle Assemblage pottery numbered 31, or 35% of IA habitation sites. The final occupation at these sites can be situated at the end of the first millennium AD or the beginning of the second millennium AD. This is indicated by the series of radiocarbon dates, 648±48 BP (cal AD 1274-1401), 910±50 BP (cal AD 1024-1183), and 1160±100 BP (cal AD 780-1100) associated with Middle Assemblage levels and obtained in the upper levels at AK1, AK4, and AK3, respectively. A thirteenth century AD date was also obtained from the uppermost levels of Kolima located in the eastern part of the survey area by Fontes et al in 1980 (1980; 1991: 35). As most Middle Assemblage sites were large mounds extending to several hectares, a progressive abandonment spanning several centuries is hypothetical, but has yet to be substantiated by more excavations.

Late Assemblage sites, the least numerous, numbered eight sites. Because of the presence of numerous fragments of tobacco pipe on their surface, these sites were dated to the post-sixteenth century. As already noted, the tobacco pipe was introduced in the Western Sudan only after 1591 (Mauny 1961). The shallowness of the cultural deposits at Late Assemblage sites indicated a short period of occupation for those sites.

Clustered sites

The phenomenon of site clustering appears to be prevalent in many regions of the Middle Niger. It has been reported from the Lake region since the turn of this century by

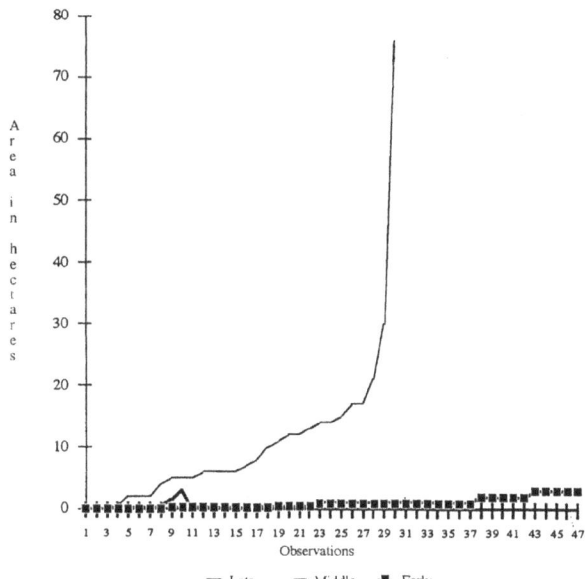

Figure 3.2. Méma site size distributions

Desplagnes (Desplagnes 1907: 55), and in recent decades by several authors (Mauny 1961: 104-107; Dembelé 1991: 63, 174-184; Schmit 1986: 4). It has also been signaled from the southern Middle Niger by Szumowski (Szumowski 1954: 107) and more recently by the McIntoshes (SKMcIntosh & RJ McIntosh 1980; Haskell et al, 1988).

In the Méma, clustering was a notable aspect of site distribution. Over 3/4 or 88 of the IA sites encountered during the survey occurred within 13 clusters or groups of sites, compared to 20 isolated IA sites. This phenomenon of site clustering in the Méma was already in expression during the LSA (Figure 3.2). Within clusters, each component was spatially separated from the other members. Each component was recorded as a separate site. This method, already employed by the McIntoshes in their reconnaissances in the Inland Niger Delta and the Niger Bend (SK McIntosh & RJ McIntosh, 1980; 1986; Haskell et al. 1988), facilitates the examination of the interrelationship between the different members of a cluster in terms of size, chronology, and function.

The various site clusters encountered during the Méma survey are presented in Table 3.1. This table, however, provides only the number of sites, with no chronological differentiation between sites within the clusters. Those data are presented in another section of this chapter. Among the Méma site clusters, the most common expression tended to consist of a major site surrounded by smaller satellite mounds. This was encountered in six clusters, Goudourou, Akumbu (Figure 3.3), Bourgou Silatigui (Figure 3.4), Toulé and Boundou Boubou North (Figure 3.5), and Toladié and Kolima (Figure 3.7). A second tendency of clustering was a constellation of several small mounds all of roughly the same size. Examples of this expression was found at Niakaré Dndondi (on the Bras de Nampala), Niessouma (Figure 1.2), and Boundou Boubou South. A third model also encountered was the pairing of two sites of almost

The Regional Site Survey

Clusters	< 1 ha	1-5	6-10	10-20	> 20	Total	Landforms/soil types
Goudourou	2	2	-	1	-	5	Bras de Nampala
T. Famé	-	2	-	-	-	2	Longitudinal dunes
Toulé	-	3	1	1	-	5	Degraded dunes
Akumbu	5	1	1	-	1	8	Niakane Maudo
N. Ndondi	3	3	-	-	-	6	Bras de Nampala
Bourgou S	4	1	-	1	-	6	Bras de Nampala
874 - 1&2	-	2	-	-	-	2	Iron pan peneplain
BB south	4	6	-	-	-	10	Iron pan peneplain/Niakéné Maudo
BB north	11	9	-	1	-	21	Niakéné Maoudo/iron
Bérétouma	1	-	-	2	-	3	Bras de Nampala
Niessouma	3	6	-	-	-	9	Niakéné Maoudo
Kolima	3	-	1	1	-	5	Bras de Nampala

Table 3.1. Various Iron Age site clusters

equal size. This model was represented by Tiabel Famé (consisting of two post 16th century small sites located within the longitudinal dune system), and 874-1 and 874-2 (within the iron pan peneplain).

Among the different components of most clusters, the broad period of abandonment, suggested by surface materials, appeared to have been generally, but not entirely, contemporaneous. Within clusters, the larger sites appear to have been abandoned at a later time than the small ones. This was particularly true for the Kolima, Goudourou, and Toulé clusters. Within each of these clusters, one to two small sites tended to have been abandoned early, as they displayed Early Assemblage pottery at their surface (Table 3.2). Opposed to this model however were the Akumbu, Toladié and Bérétouma clusters, where all the sites (small and large) had some Middle Assemblage material on their surface. The number of sites abandoned during the period of Early Assemblage increases strikingly to nearly 4/5 within the clusters of Bourgou Silatigui, Boundou Boubou south, Boundou Boundou north and Niakaré Ndondi. At Niessouma, all the sites were abandoned during that period. Again, within the first three clusters, only the relatively large sites appear to have been occupied after the period of the Early Assemblage. The case of Niakaré Ndondi is particularly interesting. Within this cluster, only one site, Niakaré Ndondi A, displayed Late Assemblage pottery, dated to the post sixteenth century. This was certainly the result of a reoccupation of the site after its abandonment during the period of the Early Assemblage. The paired sites of Tiabel Famé, appear to be contemporaneous, as they both displayed Late Assemblage pottery, associated with fragments of tobacco pipe. The other paired sites, 874-1, and 874-2, both with Early Assemblage materials, also appeared to have been abandoned roughly simultaneously.

With the exception of iron smelting sites (discussed further in this chapter), site function within clusters was not revealed by surface artifacts. Unexpectedly, surface material, with the exception of ceramics, ground stones, and slag, was light in distribution (see Appendix 2). This situation is similar to the Timbuktu and Dia regions, but fundamentally different from the Jenné region, where overall surface artifacts and features indicated functionally distinct sites within clusters. In that region, the pattern is interpreted as evidence that small sites were occupied by different ethnic or specialist groups and larger sites by several integrated specialist or corporate groups (RJ McIntosh & SK McIntosh 1983: 42-44; SK McIntosh & RJ McIntosh 1984: 89). R.J. McIntosh (1991) argues that this spatial separation may have been a means of dealing with the pluralism (presence of several corporate or specialist groups) and ethnic heterogeneity in the region, and the conflicting needs for functional integration by an increasing number of specialist groups. The occupation of physically separate sites would have enabled specialist communities to maintain their own identities and exploit the proximity to their clients and suppliers (RJ McIntosh & SK McIntosh 1988; RJ McIntosh, 1991). Unfortunately, the scarcity of surface remains (other than pottery, groundstone and slag) sites does not allow us to extend this hypothesis to the Méma surveyed sites.

Site size distributions

A comparison of site size distributions for each assemblage period reveals remarkable shifts in site sizes through time (Figure 3.2). Occupation of small settlements appeared to have been the rule during the period of Early Assemblage. Sites dated to that period, generally measuring less than 1 ha, are commonly found within packed clusters, such as Boundou Boubou south, Boundou Boubou north, Niessouma (along the Niakéné Maoudo or at its contact with the iron pan peneplain), Niakaré Ndondi, and Bourgou Silatigui (along the Bras de Nampala). In the period of the Middle Assemblage, settlements became more concentrated and restricted to relatively large mounds. Most sites dated to that period fall within the range of 10-20 ha (Figure 3.2). Toladié A, by far the largest site, measures nearly 80 ha. It is followed by Péhé (on the bank of the Fala de Molodo),

Archaeological Investigations of Iron Age Sites in the Mema Region, Mali (West Africa)

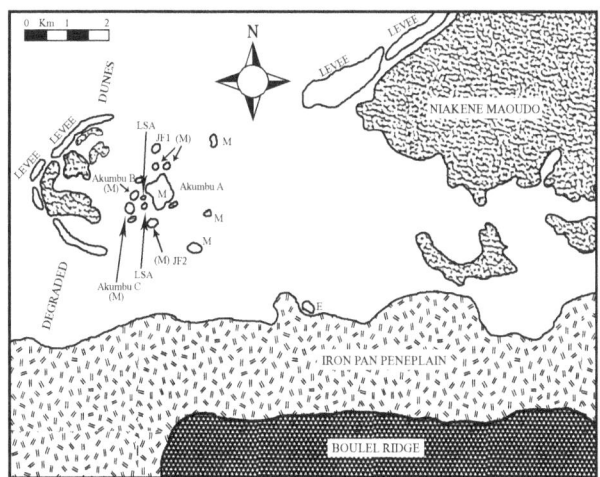

Figure 3.3. Sites and landforms on air photo MAL.75 IGN 872.

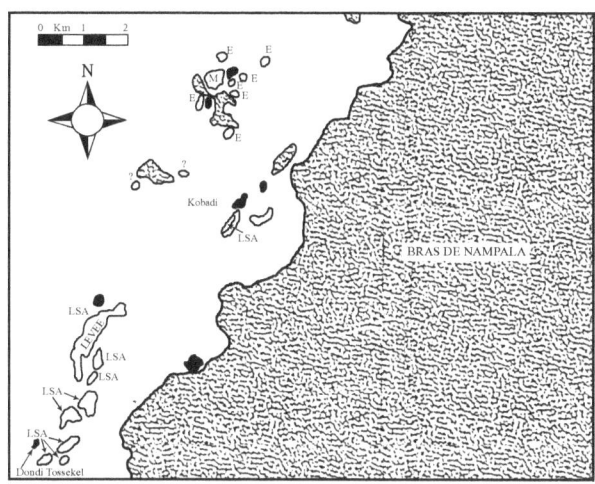

Figure 3.4. Sites and landforms on air photo MAL.75 IGN 1119.

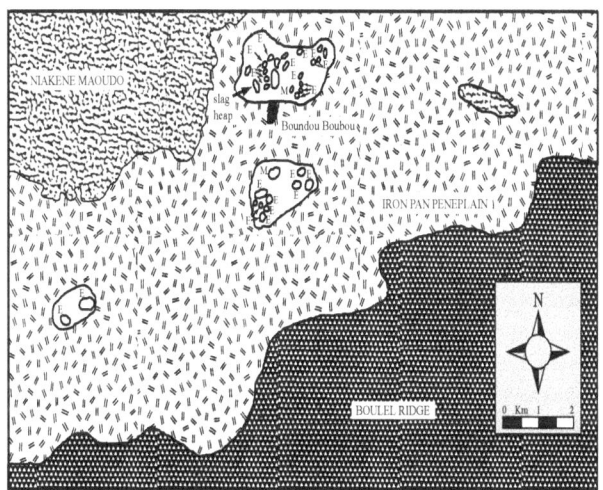

Figure 3.5. Sites and landforms on air photo MAL.75 IGN 874.

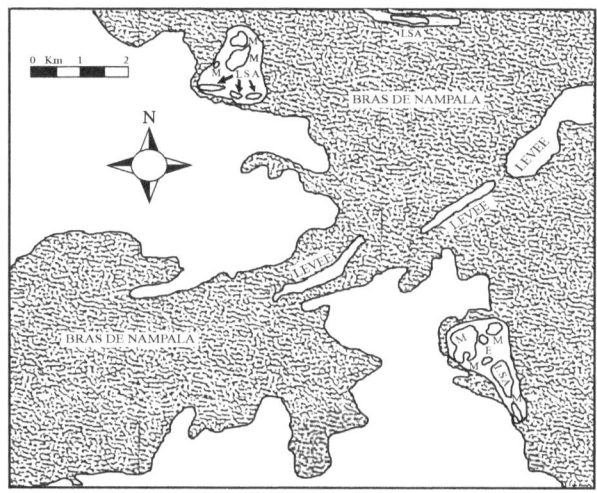

Figure 3.6. Sites and landforms on air photo MAL.75 IGN 1121.

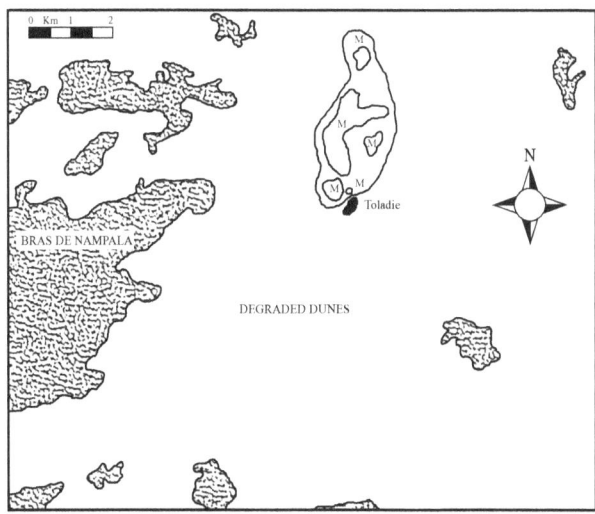

Figure 3.7. Sites and landforms on air photo MAL.75 IGN 998.

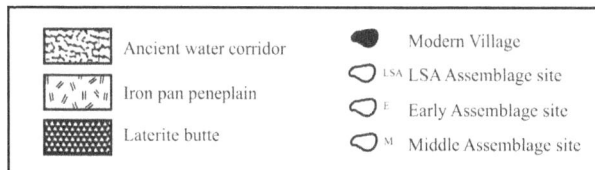

The Regional Site Survey

Table 3.2. Site chronology within site clusters

Clusters (ha.)	Late	Middle	Early	Uncertain
Goudourou				
<1	-	-	1	1
1-5	-	2	-	-
6-10	-	-	-	-
11-20	1	-	-	-
>20	-	-	-	-
Tiabel Famé				
<1	-	-	-	-
1-5	2	-	-	-
6-10	-	-	-	-
11-20	-	-	-	-
>20	-	-	-	-
Toulé				
<1	-	-	-	-
1-5	-	4	1	-
6-10	-	-	-	-
11-20	-	-	-	-
>20	-	-	-	-
Akumbu				
<1	-	3	-	1
1-5	-	1	-	-
6-10	-	1	-	-
11-20	-	-	-	-
>20	-	1	-	-
Niakaré Ndondi				
<1	-	-	2	1
1-5	1	-	2	-
6-10	-	-	-	-
11-20	-	-	-	-
>20	-	-	-	-
Bourgou Silatigui				
<1	-	-	5	1
1-5	-	-	-	-
6-10	-	-	-	-
11-20	-	1	-	-
>20	-	-	-	-
874-1 & 874-2				
<1	-	-	-	-
1-5	-	-	2	-
6-10	-	-	-	-
11-20	-	-	-	-
>20	-	-	-	-
BB north				
<1	-	-	10	1
1-5	-	-	8	1
6-10	-	-	-	-
11-20	-	1	-	-
>20	-	-	-	-
BB south				
<1	-	-	4	-
1-5	-	1	5	-
6-10	-	-	-	-
11-20	-	-	-	-
>20	-	-	-	-
Bérétouma				
<1	-	1	-	-
1-5	-	-	-	-
6-10	-	-	-	-
11-20	-	2	-	-
>20	-	-	-	-
Niessouma				
<1	-	-	3	-
1-5	-	-	6	-
6-10	-	-	-	-
11-20	-	-	-	-
>20	-	-	-	-
Kolima				
<1	-	-	1	2
1-5	-	-	-	-
6-10	-	1	-	-
11-20	-	1	-	-
>20	-	-	-	-
Toladie				
<1	-	1	-	-
1-5	-	-	-	-
6-10	-	2	-	-
11-20	-	1	-	-
>20	-	1	-	-

measuring 30 ha, and Akumbu A (at the westernmost end of the Niakéné Maoudo) measuring 21 ha. During the Late Assemblage period, occupation in the Méma was the most reduced. Only a handful of small sites, measuring between 0.1 ha to 3 ha, show indication of ephemeral occupation.

Surface artifacts and surface features
The various artifacts types and features occurring at the site surface are listed by site in Appendix 2. As already noted, pottery, iron slag, and groundstones were the most common artifacts and found at the surface of virtually all the IA sites. Despite the high frequency of slag, no direct evidence of iron smelting or smithing in form of furnace remains or tuyeres was found on any of the habitation mounds. However, as discussed below, a total of nine mounds or mound clusters were associated with iron smelting sites, characterized by slag concentrations and furnace remains. Miscellaneous artifacts, such as iron objects, copper, spindle whorls and beads (all present in the excavations at Akumbu mound complex) were less common (see Appendix 2). The spotty distribution of these artifacts may be partly attributable to the widespread looting by modern populations, especially the Fulani and Maure herders, who use many of the mounds as camp sites during the rainy season. Fragments of tobacco pipes, historically known to have been introduced in the Western Sudan in late sixteenth century AD, were found on the surface of only eight sites.

The various features recorded included burnt clay structures, outlines of mud walls, and urn remains. The burnt clay structures, the most significant feature, were circular or semi-circular structures (1.50-2.00m in diameter approximately), with short burnt clay or brick wall always associated with demarcated burnt and hardened soil. They clustered or occurred in isolation at the surface of 24 (<25%) of the surveyed habitation mounds. Two examples of these structures, excavated at the site of AK4, and in Unit AK1, were radiocarbon dated to cal AD 985-1160 and cal AD 1024-1183, respectively. These two excavated burnt clay structures were interpreted as ovens or hearths because of the thick ash deposit filling their interior and the deliberate firing and hardening of their floor. The correlation between absolute site size and presence of burnt clay features was not discernible. However, larger mounds tended to have more of these features than small ones. Of the 24 mounds with burnt clay structures, there were 16 Middle Assemblage sites and eight Early Assemblage sites. No Late Assemblage site yielded a burnt clay structure, suggesting that the tradition of building these structures ended with the abandonment of the Middle Assemblage sites. Burnt features have also been signaled from the funerary tumuli Koy Gourey, El Oualaji (Desplagnes 1907), Kouga (Mauny 1961), and more recently from the tumulus associated with the megalith concentration of Tondidarou (Fontes et al. 1991), and many of the habitation mounds surveyed by the *Projet Inventaire des sites archaeologiques du Mali* (Dembélé 1986, 1991; Schmit 1986; Raimbault and Sidibé 1991).

Remains of urns were visible at the surface of only six mounds. The two sites with the most significant number of urns (Akumbu jar field #1 and Akumbu jar field #2) had suffered severe damage because of pot hunting or recent use as a seasonal cattle kraal. At the remaining four, Toulé B, Akumbu C, Boundou Boubou north K, and Péhé, the urns were rather occasional and were always eroding from ravines.

Only seven habitation mounds displayed architectural remnants at their surface (Appendix 2). Most of these consisted of outlines of rectilinear mud walls or rounded house foundations. Four mounds (all within the Niessouma mound complex) were distinctively surrounded by the foundations of serpentine mud walls. Given the small size of these sites (>2 ha), these serpentine walls may be compound walls. The scarcity of architectural remains was certainly due to weathering, especially melting of mud walls, which, as indicated by the excavations at Akumbu mound complex, were probably prevalent. Abundant laterite pebbles covered the surface of many of the mounds within the Niessouma, Boundou Boubou south, Boundou Boubou north, and 874-1 and 874-2 clusters. These pebbles were probably deposited after the matrix of the mud walls in which they were placed had been melted by rain. Presence of similar gravel concentrations has been reported from Hamdallahi (Gallay et al. 1990), and many of the habitation sites of the Middle Sénégal Valley (Chavane et al. 1986; S.K. McIntosh, personal communication).

Site function and industry
It was difficult to discern site function because of the paucity of small finds (other than the common artifacts such as grinding stones and iron slag). Notable exceptions, however, were two urn fields and 15 iron smelting sites. The two urn fields (872-9 and 872-11), both encountered in the vicinity of Akumbu A, consisted of small, low mounds exhibiting at their surface the remains of large vessels with thickened walls. Though there was no evidence in the form of human bones, both sites are interpreted as cemeteries.

All the 15 iron production sites recognized during the survey were characterized by slag concentrations, associated with remains of furnaces, and tuyeres. Most of these sites were found on the outskirts of mounds or mound clusters such as Boundou Bounbou north (with three), Akumbu (with two), Kolima (with two), Goudourou, Bourgou Silatigui, Niakaré Ndondi, and Ndoupa (each with one). The remaining four were isolated, with no apparent association with any habitation mound. All of these iron producing sites consisted of clusters of crescentic lumps of slag, associated with tuyere remains and the remnants or the outline of the furnace at the center. The two largest iron producing sites, 874-30 (near Boundou Boubou mound complex), and 913-1 (near the village of Boulel) covered roughly 1 ha, and 7 ha, respectively. At each of these sites, the remains or outline of more than 100 furnaces were visible. The slag remains at those two sites were very distinctive. Instead of occurring in bits and pieces like at the other sites, slag was massive (approximately 0.50m in diameter) and hemispherical and appears to fit the bottom of the furnace. Though this may indicate that different types of furnace or smelting techniques were present in the Méma, it cannot be substantiated without excavations.

Both the number of sites, and the considerable dimensions of the slag concentration at some of them, denote large-scale iron production. This extensive iron production, also documented at site B-E on the bank of the Fala by Randi Haaland, was certainly due to proximity of the Boulel Ridge, a laterite ferrigenous butte that crosses the southern part of the Méma. Excavation at the Akumbu mound complex showed that iron technology was already in place in the the Méma by the mid-first millennium. Pieces of slag were present in the lower excavated levels of AK3 and associated with the earliest radiocarbon date (cal AD 342-442) obtained during the excavation. All Early Assemblage sites were also covered with slag. However, the beginning of iron production in the Méma, and its chronological evolution to an industrial scale have still to be demonstrated.

This intensive iron industry certainly played an important role in the Méma economy. Randi Haaland (Haaland, 1980) hypothesizes that the growth of the empire of Ghana, a political authority that flourished at the end of the first millennium AD and which vassalized many regions of the Western Sudan, including the Méma, helped stimulate the Méma industrial iron production. Other forces behind the large scale iron production of the Méma may be found in the cultural connection and regional trade developed in the Middle Niger as early as the mid-first millennium AD (SK McIntosh & RJ McIntosh 1980). The participation of the Méma in this formal interaction between the various regions of the Middle Niger is now demonstrated. Many of the same ceramic attributes (in particular the braided twines, and polychrome painted wares) of Jenne-jeno Phase III and Phase IV, and the 4th-8th century sequence of KNT 2 in the Lakes Région are present in the Méma Middle Assemblage. Because of the presence of the laterite and ferrugeneous deposits of the Boulel Ridge, the Méma may have specialized in industrial iron production and interacted formally with other regions of the Middle Niger. For example, nowhere in the deltaic plain of the Upper Inland Delta is there a deposit of high grade iron ore (SK McIntosh & RJ McIntosh 1980).

Correlation between landforms and site distributions
A correlation between landforms and sites shows that, chronologically, there was a great difference in occupation within the various landforms (see Figure 1.2). During the period of Early Assemblage, the bank of water corridors or their juncture with other landforms appeared to have been the most favored by human occupation. Most Early Assemblage sites (75%, n=36) were found narrowly concentrated within a distance of 2km from the Niakéné Maoudo (see Fig.1.1). A total of 11 other sites from that period were found on the bank of the Bras de Nampala, further north. Although the evidence is yet lacking, the preferential location of these many Early Assemblage sites along water corridors may be linked to the availability of permanent water or farmland for rice cultivation. The two large clusters of Boundou Boubou south and Boundou Boubou north, which comprises the majority of the Early Assemblage sites, may also have enjoyed both the water resources of the now defunct Niakéné Maoudo and the iron ore deposits of both the iron pan peneplain and the nearby Boulel Ridge.

During the period of occupation of these sites, the water corridors whose banks they lined certainly carried water permanently. The abandonment of these many Early Assemblage sites around the mid-first millennium may be a hint of early desiccation or strangulation of some of the waterways. The Niakéné Maoudo, with the highest number of Early sites, seems to have been the most affected by this phenomenon. Further indication in support of this hypothesis is provided by the absence of any fishing implements (net weight), the puzzling paucity of fish and other aquatic animal remains (see Appendix 1) from the sites referable to the period from the fifth century AD to the fourteenth century AD of the reconstructed occupation sequence from the Akumbu mound complex located at the westernmost end of the defunct Niakéné Maoudo. The one plausible explanation regarding this unexpected finding is that the onset of more humid conditions around 300 AD (Brooks 1986; McIntosh 1983), possibly accompanied by destructive flooding, may have led to the blocking up of the bed of the Niakéné Maoudo. Unlike the Bras de Namapala to the north, there is no visible connection between the Niakéné Maoudo and the Fala de Molodo, the feeder of all the waterways of the whole region (Figures 1.1; 1.2).

With the Middle Assemblage period, the banks of the water corridors, with 26 sites (more than 80% of the Middle Assemblage sites) remained the most populated. However, many of these, like those of the Akumbu cluster (at the westernmost end of the Niakéné Maoudo), the Toladié, Goudourou, Kolima clusters, Bourgou Silatigui A, Ndoupa (all along the Bras de Nampala) and Tissilit (on the north channel) appeared to have also been tied to the degraded dune system (Figure 1.2). This environmental zone, with only one Early Assemblage site, became more colonized. It contains six Middle Assemblage sites including four within the Toulé cluster and the large isolated site of Boundou Sekou. This might be an indication that the hypothetical strangulation of some of the waterways, or the population explosion during the Middle Assemblage, or the combination of both possibly led to the development of rain-based farming activities, i.e. millet cultivation to which the degraded dunes would be suited perfectly. This hypothesis is further corroborated by the notable quantity of "millet stalks" (described in details in Chapter 7) uncovered during the excavation at Akumbu mound complex. Another *raison d' être* for some the Middle Assemblage large settlements might have been their involvement in regional or long distance trade. Athough this is not substantiated by overall surface artifacts, the excavations at Akumbu, and earlier investigations at Kolima and Péhé (Mauny 1961) have yielded important trade goods, including cowrie shells, and copper objects. The environmental zones that appear to have been avoided for occupation during the Middle Assemblage period are the Boulel Ridge and the Pleistocene dune field (Table 3.2)

During the Late Assemblage, occupation in the Méma is the most reduced. During that period, only eight small sites, scattered within the longitudinal dunes or at its contact with the degraded dunes, show indication of ephemeral occupation. As already noted, oral accounts attribute the founding of some of these Late Assemblage sites to Bamanan populations who apparently penetrated the Méma during the hegemony of the Bamanan kingdom of Segou. The Bamanan expansion during that period extended as far north as the commercial center of Timbuktu (Monteil 1929).

III: CONCLUSIONS

Overall, the survey data indicate that a millennium ago, substantial permanent settlements were spread throughout the Méma. Although the transition between the IA and the LSA has yet to be pinpointed chronologically, one can hypothesize that the thriving occupation of the last two millennia forms a continuum with the LSA. Numerous sites dated to that period are narrowly concentrated on ancient levee slopes. In the intensive survey area, the chronology of IA occupation appeared to have been thus:

(1) Densely clustered small settlements flanking the banks of water corridors during the period of Early Assemblage;
(2) Large settlements (often surrounded by smaller and satellite settlements) distributed both along water corridors and within the degraded dunes during the period of Middle Assemblage.
(3) A handful of small settlements with shallow deposits (indicating an ephemeral occupation) mostly distributed within the longitudinal dunes during the period of Late Assemblage.

The most intensive IA occupation in the Méma appeared to have occurred during the periods of the Early pottery Assemblage (mid-first millennium AD) and the Middle Assemblage (seventh century AD to twelfth to fourteenth century AD). During that time span, the density and sizes of sites in the Méma are comparable to those in the Jenné and Dia hinterlands, where intensive regional surveys were conducted by the McIntoshes in the late1970s and1980s (SK McIntosh & RJ McIntosh, 1980; Haskell et al. 1988). They also suggest that patterns of occupation dynamics in the Méma were broadly similar to the ones in those regions during the period spanning the mid-first millennium AD and early second millennium AD. The strongest testimony of this similarity of occupation dynamics is the presence in each of these regions of densely and contemporaneously occupied clustered settlements. In addition, the population explosion during Jenné jeno Phase III (AD 400 - AD 850) (SK McIntosh & RJ McIntosh 1980) and Timbuktou Middle assemblage (SK McIntosh & RJ McIntosh 1986), characterized by the growth of many settlements to urban size is reflected in the Méma Middle Assemblage. During that period, large settlements averaging 10-20 ha in area lined the banks of now relict waterways or were located within the degraded dunes.

The archaeological evidence does not reveal the cause of abandonment of the many Middle Assemblage sites by AD 1200 or 1400. However, this was probably related to the onset of climatic decline around 1100 (Brooks 1986; McIntosh 1983) or to political turmoil, or the combination of both. It corresponds to a general depopulation around Jenné, Dia, and in the Niger Bend. In those regions, a widespread abandonment of crowded hinterland settlements occurred in early to mid-second millennium AD, and a more reduced population concentrates at a few large sites such as Jenné jeno, or Mara, also abandoned around 1400 AD or shortly after (SK McIntosh & RJ McIntosh 1980, 1986; Haskell et al. 1988).

The discovery of numerous smelting sites, some of which are associated with extensive slag heaps, is of considerable interest. Both, the number and volume of these slag heaps suggest that the Méma, at some point during the IA, specialized in industrial iron production. This commodity was probably traded to neighboring regions, such as the political authority of Ghana, or the Inland Niger Delta to the east.

CHAPTER 4
EXCAVATIONS AT THE AKUMBU MOUND COMPLEX

I: SITE LOCATION AND DESCRIPTION

Akumbu is a cluster of four settlement mounds (referred to as Akumbu A, B, C and D) and two potential cemeteries, where remains of large vessels (assumed to be funeral urns) were visible on the surface. It lies within the degraded dune system of the Méma and outside the modern and seasonally inhabited hamlet of Akumbu. It is located approximately 25 km south-west of the town of Nampala, our base camp.

The mound cluster of Akumbu was first reported in an inventory of archaeological sites in the Méma, executed by the DPC in 1984. As already noted, elements of the Soninké oral traditions collected during this inventory mission linked it to the founding and rise of the medieval Soninké empire of Wagadu (DPC1985; Raimbault and Togola 1991).

Significant features related to Akumbu's location include the presence of three seasonal ponds and its position close to the former bed of the now defunct Niakéné Maoudo water corridor. These ponds, oasis-like in the dry and almost naked sahelian landscape, surround the mound complex. They are focal points for Fulani pastoralists and their herds of cattle, sheep and goat during the rainy season and early months of the dry season, when they hold water. This type of preferential location near seasonally flooded ponds, is charactistic of most of IA settlement mounds and nearly all LSA sites surveyed in the regional site survey.

The relict Niakéné Maoudo water corridor runs east of the site cluster and skirts the northern edge of the iron-pan-peneplain, which turns about the Boulel ridge. Its westernmost levee is approximately two km to the west of Akumbu mound complex. The remains of a now stabilized longitudinal dune, covered with vegetation, runs roughly east-west a few kilometers to the south of the Akumbu mound cluster.

Roughly rounded in plan, the main mound, Akumbu A, measures 21 ha in surface area (Figure 4.1). It was the third largest mound in the survey area, after Toladié A and Péhé, and one of the highest identified during the 1989/90 Méma regional site survey. The easternmost of three nearby seasonal ponds almost touches its southeastern edge. To retain water longer for Fulani pastoralists and their herds, this pond was dredged by the *Office de Developpement de l'Elevage de Mopti* (ODM) in the mid 1980's. Akumbu A rises six to seven meters above the surrounding plain and presents a tabular surface, with three mounded areas, and a depression (located in the mid western section of the site) now occupied by a small grove of trees. The mounded areas seem to consist primarily of midden deposit (at least at their top). At the surface, they are characterized by dark grey, friable soil and are favored by burrowing animals. A number of circular or semi-circular burnt clay structures and several sand stone or laterite blocks are visible on the surface. Three to four ravines, several meters deep, undercut the cultural deposit and run from the top of the mound toward the ponds and the surrounding plain.

Akumbu B, also rounded but steeper than A, is located 300 to 400 to the south west of Akumbu A. Standing approximately 7-8 m. high and covering 8 ha in surface area, it was the highest and second largest mound of the complex. Its additional height is perhaps attributable to the remains of the dune on top upon which both mounds B and C rest. This dune begins from a low-lying area with a few small acacia groves to the west of Akumbu A. Dense concentrations of LSA materials (particularly pottery) were found on the northwestern and eastern slopes of this ancient dune.

Akumbu C, the third largest mound of the complex, was a free standing mound, similar in shape to Akumbu B. It extends over 3 ha in surface and rises approximately 7 m. in height.

Although artifacts, especially domestic pottery, from the surface of both Akumbu B and C generally parallel those of Akumbu A, these mounds appeared to be more ancient in occupation than Akumbu A, as they yield at their flanks mostly LSA material and a few elements characteristic of the Early Assemblage. The circular or semi-circular burnt clay structures so numerous on the surface of Akumbu A were absent from B and C.

Two small and very low mounds a few hundred meters to the north and south of Akumbu A had remains of large vessels with thickened walls (believed to be funerary urns) on their surface. These two urn field sites were the most damaged sites of Akumbu mound complex. The one to the north side was almost completely destroyed by treasure seekers who have recently dug large looting holes in its surface. The one to the south was used by Fulani pastoralists as seasonal kraal, with the result that the surface material (especially pottery) was badly crushed.

Two concentrations of slag, associated with furnace remains, of approximately 0.1 ha each, were also present on the eastern and northern edges of the mound complex. These slag concentrations were rather small, compared to the ones found in the southern part of the survey area and discussed further in the chapter on the survey.

II: EXCAVATION METHODS

Excavations commenced at Akumbu mound complex in early March and continued until early May 1990, after a two week interruption in April. Three experienced excavators (Helen Haskell, a Rice University graduate student, Kevin C. MacDonald, a Cambridge University graduate

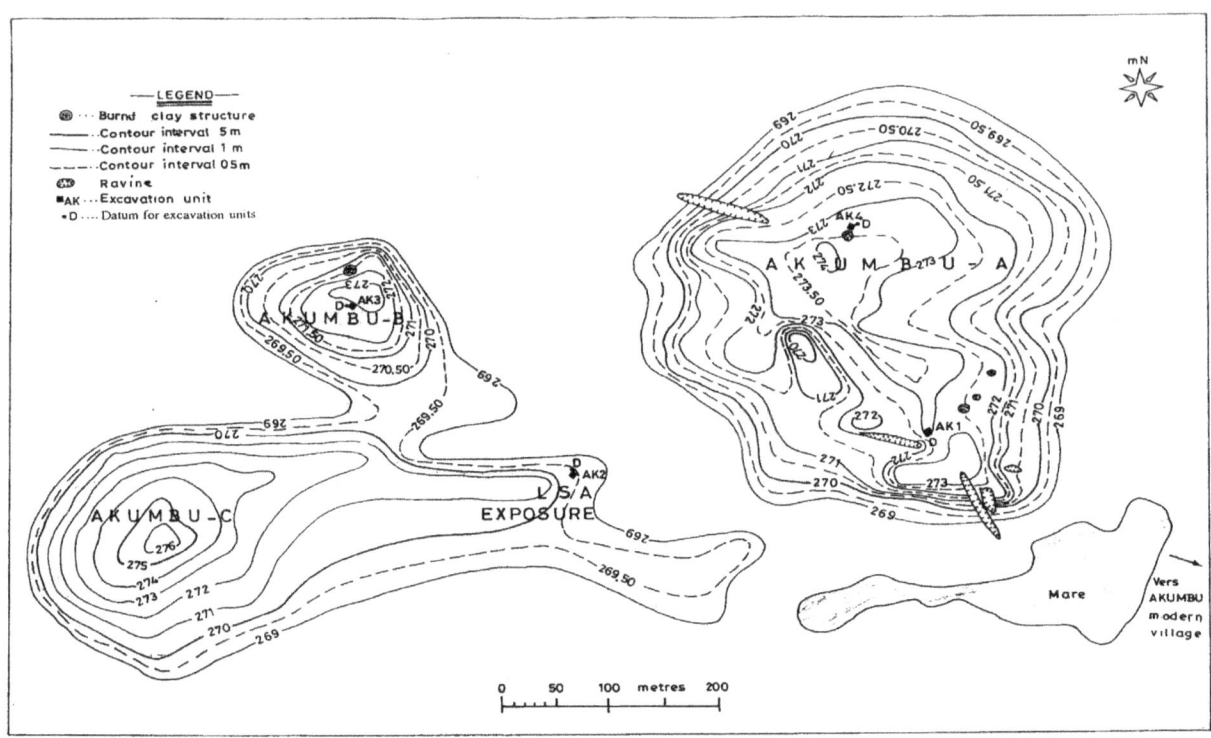

Figure 4.1. Map of Akumbu A and Akumbu B

student, and myself) were responsible for supervising the excavation units. Karina Macovat and Sandra Poznikoff (two Canadian students) spent three weeks with us in March and participated in the excavations. Nafogo Coulibaly and Kéchéry Doumbia (both from the ISH) also assisted during the last two weeks of excavations. A total number of eight workmen, recruited in the villages of Nampala and Toulé (located mid-way between Nampala and Akumbu), were employed as laborers.

As already noted, a total of four test pits were opened at various locations of Akumbu mound complex. In each excavation unit, all levels were excavated, using either trowels or the traditional implements (*daba* or hoes) favored by Malian laborers for digging. Particular care was taken to follow natural stratigraphic levels as closely as possible. A new level was opened whenever changes in the soil texture, degree of compaction, or color were observed. If, however, these changes became less apparent and more difficult to discern, excavation levels were arbitrary changed. As a result, natural stratigraphic levels (Figures 4.2, 4.6, and 4.9) do not always correspond to excavated levels (Figures 4.3, 4.7, and 4.10). Each archaeological feature (burial, wall, trash pit or midden deposit, hearth, concentration of pot sherds...etc), encountered was excavated as a separate level.

All excavated soil was screened with a 0.5cm window screen for artifacts and faunal material. Artifacts were bagged by excavated level and transported to Nampala, our camp base. Faunal remains were bagged separately from pottery. All other artifacts, considered as Small Finds, were bagged together. Recording and preliminary analysis of the pottery from the survey and from unit AK1 (the largest and only unit of the IA mounds dug to sterile soil) were accomplished in May and June 1990 by myself in Bamako. With the exception of a small study collection (brought to Rice University, Houston), all the pottery (from both excavations and survey), was placed in the care of the ISH in Bamako. The faunal remains, as well as the Small Finds referred to above, were brought to Rice University for analysis. The Small Finds were counted, weighed, and described in detail. They have since been returned to the ISH in Bamako. Flotation samples (for botanical analysis), averaging four liters in volume were taken consistently from archaeological features such as hearths, trash pits or midden deposits, and burnt areas (which were more likely to yield charred seeds) and periodically from others levels. Floatation of the samples was undertaken by Cecilia Capezza in March 1993, and the floats await study in Bamako. Soil samples were periodically taken in order to illuminate the nature and origin of specific and unusual deposits. Numerous charcoal samples for radiocarbon dating were collected using tweezers, a knife, or the tip of a trowel. They were each placed in an envelope of aluminum foil, which was subsequently sealed in a plastic bag.

III: DISCUSSION OF THE EXCAVATION UNITS AND CHRONOLOGY

As mentioned above, only four small test units (referred to as AK1, AK2, AK3 and AK4) were excavated during the 1989- 90 exploratory mission. All these excavation units were specifically placed at various parts of the mound complex, taking mainly into account the presence of surface features (possible indication of function) and the range of artifacts (in particular the pottery) believed to indicate a long chronological span. None of the excavation units exhibited sterile layers that might indicate a temporary abandonment of the site.

AK1, the largest unit, measured 2×3 m. It was placed in the immediate vicinity of the highest point of Akumbu A, in an area with relatively hard and compacted soil, assumed to be a residential sector. The highest point itself, believed to be primarily a midden deposit because of the extreme softness and friability of its surface soil, was avoided. This highest area was also heavily disturbed by burrowing animals. We hoped that AK1, located at one of the most deeply stratifed areas of the mound would, at the bottom, yield evidence for the initial occupation of Akumbu A (the largest mound of the complex) and also produce stratified and dated artifact sequences (in particular pottery). Concentrations of Middle Assemblage pottery, recognized during the regional site survey, were present in the sector where the unit was opened.

AK1 was dug through 69 levels, to a depth of 7.50 m. Its original size of 2×3 m. was reduced to 2×2 m. in level 31 at the depth of 3 m. (Figures 4.2, 4.3). The Point of Origin, from which all measurements inside the unit were executed, was located at the south-west corner.

The excavated levels of Unit AK1 are shown in Figures 4.3, while Table 4.1 reconstructs the depositional processes and related events of the various individual excavated levels. The natural strata (Figure 4.2) are discussed in order of discovery and thus in the reverse of correct chronological order.

Three occupation levels were identified in unit AK1. They were marked by the presence of archaeological features, such as stumps of mud structure or burnt hearth floors associated with horizontal ash lenses. These occupation levels were separated by thick strata of clay or loam (primarily accumulated by the collapse of mud structures), and middens (mostly deposited in disposal pits). The sterile soil, consisting of a compacted laterite concretion, yellowish in color, was encountered at a depth of 7.5 m, below the surface.

The most recent occupation level before the abandonment of the site was encountered in levels 5, 6, and 7, at the depth of approximately 0.5 m, immediately underlying a stratum of wall collapse (levels 1, 2, and 4) with clearly discernable brick rubble. It was characterized by the presence of the stump of a rectilinear mud structure (Figure 4.4), which appeared to be the most recent architectural remain in Unit AK1. This structure, located on the eastern part of the unit, ran 0.5 m. parallel to the north wall of the unit. It was made of irregular, crude rectangular mud bricks, with only one brick in width and one brick in depth. This strucure was plausibly a partition wall, as on both sides an apparent "living" floor was marked by the presence of small burnt hearth floors, associated with horizontal ash deposits. Several large horizontally-oriented sherds, four complete and semi-complete vessels, seven grinding stones and grinders, four decorated spindle whorls and a few ornamental and élite objects (such as clay beads, fragments of eggshell and cowrie shells) were uncovered in this occupation level. Charcoal collected from level 6 yielded a radiocarbon date of 640 ± 70 BP (Beta 10441). Using Stuiver and Pearson' s calibration curves at one standard error (Stuiver and Pearson 1986), this data calibrates to AD 1274-1401. Pottery from this first occupation level belong to the Middle Assemblage material, described in Chapter 6.

This first occupation level was underlain by a thick stratum of heterogeneous but firm loam consisting of light clay, sand and ash mixed with charcoal lenses (levels 9, 11, 12, and 14). This stratum seems to represent a slow accumulation over a long period of time. It was interrupted in the southern and western parts of the unit by a large disposal pit, which occupied nearly one third of the unit and stretched along the southern and western walls. This disposal pit extended through four levels (levels 8, 10, 13, and 15), from 0.80 to 1.60 m. depth. It was filled with alternating layers of very friable loam, loosely compacted sand, and soft ashy soil, intermixed with charcoal. Archaeological materials uncovered from this disposal pit included large pot sherds, a significant amount of non-ceramic material such as animal bones, numerous rusted iron objects and iron slag, millet "stalks" and a few élite objects (two cowrie shells, one crumbling copper object), and two bone artifacts). Radiocarbon samples collected from charcoal taken in level 10 and near the top of this trash pit produced a date of 750 ± 70 BP (Beta 40442). Using Stuiver and Pearson' s calibration curves at one standard error (Stuiver and Pearson 1986), this date calibrates to AD 1225-1288. Pottery from this trash pit paralleled that of the upper levels.

Beneath the disposal pit was another stratum of firm heterogeneous loam, which was excavated as levels 14 and 16. It resembled the loamy stratum excavated as levels 9, 11, 12, and 14, described above. However, it contained a higher clay component and was often green-stained, especially in its lower levels. Intrusive within this firm heterogeneous loam was a pit filled with pure clay, also green-stained. This pit, located in the south east corner of the unit, was excavated as levels 22 and 26. It was roughly circular in plan and measured approximately 0.5 m. in diameter. It extended from 2.18 m. to 2.70 m. in depth. The function of this pit was unknown. However, the unusual

Excavation at Akumbu Mound Complex

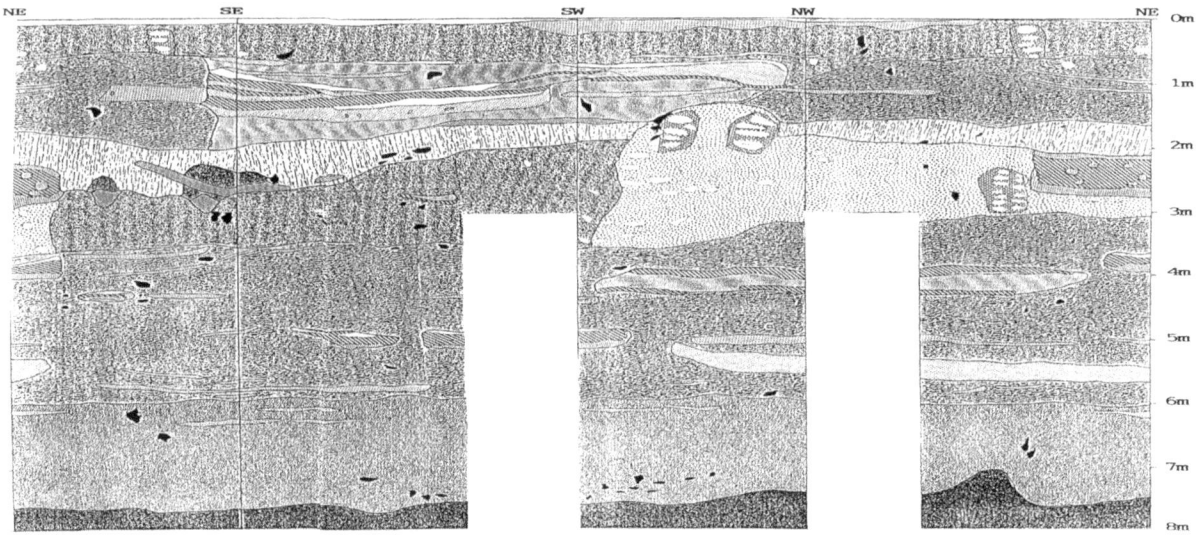

Figure 4.2. AK1. Natural strata

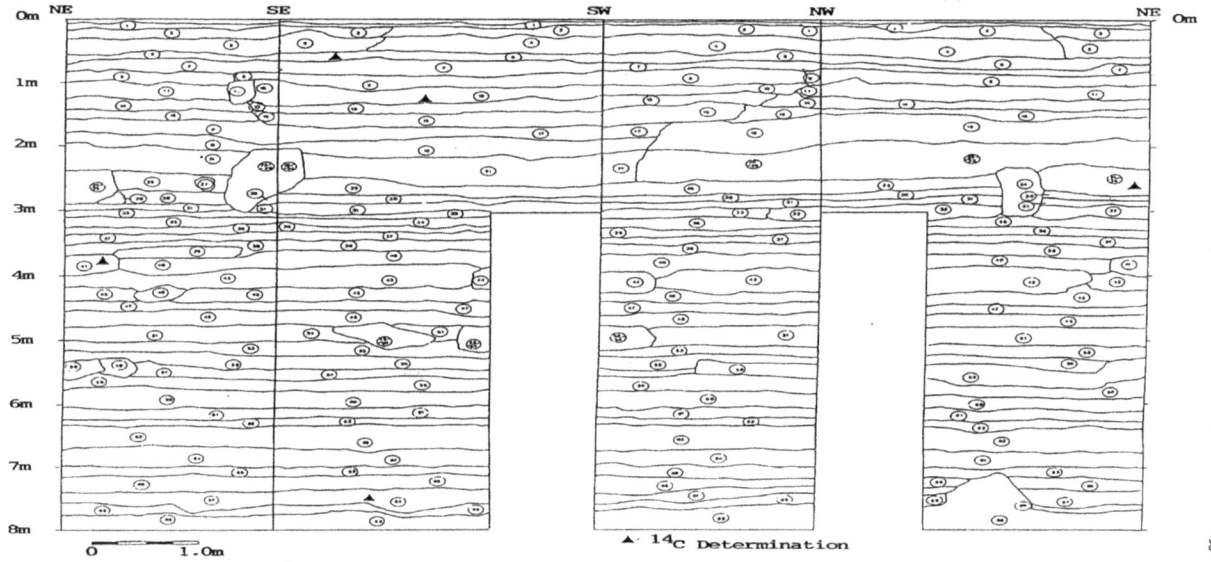

Figure 4.3. AK1. Excavated levels

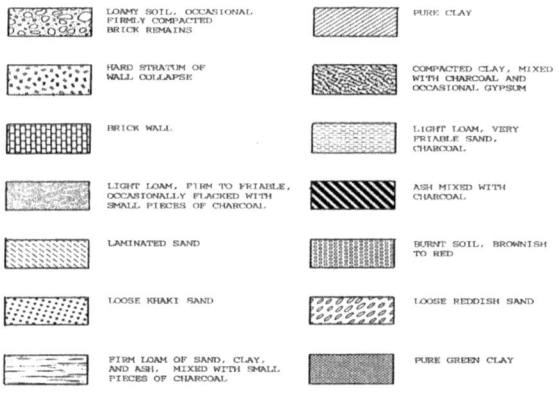

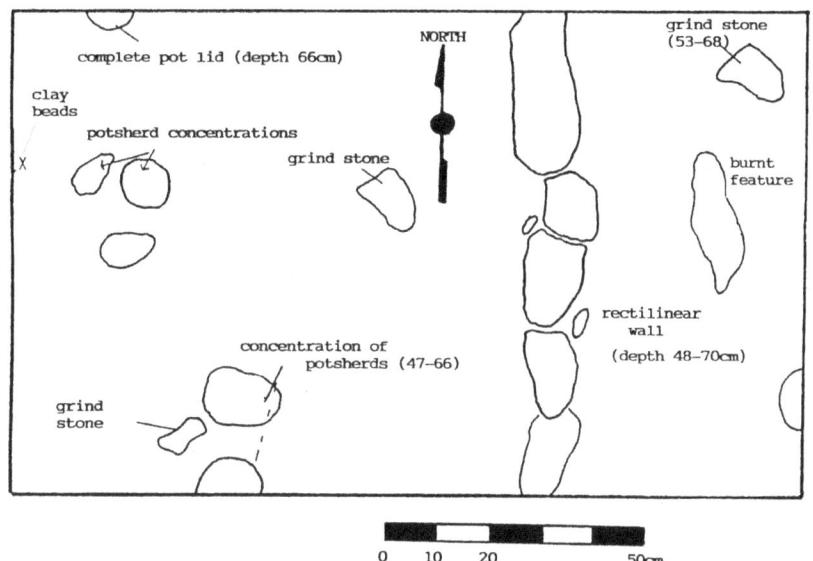

Figure 4.4. AK1. Levels 6 and 7

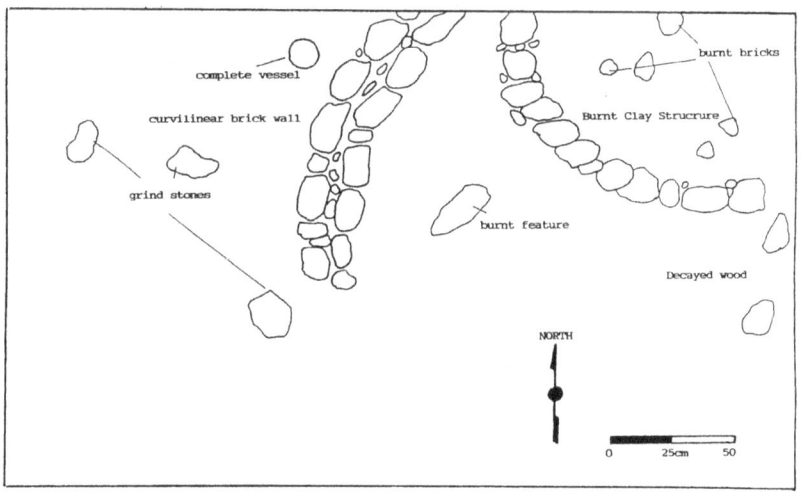

Figure 4.5. AK1. Levels 24, 29 and 34

Table 4.1: Reconstruction of depositional sequence in Unit AK1.

Level	Excavated Depositional events
1/2	Surface deposits
3/4	Wall collapse with discernible whole bricks
5	Burnt soil. Possible hearth. Associated with horizontal ash deposits.
6a/6b/7	'Living surface'? with horizontally positioned objects. Stump of rectilinear mud brick wall. [Beta 40441 cal AD 1274-1401]
8/10	Disposal pit filled with alternating layers of loosely compacted sand mixed with ash and small pieces of charcoal.[Beta 40442 cal AD 1225-1288]
13/15	Disposal pit filled with alternating layers of loosely compacted sand mixed with ash and small pieces of charcoal.[Beta 40442 cal AD 1225-1288]
9/11	Heterogeneous loam of light clay, sand, and ash mixed with small pieces of charcoal.
12	Wall collapse with brick rubble.
14/16	Similar to 9/11
17	
18	
19	Similar to 9 and 11 but with a higher clay component.
20	Rapid wall collapse. Occasional whole yellowish bricks.
21	
22/26	Drainage pit? Filled with green stained pure clay
23	
24	Interior of burnt clay structure [Beta 40443 cal AD 985-1160]
25	
27/28	Pieces of decayed wood associated with burnt clay structure
29	Wall of burnt clay structure
30	'Living surface'. Possibly interior of circular house.
31	
32	
33	Wall collapse with occasional brick rubble.
34	Stump of curvilinear mud wall.
35	
36/37/ 38/39	Light sandy loam occasionally mixed with ash and small pieces of charcoal
40	shallow disposal pit.
41	Small open hearth associated with ash deposits [Beta 40444 cal AD 548-661]
42	Shallow disposal pit
43/45	Light loamy soil of sand mixed with small pieces of charcoal
44	Small hearth associated with ash deposit
46	Small hearth associated with sherd concentration
47/48/51	Light loamy soil Similar to 43/45
49/50	Small hearth similar to 44
52/54	Small hearth, next to 49/50
53/55/56	Light loamy soil with occasional laminated sand
57/59/60	Loamy soil similar to L. 53/ 55/56
58	Loose sand deposit
61	
62	Upper levels of disposal pit.
63	Clayey loam mixed with domestic refuse. Occasional gypsum crystals.
64	
65	
66	Lower levels of disposal pit. Similar to 61 through 64. Also
67	occasional gypsum crystals [Beta 40445 cal AD 604-681]
68	Sterile yellowish laterite concretion.
69	

greenish color of the clay filling it suggests that it had once been filled with stagnant water.

At 2.25 to 3.25 m. depth, was a thick clay stratum of wall collapse, yellowish in color, and very hard to dig. This yellowish wall collapse occupied the northern half of the unit (Figure 4.2). It was excavated as levels 18, 20, 23, and part of level 25. It contained numerous compacted brick fragments and represented the debris of the rapid collapse of two mud walls. These mud walls, constructed with roughly rectangular bricks, were undetected during excavations. However, their outlines were clearly visible in the western profile of the unit. This yellowish wall collapse was very hard and almost sterile, containing only small pieces of pot sherds and very few other archaeological materials.

Adjacent to the yellowish wall collapse and occupying the southern half of the unit was a featureless deposit of wall collapse/wall melt deposit which was excavated as 17, 19, 21, and part of level 25. Protruding within the yellowish wall collapse and approximately between the depth of 2.75 m. and 3.00 m. were two clearly defined mud structures: the rubble of a burnt clay structure and the stump of curvilinear mud brick wall (Figure 4.5).

The burnt clay structure (levels 19 and 24) was semi-circular in outline. It was located in the north-east corner of the unit, with its northern and eastern ends obscured by the north and east walls. It averaged 1.50 m. in diameter and extended from 2.75 to 3.00 m. in depth. It was constructed with irregular cylindrical mud bricks. Both the wall and the floor were dark grey to dark orange in color and were hardened by evident firing. The floor was covered with a thick blanket of ash and charcoal mixed with several fired brick chunks which were also dark grey to dark orange in color. With the exception of a few pot sherds, no artifacts were recovered from the burnt clay structure. However, the evident firing of its wall and floor, and the thick deposit of ash and charcoal, strongly suggested that it was used as a hearth or oven. The firing of the wall and floor seemed to have occurred during its continuous use as hearth or oven. Charcoal collected from the floor produced a radiocarbon date of 980±70 B.P (Beta 40443). Using Stuiver and Pearson's calibration curves at one standard error (Stuiver and Pearson 1986), this calibrates to AD 985-1160. A significant archaeological feature associated with the burnt clay structure was a piece of decayed wood. This feature, found in two spots, was separately excavated as levels 27 and 28. The first spot, level 27, was located 0.50 m. from the structure, while the second spot, level 28, was just at the opening of the burnt clay structure.

The base of the curvilinear mud brick wall was excavated as level 34. It extended from 2.75 to 3 m. depth and was 0.80 m. in length. Its northern end was obscured by the north wall of the unit (Figures 4.3 and 4.5). It was constructed with two courses of roughly rectangular yellowish bricks. Given its curvilinear outline, this mud brick wall was interpreted as the plausible foundation or base of a circular house. To the west of this curvilinear mud brick wall was an apparent living floor (part of level 25, 30, and 31). This apparent living floor consisted of very compact and yellowish loam. Like the layer of yellowish wall collapse, it was very hard to dig. Possibly, it represented the interior of the circular house. It was marked by the presence of a complete pot (see Figure 6.26) and two sandstone grinders (Figure 4.5).

The above series of archaeological features (the clay filled pit, the burnt clay structure, and the curvilinear mud brick wall along with the adjacent living floor) were clearly associated. They were all located between 2.25 m. and 3.00 m. of depth. Together, they indicated an intense cultural activity and the second occupation horizon encountered in Unit AK1. Pottery in this occupation level was very similar to that of the upper levels and belonged to the Middle Assemblage.

Levels 32 through level 39, beneath the second occupation level, consisted of wall melt deposit. This deposit of wall melt, far below the bases of the structures encountered in levels 24/29 and level 34 was difficult to interpret. Nonetheless, it contained numerous yellowish brick fragments, particularly in level 32.

Beneath this level of wall melt, the remaining deposits were constituted of a thick stratum of sandy loam (3.75 to 6.00 m), and a stratum of compacted clayey loam, mixed with abundant domestic refuse (6.00 to 7.50 m), which contrasted sharply with the upper strata. These two strata (individually discussed below), with no architectural remains, appeared to have been deposited in a very short period of time, between calibrated radiocarbon date AD 985-1160 (obtained from the burnt clay structure and a few centimeters above the stratum of sandy loam) and calibrated radiocarbon date AD 604-681 (obtained in level 67). This rapid accumulation was partly attributed to the huge refuse layers (discussed further below) that constituted the 1.50 m. bottom-most cultural deposits of the unit.

The stratum of firm sandy loam extending between 3.75 m. and 6.00 m. was often intermixed with ash containing charcoal lenses. As already noted, it contained no architectural remains and archaeological features uncovered within it were limited to a shallow trash pit and a series of four small hearths. The shallow trash pit was excavated as level 42. It averaged 0.40 m. in depth, 0.50 m. in width, and extended along the north and west wall of the unit. It was filled with very friable loam of sand and ash mixed small pieces of charcoal. The five small hearths were excavated as levels 41, 44, 49/50, 52/54 and 58. They all consisted of dark grey to brown burnt soil, associated with greyish ash horizons. Occupation was possibly very light in character within this thick layer of sandy loam. This interpretation is based on both the lack of architectural remains and the low level of artifacts, and faunal materials. Wood charcoal collected from the small hearth of level 41 was dated to 1430 ± 70 BP (Beta 40444). This radiocarbon date calibrates to AD 548-661 using Stuiver and Pearson's calibration curves at one standard error (Stuiver and Pearson 1986).

The bottommost stratum of featureless compacted clayey loam, mixed with abundant domestic refuse, was encountered in level 61, at approximately 6 m. depth. This mixture of clayey loam and domestic refuse (composed of greyish ash flecked with small pieces of charcoal large pot sherds, chunks of fired and reddish bricks, animal bones, and oyster shells) characterized the remaining 1.5 m. of the archaeological deposits. As already noted, it seemed to be the result of a rapid accumulation and appeared to represent the fill of a low lying terrain or basin. This low lying terrain or basin was possibly periodically flooded, as indicated by the presence of sand lenses often made up of rounded sand grains and occasional river pebbles in quartz (all possibly water deposited), and by abundant gypsum crystals throughout this stratum of clayey loam. These gypsum crystals, which clearly formed in the cultural deposits, most likely after deposition, indicate an increasing dessiccation. Gypsum is an evaporate sedimentary mineral that originates from water strongly impregnated with salt. Groundwater dissolves calcium-sulfates or salts that are brought by rainwater as it passes through rocks or areas containing them (Blatt et al. 1980). Evaporation increases the concentration of these salts to the point that gypsum is precipitated (Blatt et al. 1980). A possible area where rainwater could became saturated with salt before flowing into adjacent potential low lying terrain is the settlement itself. According to Fulani pastoralists, soil of ancient settlement mounds has a salty taste and is relished by animals, especially cattle. This stratum of clayey loam was dated to 1390±80 BP from charcoal collected in level 67 a few centimeters above the natural deposit (Beta 40445). This calibrates to AD 604-681, using Stuiver and Pearson's calibration curves at one standard error (Stuiver and Pearson 1986). The extension of archaeological deposit in Unit AK1 to a depth of 7.50 m, compared to the maximum height above the surrounding surface of 6 m. for the mound, was likely due to the presence of the lying terrain which was possibly subject to flooding and perhaps erosion and would necessarily have to be filled before occupation.

AK2, a unit of 1×1 m. in area, was placed on the eastern flank of the ancient dune beneath Akumbu B and C, which exhibited concentrations of LSA artifacts. It was opened in the hope of illuminating LSA occupation in the area. The results of AK2 are being treated by Helen Haskell in a report on LSA sites (Haskell in preparation) and will not be included in this discussion. Unit **AK3** measured 2×2 m. in area. It was placed at the center near the summit of Akumbu B. Due to the presence of LSA artifacts on the dune underlying Akumbu B, it was hoped that the site would yield continuous stratigraphic deposits stretching from the LSA to the IA.

The point of origin was located at the northwest corner of the unit. The excavated levels of Unit AK3, are illustrated in Figure 4.6 while Table 4.2 reconstructs the depositional

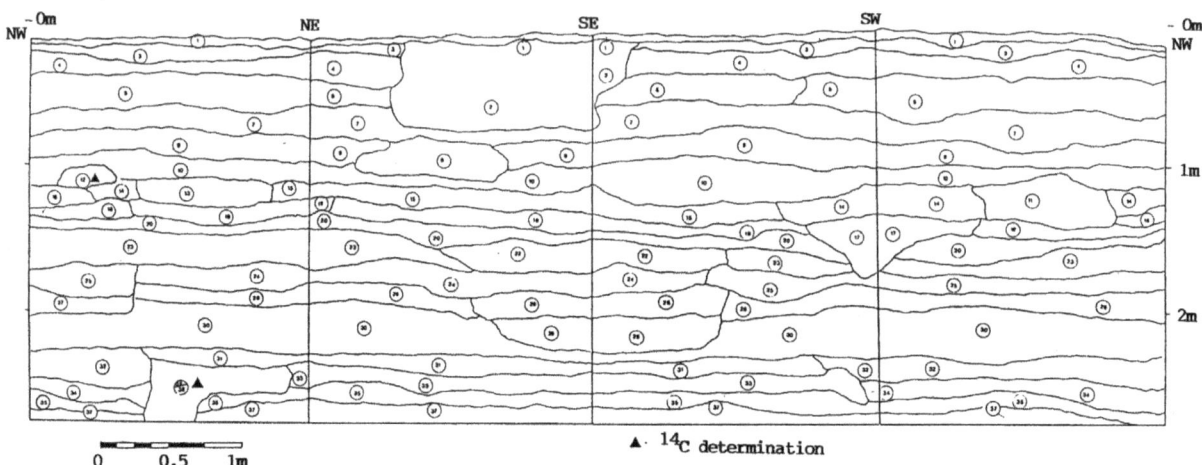

Figure 4.6. AK3. Excavated levels

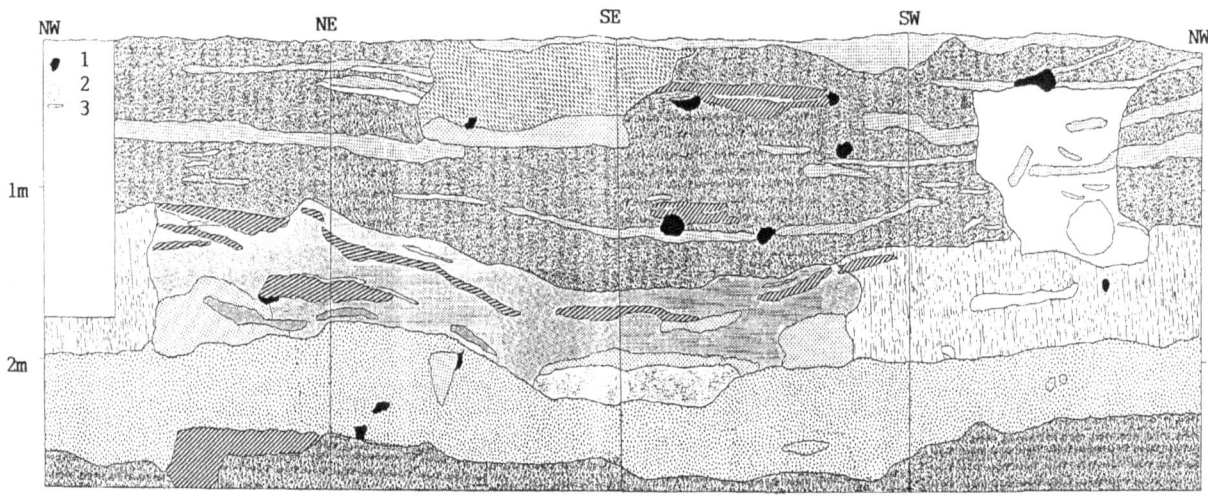

1: animal burrow
2: brick
3: ash deposit

Figure 4.7. AK3. Natural strata

processes represented by the excavated levels. The natural strata (Figure 4.7) are discussed in order of discovery (reverse of correct chronological order). Because of time limitations, AK3 was not dug to sterile. Excavation stopped at 2.75 m. depth (level 38) and the excavation unit was covered to protect the deposits from erosion. AK3 was the only unit to display two distinct pottery sequences, Early and Middle Assemblages, both known from survey. The stratigraphy in Unit AK3 was extremely complex. This was due to the presence of two burial pits, which had disturbed the deposits.

Beginning near the surface and extending to approximately 1.25 m. of depth was a thick stratum of hard, heterogeneous loam. This stratum of hard and heterogeneous loam contained a few brick fragments and appears to have been primarily accumulated by wall collapse and wall melt materials. It was much thicker along the east and south wall of the unit where it extended up to 1.40 m. This stratum appeared to reflect a period of intensive occupation in the area of AK3. However, the presence of thin layers and horizons of yellowish sand (Figure 4.6) suggested periods of exposure during deposition. It was intruded by a series of six pit-like features (levels 2, 6, 8, 11, 12, and 13) of varying sizes and depths. Level 2, encountered only a few centimeters below the surface in the eastern part of the unit, was a huge pit 1.50 m. wide and 0.75 m. deep. It was filled with laminated reddish sand flecked with ash patches and small pieces of charcoal. Levels 6 and 8, encountered at 0.50 m. and 0.85 m. respectively, were both shallow domestic refuse pits filled with ash, charcoal lenses and sand. The most prominent of these pit features was the interment pit for an extended human burial. This pit remained undetected during excavation until the depth

Table 4.2: Reconstruction of depositional sequence in Unit AK3.

Levels	Excavated Depositional events
1	Surface deposits
2	Reddish sand deposits. Very friable
3/4/5/7	Hard stratum of loamy soil with few discernible brick fragments
6	Pit like feature filled with ash, charcoal lenses and friable sand.
8	Pit like feature, similar to that of level 6.
9/10	Continuation of the hard stratum of loam of levels 3/4/5 Presence of brick fragments.
12	Small open hearth associated with white ash deposit and charcoal [Beta 49720 cal. AD 780-1100]
11	Upper level of burial pit.
21	Bottom of burial pit. Extended human burial.
13	Small pit like feature, similar to level 6 and level 8
14/15/16	Heterogeneous loam, similar to level 9/10; but with a higher clay component.
17	Patch of ash and soft friable sand, associated with a semi complete vessel.
18/19	Expansion of the pit feature of level 13. Ashy soil.
20	Heterogeneous loam extending below the various pits excavated in levels 13, 18, and 19.
22	Patch of ash and soft friable sand, very similar to level 17. Possible disposal pit.
23	Compacted loamy soil, with some brick fragments. Adjacent to the pit feature of L. 22.
24	Expansion of L.22. Contains lots of charcoal, and dark organic soil sometimes green stained.
25	Loamy soil similar to L.23.
26/27	Loamy soil similar to L. 23 and level 25. But with occasional laminated sand.
28/29	Burial pit. Contains a disintegrated child burial.
30/33	Hard stratum of wall collapse with brick remains. Intruded by burial pit of L. 28/29.
32/34	Putative mud brick wall
35/37	Similar to level 30/33
36/38	Open hearth. Associated with ash deposits. [Beta 40446 cal. AD 342-442]

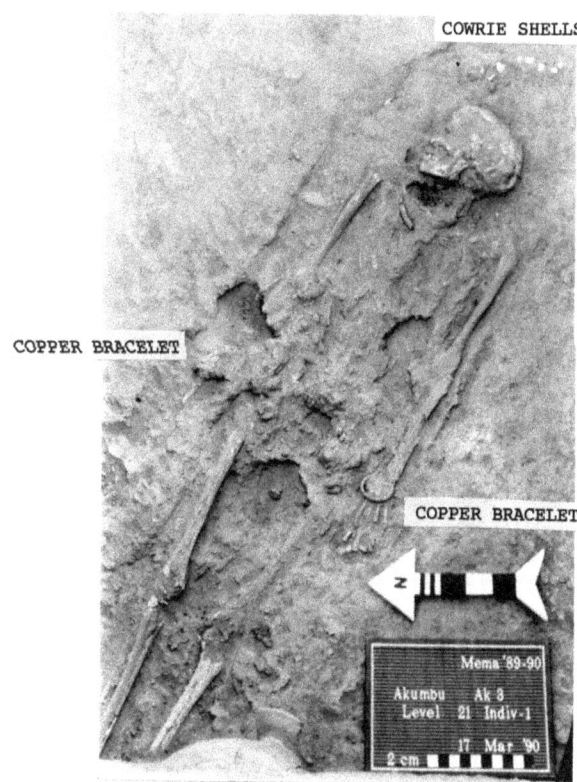

Figure 4.8. AK3. Extended Burial

of 1.00 m. However, its entire outline is clearly visible in the profile of the west wall of the unit. The extended human burial, excavated as level 11, was found in its lower part, between 1.36 m. and 1.40 m. of depth. It was accompanied by a complete *Jidaga* (water jar), two copper bracelets (oneat each wrist), 13 cowrie shells and 13 stone beads made from white and coral quartzite (Figure 4.8). Levels 12 and 13 were small patches of loose ashy sand mixed with small pieces of charcoal. They were both situated in the eastern sector of the unit and at the same depth as the bottom of the interment pit. Charcoal collected from level 12 was dated to 1130±100 BP (Beta 49720). This calibrates to AD 780-1100, using Stuiver and Pearson's calibration curves at one standard error (Stuiver and Pearson 1986).

Beneath the strata of hard and heterogeneous loam and at the depth of 1.25 m, the soil changed to a firm heterogeneous clayey loam which extended up to approximately 2 m. of depth. Sherds with characteristics of the Early Assemblage material known from the survey seemed to be abundant in this deposit. The most important disturbances and cultural activities within this layer were a huge domestic refuge pit and an apparent interment pit. The domestic refuge pit (levels 17, 22, and parts of levels 24, 25 and 26) occupied nearly one half of the unit and stretched along the southern and eastern walls. It was filled with alternating layers of very friable loam dark grey in color, and soft ashy soil flecked with small pieces of charcoal. It also contained patches of loosely compacted sand, mixed with small pieces of charcoal. Archaeological materials uncovered from this pit uncluded large pot sherds, a significant amount of faunal materials and iron slag. The apparent interment pit (levels 28 and 29) was located just beneath the domestic refuse pit and between 2-2.25 m. of depth. It contained in its bottom a small amount of the almost completely disintegrated bones (part of the cranium bone and teeth) of a 3-4 year old child, scattered within a matrix of loosely compacted yellowish sand. No grave goods were present.

Immediately underlying the huge domestic refuse pit and the apparent interment pit was another stratum of wall collapse and wall melt materials (levels 30, 35 and 36). Intruding in this layer of wall wall collapse and wall melt were a putative mud wall and an evident open hearth. The putative wall (levels 32 and 34) was rectilinear in outline and appeared to have been constructed with irregular mud brick. It extended along the western edge of the unit and between 2.25 m. and 2.50 m. The open hearth (level 36 and 38) occupied the center of the unit. It was associated with grey and white ash horizons and brown burnt soil. These two archaeological features (the putative mud wall and the hearth) clearly indicated an occupation level, which dated to 1630±60 BP (Beta 40446) on charcoal collected from the hearth. This calibrates to AD 410 - 431, using Stuiver and Pearson's calibration curves at one standard error (Stuiver and Pearson 1986). Pottery in this occupation level consisted of Early Assemblage pottery. Level 38 was closed with artifacts still occurring.

Unit **AK4** was located near the second highest point of Akumbu A, almost at the northern edge of the mound and situated on the site of a burnt clay structure, which was believed to be an indication of a "residential area." Our principal motive in focusing excavation Unit AK4 on the site of a burnt clay structure was to illuminate the nature and function of this structure. Many examples of this type of structure were present either isolated or clustered on the surface of Akumbu and most major IA settlement mounds of the Méma. Unit AK4, initially measuring 2×2 m. in area, was extended an additional 20cm to the south to encompass the total extent of the burnt clay structure. This southward extension was closed immediately after excavations reached a hard clay stratum of wall collapse with yellowish brick rubble beneath the burnt clay structure at 0.40 m.

The point of origin of Unit AK4 was located at the south east corner of the unit. The unit was excavated through 27 levels and to the depth of 2.20 m. Unfortunately, excavations did not reach the sterile and natural deposit. Like AK3, it was covered, awaiting a second field season. The excavated levels are shown in Figure 4.10, while Table 4.3 reconstructs the depositional process represented by the individual excavated levels. The burnt clay structure, which occupied the southwestern corner of the unit, was excavated as levels 1, 2, 6 and 7. It was roughly a triangular structure, which extended from 0.10 to 0.45 m. in depth (Figure 4.11). Although different in plan, it was similar in construction with the one in levels 24 and 29 of Unit AK1. Its wall, made with one seating of irregular rectangular clay bricks, had been hardened by evident firing. Its interior was filled with a thick deposit of dark grey ash, mixed with charcoal. This ashy deposit covered a compact and brownish floor, also hardened by firing. Like the one of levels 24 and 29 in Unit AK1, this burnt clay structure was clearly used as an oven or hearth. It marked the last occupation level of Unit AK4. It was radiocarbon dated to 970±50 BP (Beta Analytic 40447) from charcoal collected from the ashy deposits inside the burnt clay structure. Using Stuiver and Pearson's calibration curve at one standard error this date calibrates to AD 1024-1183 (Stuiver and Pearson 1986). This same occupation level in Unit AK4 is approximately contemporaneous with the second level occupation in Unit AK1, which also witnessed building of burnt clay structure, and was dated to calAD 985-1160.

Beneath the burnt clay structure and extending from only a few centimeters below the surface to approximately 1.00

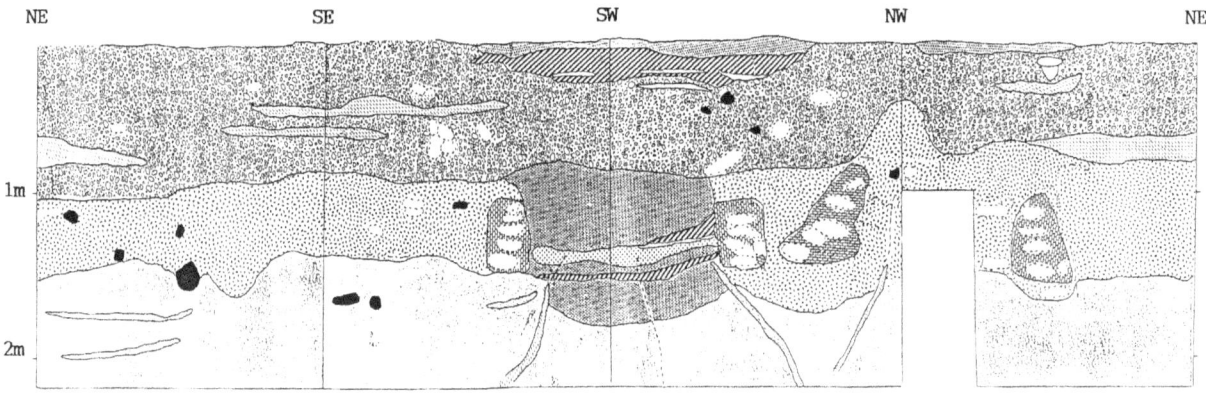

Figure 4.9. AK4. Natural Strata

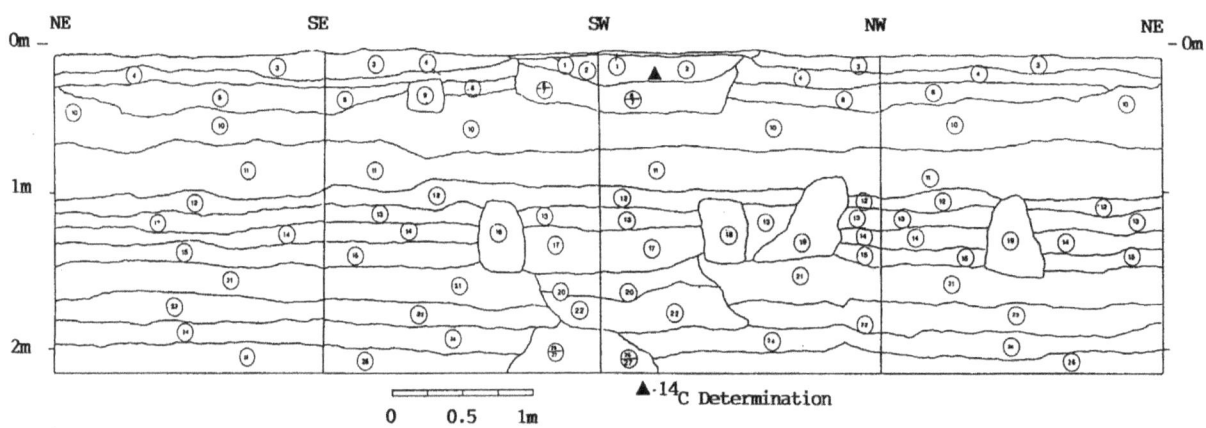

Figure 4.10. AK4. Excavated levels

Figure 4.11. AK4. Burnt clay structure

m. of depth was a stratum of firm loam, representing wall collapse and wall melt. This stratum was excavated as levels 3, 4, 5, 8 and 10. It seemed to have been exposed during accumulation as suggested by the presence of pockets and microlayers of laminated yellowish to khaki sand. At a depth of 0.50 m. and extending from the east wall toward the center of the unit was a concentration of yellowish clay bricks. This concentration of bricks, thought to indicate a wall, was excavated as level 9.

This layer of wall melt deposit was underlaid by a stratum of hard and yellowish clay, which was excavated as levels 11, 12, 13, and 15 (Figures 4.9 and 4.10). This stratum contained a profusion of brick rubble and brick chunks and seemed to have been accumulated in a short period of time by the rapid collapse of a series of mud structures, which were excavated as levels 16, 18, and 19. The first of these structures was the stump of a curvilinear mud brick wall, which possibly belonged to a round house. It was constructed with a single seating of roughly rectangular bricks. It protruded between 1.20 m. and 1.40 m. of depth and extended from the south wall to the west wall of the unit. The second was the base of a rectilinear mud brick wall which extended from the north wall of the unit and almost abutted the curvilinear wall. It was only one brick thick and also constructed with irregular rectangular bricks. The remaining two mud brick walls (Figure 4.10) were very similar to the second, just described above. These mud structures marked another occupation level, the second encountered in Unit AK4. Between 1.0 m. and 2.15 m. of depth and occupying the southwest corner of the unit was a disposal pit which was excavated as level 17, 20 and 22. This disposal pit (Figure 4.10) was filled with alternating layers of loose sand and dark ashy deposits mixed with pieces of charcoal, large pot sherds, and animal bones. At 1.80 m. of depth and underlying both the stratum of rapid wall collapse and the disposal pit was a layer of light loam which was excavated as levels 21 through 27. This layer seemed to contain no archaeological features. The unit was closed in level 27, with cultural material still occurring.

IV: SUMMARY OF OCCUPATION AT AKUMBU MOUND COMPLEX

The examination of the stratigraphy, artifact sequences and the seven radiocarbon determinations permit some general and preliminary conclusions on the chronology of occupation at the Akumbu mound complex. The seven radiocarbon dates obtained from the excavations fall between the fourth and fourteenth centuries cal AD (Table 4.4).

The three excavation units, AK1, AK3, and AK4, appear to have been in "residential" sectors of Akumbu A and Akumbu B. This was indicated by the nature of the archaeological deposits, which in each of the excavated units consisted primarily of domestic remains including the decay of mud structures, hearths, ceramics, animal bones, and ash. The three excavation units revealed dissimilar occupational histories, with archaeological levels or artifact series present in one and absent from the others. This was supported by the radiocarbon determinations, which showed that occupation in the three units did not always coincide (Figure 4.12). The earliest radiocarbon determination, in the fourth-fifth century AD, was obtained on wood charcoal, collected from a hearth feature and at approximately 2.75 m. of depth in Unit AK3, situated on the summit of Mound B. This hearth feature (L 36 and 38) was found within a deposit defined by the presence of numerous fragments of pottery with characteristic features of the Early Assemblage and that of permanent architectural remains, notably mud brick walls and mud wall collapse. However, given the presence of LSA artifacts on the flank of the dune beneath Akumbu B, there are strong possibilites that occupation at this mound might extend back to the LSA. As noted above, excavations at AK3 did not reach the sterile deposit. Therefore, further investigations are necessary to confirm this hypothesis and to pinpoint the plausible transition between LSA and IA deposits. The upper strata of AK3, for which a tenth century AD date is available, were associated with the

Table 4.3: Depositional Sequence in Unit AK4.

Levels	Excavated Depositional events
6	Burnt clay structure [Beta 40447 cal. AD 1024-1183].
4	Hard strata of wall collapse with discernible brick rubble.
8/10	Hard strata of wall collapse. Similar in texture to levels 3/4/5
9	Putative mud brick wall
11/12/13	Hard stratum of wall collapse. Profusion of yellowish clay bricks. Decay of mud brick walls excavated in Levels 16, 18, and 19.
14/15	Continuation of wall collapse of levels 11/12/13. Still contains abundant yellowish brick rubble
16	Mud brick wall. Constructed with irregular rectangular bricks.
18	Mud brick wall, similar to that of level 16.
19	Mud brick wall. Also constructed with irregular rectangular bricks. Curvilinear in plan
17/12/22	Disposal pit. filled with alternating layers of loosely compacted sand mixed with ash and small pieces of charcoal.
21/22/23	Light loamy soil, occasionally flecked with small pieces of charcoal
24/25/26	Continuation of the loamy soil of levels 21/22/23
27	Disposal pit with abundant charcoal and animal bones

Table 4.4: Radiocarbon dates obtained from the excavation at Akumbu

Lab no. (Beta)	Sample no.	C-14 Age years B.P	Calendar years (calculated)
40441	AK1 L6	640 ± 70	AD 1274 - 1401
40442	AK1 L10	750 ± 70	AD 1205 - 1288
40443	AK1 L24	980 ± 70	AD 985 - 1160
40444	AK1 L41	1430 ± 70	AD 548 - 661
40445	AK1 L67	1390 ± 80	AD 604 - 681
40446	AK3 L38	1630 ± 60	AD 342 - 442
40447	AK4 L1	910 ± 50	AD 1024 - 1183
49720	AK3 L12	1130 ± 100	AD 780 - 1100

Middle Assemblage pottery. This Middle Assemblage deposits contained a rich and extended burial whose offerings included two water jars and traded goods such as cowrie shells, copper bracelets, and stone beads. As discussed below, these artifacts were also characteristic of the most intensive occupation period at Akumbu A.

The radiocabon determinations obtained from AK1 indicated that Akumbu A, the largest mound, was occupied between the seventh and fourteenth century AD. The entire 7.5 m. cultural sequence of Unit AK1 and the 2.20 m. excavated strata of Unit AK4 were characterized by the Middle Assemblage pottery, mixed in the lower levels of AK1 with few elements characteristic of Early Assemblage. Both the stratigraphic information and radiocarbon determinations from Unit AK1 allow me to suggest two broad occupation periods.

The earliest of these occupation periods (seventh century AD to early twelfth century AD), defined by the absence of any evidence for mud architecture, was a period of rapid accumulation. The approximately 4 m. (3.75 to 7.50 m) of cultural deposits during this period appear to have been deposited in a maximum of five centuries. This rapid accumulation was certainly due to the presence at the bottom of the unit of a low-lying terrain or basin which was filled up with a mixture of clayey loam and large amounts of domestic debris. The only indications of a 'living surface' within these 4 m. of cultural deposits were a series of small hearths (between approximately 3.75 m. and 6.00 m) often associated with ash horizons. Occurrence of non ceramic artifacts was erratic, compared to the upper strata.

The second occupation period (late twelfth - fourteenth century AD), encountered in the upper 3 m. of deposits, was the most intensive. It was defined by the presence of permanent architectural remains in the form of wall collapse material and a series of mud structures including the foundation of a curvilinear house (L. 34), the remains of burnt clay structure (L. 24 and 29) and a rectilinear mud brick wall (L. 6). In addition, non-ceramic artifacts were abundant during this period of most intensive occupation and included iron slag, iron artifacts, cooper objects, cowrie shells, a few bone artifacts, spindle whorls, and numerous clay beads. Akumbu's people were certainly prosperous during this period of intensive occupation, given the presence of luxury goods such as copper and cowrie shells.

This period of intensive occupation at AK1 was paralleled in the 2.20 m. excavated strata of AK4, which revealed similar artifacts and stratigraphic levels including mud walls, layers of wall collapse, and a burnt clay structure. This burnt clay structure was contemporaneous with the one in levels 24/29 of AK1 (Figure 4.12). The area of AK4 on the northern edge of Akumbu A was abandoned around twelfth century AD.

In summary, the expanded mound complex of Akumbu, which extended more than 30 ha, appears to have developed out of the relatively small mound of Akumbu B, from which the earliest radiocarbon dates came. Population transfer from this mound to nearby Akumbu A likely occurred around the seventh century AD. The accumulation of the 7.50 m. cultural deposit in the area of AK1, near the highest point of Akumbu A, seems to have occurred in a maximum of seven centuries. This time span of occupation is very constricted, compared to that for mound expansion at Jenne-jeno, Shoma and Mara (in the current Inland Niger Delta), which were all occupied for at least a millenium and half, between the the third century BC and the fourteenth century AD (McIntosh and McIntosh 1980, SK McIntosh in press; Haskell et al. 1988). Of the IA settlement mounds of the Middle Niger for which complete stratigraphic information is known only Mouyssam (KNT 2) near Sumpi in the Lakes Region (Dembélé 1986; Raimbault 1991), and Mound B on the bank of the Fala de Molodo (Méma) (Haaland 1980), have a period of occupation shorter than that of Akumbu A. These two sites were respectively inhabited between AD 300 and AD 680 (Dembélé 1986; Raimbault 1991) and the eighth and twelfth centuries AD (Haaland 1980). The stability seen in the pottery of AK1 is certainly consistent with this short time span of occupation. A radiocarbon date of 665±40 BP (calibrated 1280 -1310) runs on charcoal collected near the surface and is also available for the mound of Kolima, in the easten part of our survey area and 22km east of Nampala (Fontes et al. 1980, 1991). This date and the presence of similar artifact assemblages (in particular Middle Assemblage pottery) suggests that Kolima and Akumbu were both abandoned at about the same period. It is interesting to note that the period of abandonment of these two mounds in the Méma for which C14 dates are available corresponds to the end occupation at Jenné-jeno and Shoma (in the current Niger Delta) during Phase IV (1200-1400 AD) (McIntosh and McIntosh, 1980, 1190; Haskell et al. 1988). Site abandonment in many regions of the Middle Niger, which implies depopulation, appears to be a widespread phenomenon during that period.

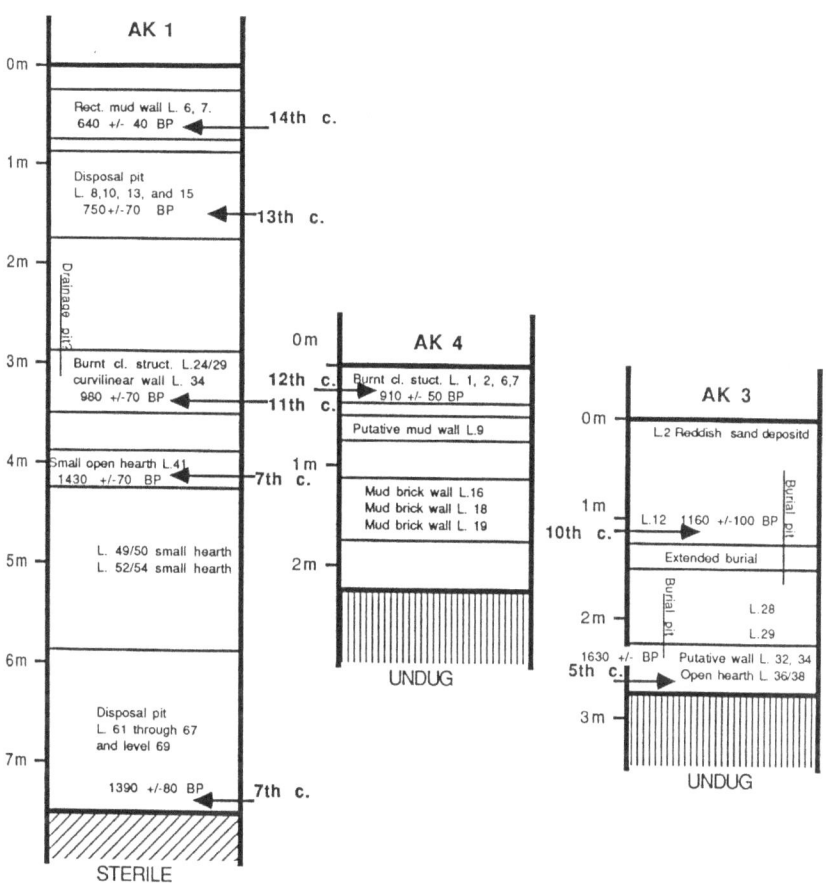

Figure 4.12. Chronological relationship between excavation units AK1, AK3, and AK4

CHAPTER 5
EXCAVATED MATERIALS OTHER THAN POTTERY

The first section of this chapter is devoted to the description of artifacts, other than pottery, retrieved from the excavations at Akumbu A and Akumbu B. These artifacts, labeled as Small Finds, fall into 17 artifact categories. Short summaries for human skeletal remains and botanical materials recovered follow in the final sections of the chapter. Faunal remains were studied by K. MacDonald, whose report is presented in Appendix 1.

I. METALLURGICAL REMAINS.

Iron slag

Iron slag was by far the most common category of the artifacts, other than pottery. In total, 208 pieces of iron slag weighing over two kilograms were uncovered from the 1990 excavations at Akumbu mound complex. Iron slag generally occurred in isolated trace bits and pieces throughout the entire 7.5 m cultural sequence of AK1, and the excavated strata of AK3 and AK4. The slag encountered varied in texture and outer appearance. While some specimens were heavy, dark blue or black in color with a flow or glassy appearance, others also heavy were brownish with rugose surface. Lightweight, porous and greyish cinderlike examples were also present. This difference in outer appearance was difficult to interpret. However, based on Bachmann's (1982) classification the specimens with flow or glassy appearance can be considered as tapped slags and the heavy brownwish and rugous examples as furnace slag. Haskell et al. (1988) who encountered lightweight and cinderlike specimens at Shoma and Mara near Dia, qualified them as smithing slags. As no furnace remains (suggesting smelting) were found at none of the excavated mounds, it is unknown how the slag pieces found their way to the sites surface and into the deposits.

Iron objects

In total, 57 iron objects were recovered from the three excavation units. A high proportion (over 90%) of these iron objects were badly corroded and in fragmentary state, making difficult the determination of their initial appearance and use. The function of only six specimens (less than 10%) could be definitively ascertained. Among these, four were rings or fragments of rings, and two were knife blades (Table 5.1). Eighteen corroded and fragments of iron artifacts measuring between 3 and 4cm, were assumed to have been putative nails or small projectile points as they displayed a roughly rounded cross-section and sometimes a pointed end.

Copper objects

In total, seven cuprous objects were found. With the exception of two bracelets, all these copper objects were too corroded and fragmentary to be identified. The two bracelets were found on each wrist of the extended burial encountered in Unit AK3 (Figure 5.1). They were both flat in cross-section, with a maximum thickness of 1cm at the end. They measured between 6.5 and 7cm in diameter and weighed 64g and 65g. The result of the chemical analysis of one of the copper bracelet (I am grateful to Mr. Milton of the Geology Department of Rice University for having conducted this analysis) indicated that it was an alloy constituted of copper (92.29%), tin (2.12%), arsenic (5.35%), and antimony (0.03%) (Figure 5.2). The closest potential sources of these copper objects of are Nioro du Shahel in northwestern Mali or Akjoujt in Mauritania. At this latter location, archaeological investigations by Mauny (1951), followed by excavations executed by Lambert (1971) have uncovered early copper production centers dating to the fifth century BC. Nioro remains

Figure 5.1. Copper bracelet

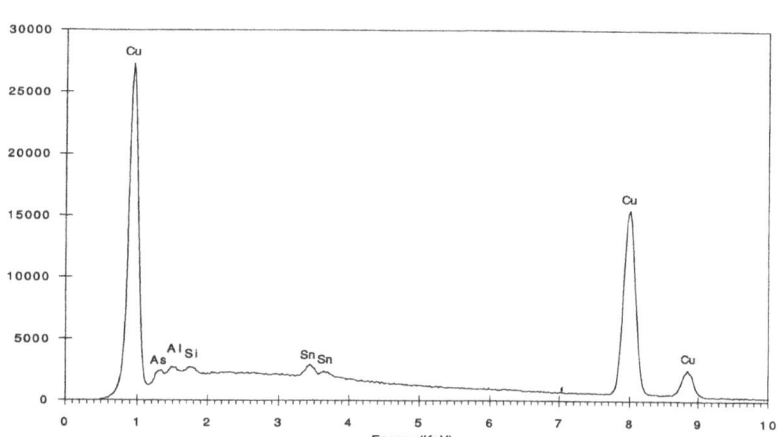

Figure 5.2. Copper analysis

Excavated Material other than Pottery

Figure 5.3. Stone beads   *Figure 5.4. Spindle whorls*

Table 5.1: Identifiable iron objects

Provenience	Description	Weight	Dimensions
AK1 L5	Ring. Roughly circular in outline. Closed. Rounded cross-section.	9.5 g	Diam: 3 cm; Section: 5 mm.
AK1 L5	Knife blade. Broken. Tang present and approximately central to the butt of the blade.	45 g.	Length of the tang: 4cm; Width of the blade: 2.5 – 3 cm
AK1 L18	Knife blade. Broken. Ancient break of tang. Tang seems to have been central to butt of blade.	23.5 g.	
AK3 L10	Ring. Broken. Circular in outline. Rounded section.	5 g.	Diameter: 4cm; Section: 3mm.
AK3 L35	Fragment of ring w/rounded section.	1.3 g.	Section l: 2mm

Table 5.2. Stone beads

Provenience	Description	Length	Maxi.	Bore	Weight	Material
AK3 (burial)	Biconical. Polished coral	10mm	9mm	1mm	1.3g	quartz
AK3 (burial)	Biconical. Polished coral	10mm	7mm	1mm	1.1g.	quartz.
AK3 (burial)	Biconical. Polished	8mm	7mm	1.2mm	1g.	white quartz
AK3 (burial)	Biconical. Polished	9mm	8mm	1.5mm	1.1g	white florescent quartz.
AK3 (burial).	Barrel shaped. Polished	8mm	6mm	1mm	0.8g	coral quartz.
AK3 (burial)	Barrel shaped. Polished	8mm	7mm	2mm	1g	white florescent quartz.
AK3 (burial)	Barrel shaped. Polished	8mm	7mm	2mm	1.9g	white florescent quartz.
AK3 (burial)	Barrel shaped. Polished	6mm	5mm	1mm	0.7g	coral quartz.
AK3 (burial)	Barrel shaped. Polished	6mm	5mm	1mm	0.7g	coral quartz.
AK3 (burial)	Barrel shaped. Polished	5mm	4mm	1.5mm	0.7g	white florescent quartz.
AK3 (burial)	?	1.5mm	6mm		1g	coral quartz.
AK3 (burial)	Disc-shaped. Polished	-	7mm	1.5mm	1g	coral quartz.
AK3 (burial)	Rounded. Polished	-	6mm	1mm	0.8g	white florescent quartz.

Table 5.3. Spindle whorls

Provenience	Description	Diam.	Bore	Length	Weight
AK1 L4	Conical. Decorated on the entire surface w/longitudinal grooves and punctuations Incising and punctations filled w/white painting.	3.5 cm	0.5cm	3.5 cm	19 g
AK1 L4	Conical. Black. Incised and punctated at the base. Incised grooves organised to form a cross. Grooves and punctations painted in white.	2.8 cm	0.5 cm	3 cm	19 g
AK1 L6	Fragment. Black. Incised grooves painted in white.	-	-		2.5 g
AK1 L6	Conical. Incised and punctated at the base. Incised grooves organised to form a cross. Grooves and punctations painted in white.	2.5 cm	0.4 cm	2.5 cm	12 g
AK1 L8	Spherical. Black. Undec.	4 cm	0.8 cm	3 cm	21 g.
AK1 L31	Broken. Brown. Undec.	2 cm	0.3 cm	2.5 cm	9 g.

uninvestigated.

II. STONE ARTIFACTS OTHER THAN BEADS

Grindstones

In total 25 grindstones or fragments of grindstones were encountered. They were found isolated throughout the deposits of the three excavation units. They were all made in sandstone and showed one or more pecked surfaces. The sandstone used was certainly brought to the site from the Boulel ridge on which various types of stone (specially sandstone and laterite) occur. Among the grindstones were four polished and phallus shaped stone grinders, made also in sandstone. They were recovered from level 37 of AK3 (n=3) and level 6 of AK1 (n=1). They measured between eight and fifteen centimeters. These phallus shaped stone grinders exhibited one convex and pecked end, suggesting that they were possibly used for pounding or hammering. Examples of these hammer stones were present at the surface of most the I.A. mounds examined during the regional survey. M. Dembélé (1986) reports similar artifacts from the IA mound of Mouyssam near Soumpi in the Lakes Region and labels them as *"pierres phalliques"*. He suggests that in addition to a utilitarian aspect, they might also have had a symbolic function because of their resemblace in shape to the megaliths of Tondidarou.

Rubbing stones

Four small stone artifacts made of were encountered. They all came from Unit AK1. One was found in the disposal pit of level 8, two in level 9, and one in the wall collapse deposit of level 21. None of them displayed any determinate shape. They weighed 21, 11.5, 25 and 24 g. They were probably used for producing a red color by rubbing them against a hard surface. Apparently as a result of such use, each specimen showed one or more flattened and polished surfaces. Similar artifacts uncovered at Jenne-jeno (SK McIntosh & RJ McIntosh 1980, SK McIntosh in press) and Mara and Shoma near Dia (Haskell et al. 1988) have been interpreted by their discoverors as "potter's ochre".

Figure 5.5. Clay beads

III. STONE BEADS

A total number of 13 stone beads were uncovered. All of these stone beads were clustered between the skull and the elbow of the extended burial uncovered in Unit AK3 (Figure 5.3). Possibly, these beads composed a single necklace which adorned the corpse before burial. They were made from white or coral quartz and basically displayed four shapes; biconical, barrel-shaped or cylindrical, rounded, and disc-shaped (Table 5.2). They were all polished and displayed a straight and well-centered bore. Stone beads are reported to have been in use in Western Sudan since the LSA (Mauny 1961). However, according to Mauny (1961) large, long and lengthwise perforated stone beads were not made until the medieval period. This was due to the fact that the length of the perforation required not only great skill, but also an efficient instrument for boring.

IV: SPINDLE WHORLS

In total, six spindle whorls were uncovered. All these specimens were found between the penultimate and final occupation levels of Unit AK1 and dated between cal AD 985-1160 and cal. AD 1274-1401. The spindle whorls uncovered at Akumbu were basically of two shapes; conical, and spherical (Table 5.3). They ranged in diameter from 2.5 to 3.0cm, with a bore diameter varying between 0.5cm to 1.0cm. They were all made with very fine paste. With the exception of one specimen, they were fired black. Two specimens were undecorated and four were decorated with incised grooves and punctuations. Both of these designs were always filled with white paint (Figure 5.4). Spindle whorls are a good indication of cotton working, especially spinning and weaving. They are pierced from top to bottom for the tight insertion of a thin wooden stick. When a spindle whorl is held at the base of a spindle, it increases and regularizes its movement. Mauny (Mauny 1961) considers their presence as one of the indications of the contact with the Arabs who introduced cotton in West Africa around AD 800. Spindle whorls have been found in abundance at the medieval entrepot cities of Koumbi Saleh, assumed to represent the capital of the Empire of Ghana, (Mauny 1961) and Tegdaoust (Chaleix 1983). They appear in Phase IV deposits (dated between AD 850 -1400) at Jenné-Jeno (McIntosh & McIntosh 1980, McIntosh in press) and Phase IV and Phase V deposit of Mara, near Dia (Haskell et al. 1988).

V. CLAY BEADS

A total number of 44 fired clay beads were recovered from the 1990 excavations at Akumbu (Figure 5.5). These fired clay beads were of five types; flat-disk shaped, cylindrical, spherical and carinated. They were all fired, black in color and undecorated. They ranged in diameter from 2 mm to1.5 mm. Their bores, averaging 1 mm in diameter, were often poorly drilled and not always centered. Average weight was 2 g. The majority of these clay beads (41) may have composed a single string, when originally deposited. They were found together in the western part of level 6 of Unit AK1. The remaining were recovered from a wall collapse/ wall melt deposit (level 1, with two) and a disposal pit (level 8, with one) of Unit Ak1.

VI. SHELL BEADS

Only three shell beads were encountered during the Akumbu excavations. They were found in levels 40 and 51 of AK1, and level 22 of AK3. All these shell beads were roughly circular in outline with an average diameter of 5 mm and a maximum thickness of 1 mm.

VII. GLASS BEADS

A single glass bead was recovered from the excavation at Akumbu A. This glass bead was half broken. It was found in level 66 of Unit AK1 and in a midden deposit, which was dated to AD 604- 681. It was poorly-made, with a roughly rounded shape and a rugose surface. It was plain and white, transluscent in color. It measured 1.5 cm in diameter, with a perforation diameter of 2 mm. It weighed 0.8g. The chronology of this single glass bead is somewhat disturbing. No historical source mentions the existence of trade in glass beads in the Western Sudan prior to the tenth century AD (Mauny 1961). However, other glass beads dated to the first mid millenium AD, have been recovered from Jenne-jeno (McIntosh and McIntosh, 1980, SK McIntosh in press) and Mara, near Dia (Haskell et al.1988).

VIII. COWRIE SHELLS

In total, 21 cowrie shells were found. More than one half (13) of these cowrie shells were found clustered near the skull of the extended burial of unit AK3 (Figure 4.8) and possibly were hair ornaments or offered as grave goods. The remaining eight were found in levels 6 through 19 of Unit AK1. The cowrie shell specimens from Akumbu are currently being analysed to determine their species and potential origin. Mauny (1961: 420) and Johnson (1970) have underlined the importance of cowrie shells as fossil types or fossiles directeurs in West African archaeology and stated that they were used as currency in West Africa as early as the eleventh century AD (Mauny1961; Jonhson 1970). Cypraea Moneta, which originates from the Maladive Islands in the Indian Ocean, seems to have been the earliest species to penetrate Sub-Saharan West Africa through the trans-Saharan trade (Mauny1961; Jonhson 1970). Several examples of this species have been recovered from Kumbi Saleh, the putative capital of the Empire of Ghana (Mauny 1961).

IX. BONE ARTIFACTS

Five specimens of bone artifacts were recovered, all from AK1. Among these, only one specimen could be determined with certainty as a pendant. It was made from the phalanx of a small bovid (gazelle, goat or sheep). It was polished and pierced in the distal end. It measured 3.5cm and weighed 1.5g. The other specimens, thought presenting evidence of reworking (cutting and polishing) were too fragmentary to be identified.

X. BOTANICAL REMAINS

A major interest of the 1989/90 excavations was the recovery of botanical materials. Accordingly, soil samples for flotation were collected from all archaeological features, especially from refuse pits and burnt areas which we believed were more likely to yield charred seeds and other botanical remains. As water was a major problem in the Méma (it had to be drawn from wells 50 to 60m deep), the flotation samples could not be processed on-site. Therefore, they were transported to the ISH in Bamako where they were processed in March 1993 by Cecilia Capezza. The processed flots await specialist study.

For the moment, the only evidence for plant remains we possess from the mound complex of Akumbu are casts of Pennisetum millet stalks. These, recovered throughout the 7.50m cultural deposits at AK1 and the excavated strata of AK3 and AK4, were easily identifiable. The interior was filled with casts of mud, possibly following termite activities. These casts, with the same shape and same size (in cross-section) of the millet stalks, were often burnt, and thus were well preserved. Before the beginning of the excavations at Akumbu, we were fortunate to observe similar casts of millet stalks in both modern millet fields and near burnt straw houses around Nampala.

The occurrence of Pennisetum millet at Akumbu is of particular interest. It implies that early as the fifth century AD, the western part of the Méma was dry enough to allow millet cultivation.

XI. HUMAN SKELETAL REMAINS

A total of three single burials were detected during the excavations at Akumbu mound complex. These skeletons, all found in Unit AK3 on Akumbu B, are referred here as skeletons 1, 2 and 3. These numbers reflect the order in which they were found. Of the three burials, only the osteological remains of skeleton one could be exposed and recovered. The bones of skeletons 2 and 3 were in completely disintegrated states and were identified (thanks to Kevin MacDonald) during the analysis of the faunal remains. Information on on these two skeleton is provided in Appendix 1.

Burial conditions and context of skeleton 1
Though its bones were crumbling to powder at any contact, skeleton 1 could be recorded and analysed *in situ* by Kevin MacDonald. It was lying in an apparent burial pit. This pit, though undetected during excavations, was clearly defined in the west section of the unit. The skeleton, found at 1.40m of depth, was oriented southeast-northwest with the head facing north/northeast. It was accompanied with a complete pot (illustrated in Figure 6.29), 13 cowrie shells, 11 stone beads, and two copper bracelets, one at each wrist (see Figure 4.8).

Description of Skeleton 1
Skeleton 1 was complete except for the distal part of the right ulna, which had been destroyed, possibly by rodents. The following notations on age, and sex of this skeleton refer to MacDonald's analysis *in situ*.

Sex. Female. On the basis of the generally slender skull and the large angle (between 100° and 110°) of the sciatic notch the sex of the individual is judge to have been female. The slender jaw, rounded at mid-point and the small mastoid process further support this assessment.

Age. Young adult. 17 - 25 years. This age was assigned with high degree of confidence based on fusion of cranial sutures and epiphyses, and on dental attrition. All long bone epiphyses were fused and M3 was recently erupted and presented little dental wear. No pathological conditions and anomalies were noted.

CHAPTER 6
SURVEY AND EXCAVATION POTTERY

I. INTRODUCTION

The principal objectives of the study of the pottery were three-fold: 1: to identify and describe in a preliminary manner the pottery assemblages recovered from different sites during excavation and survey; 2: to evaluate the chronological and spatial variability of these pottery assemblages; and 3: to compare the pottery of the Méma to that of other regions of the Middle Niger. The elucidation of these questions was of primary importance, given the lack of any previous pottery classification for the Méma. A description of 99 vessels from the 'tumulus' of Kolima (actually a settlement mound located in the eastern part of the study area) was performed by Pascale Schmit (1985). These vessels, collected from excavations by Serge Christoforoff (head hydrologist of the ON at Kolima in 1929), were exhibited at the *Exposition Coloniale* in 1931 at Paris and subsequently deposited at the *Musée des Arts Africains et Océanéens* (Schmit 1985). A brief description and photos of a few complete vessels from Szumowski's excavations at Péhé (Szumowski 1956) were also available.

The three sequential pottery assemblages, Early, Middle, and Late, were identified in the survey pottery and are described here. Each of these assemblages was established on the basis of co-occurrrence and patterning of multiple ceramic attributes (in particular rims types and decorative attributes) at a number of sites. The Early, and Middle Assemblages could be radiocarbon dated as they were also encountered at the excavations at Akumbu mound complex. The Late Assemblage, exclusively found during the survey, could be dated only by relative chronological methods.

The analysis of the body sherds and that of the rim sherds were conducted with the assistance of, respectively, the Excel and Stat View programs. The frequencies of the various attributes within site and excavated level at Unit AK1 are presented on graphs executed with Excel.

The analysis begins with an examination of the collection and recording procedures of the pottery, followed by a presentation and definition of the various variables recorded and employed in the analysis. The pottery collected during the survey is then presented, followed with that of the excavations. The last section of the study is a brief discussion assessing the affinities and divergences between the pottery of the Méma and that of adjoining regions.

II. METHODS OF RECOVERY AND RECORDING PROCEDURES

Recovery of the surface pottery
Due to time constraints and limited number of personnel, the pottery of only approximately 25% (23) of the surveyed IA sites could be recorded and included in the analysis. Two different approaches were employed for data recovery. The first consisted of collecting all pot sherds within two to three 2m x 2m squares at sites large sites, and one 2m x 2m at small sites. However, these 2m x 2m squares, called collection units, were not systematically correlated to absolute site sizes. They were judgmentally placed at different parts of the sites, taking mainly into account the density of surface scatter, and the desirability of dispersing the collection units over the site in an attempt to sample functionally or chronologically different areas. The decision to collect all sherds within each collection unit was aimed at reducing bias toward highly decorated or unusual sherds. The second approach consisted of a general surface collection in which one to two bags of preferentially selected sherds were collected from all over the site surface. Potsherds with unknown features, or features known from already surveyed sites, and/or characteristics of the well known pottery sequences from the Inland Delta were of particular interest. This general and preferential surface collection was aimed at supplementing the non-preferential collection. Pottery collected was placed in cloth bags labelled with the site name, the collection unit number or the general surface and brought to Nampala,

Table 6.1: Early Assemblage. Other decorative motifs on body sherds

Sites	Chan+ tw	Slip+ punct	Chan only	Chan+ chan	Chan+ finger	Chan+ paint	Paint over tw	tw4+ tw14	tw6+ tw14
Goud. A	-	-	4	-	1	-	-	3	1
Toulé C	2	1	6	-	-	-	-	2	-
Bourgou F	2	-	4	-	-	1	-	1	1
Bourgou C	1	-	4	-	1	-	-	-	-
BB south C	-	-	2	-	-	-	-	1	1
BB south I	3	-	3	1	-	-	-	1	-
BB north G	1	-	2	-	-	-	1	-	-
Niess. D	5	2	7	-	-	-	1	3	-
Niess. F	2	-	3	-	-	-	-	2	1
Kolima C	3	-	3	-	-	1	-	-	2

our base camp. These were subsequently transported to the ISH storage facilty in Bamako for recording.

Recovery of excavation pottery
At each of the three excavation units, potsherds were recovered from excavated soil screened through a 0.5cm screen. All the sherds from each day's excavations were placed in cloth bag labelled with the excavation unit, LRF and stratigraphic level numbers, and brought to Nampala where they were washed and left to dry by our workers. They were subsequently rebagged and, as for the survey pottery, transported to Bamako for recording. However, due to the limited number of personnel available (all recording was executed by myself) and time constraints, pottery recovered from AK3 and AK4 could not be recorded and is currently in storage at Korofina, the ISH storage facility in Bamako.

Recording Procedures
In an attempt to pursue continuity with previous ceramic studies in the Middle Niger, the recording methodology employed by the McIntoshes in the Inland Delta (SK McIntosh & RJ McIntosh 1980; Haskell et al.1988; SK McIntosh in press), was followed. This recording methodology has proved to be very useful as it has allowed, through detailed typologies, the compilation of pottery sequences and cultural phases in the Inland Delta (McIntosh and McIntosh 1980; Haskell et al.1988; SK McIntosh in press). In addition, the adoption of the standard recording systems employed by the McIntoshes, it was believed, would enhance the comparability between the pottery of the recorded pottery data of the Méma and that from the Jenné and Dia regions, the sole regions of the Middle Niger (indeed of the whole of Mali) where a pottery classification and extended pottery sequences are available. During the recording and the analysis, the rim profiles and decoratives attributes, which have proven to be the most temporally diagnostic variables around Jenné and Dia in the current Niger Delta (SK McIntosh & RJ McIntosh 1980; Haskell et al. 1988; SK McIntosh in press), were prominently featured.

For each pottery bag, the recording began by separating the body sherds from the feature sherds (rims, bases and handles). Body sherds and feature sherds were then recorded separately. For both categories, a careful search was executed to detect all the sherds belonging to the same pot. These sherds were then set aside and only one of them was retained for recording. This was intended to avoid inflating the samples with a large number of sherds from a single vessel.

Recording of the body sherds
In total, six variables were selected for recording and describing the body sherds. These variables, described below, comprised provenience, temper, and decorative motifs (slip, twine impression, plastic decoration, and paint). For each pottery bag, the body sherds with the identical single attributes were counted and recorded on a standard data recording sheet. Body sherds with multiple attributes, i.e. those with two or more decorative motifs, were recorded on a separate sheet. For each multiple attribute sherd, a sketch illustrating the various decorative motifs was executed on the far right side of the recording sheet.

Recording of the rim sherds
The rim sherds were described in much more detail than the body sherds. In addition to the six attributes (provenience, temper, slip, twine impression, plastic decoration, and paint) retained for the body sherds, each rim sherd was described and recorded in term of four other individual properties including rim profile, rim thickness, rim diameter and the position of the decorative motif. Rim angle was considered only for simple rims. Each of the rim attributes (provenience, rim form, and the various decorative attributes) was coded and entered into the computer. An example of this computer data entry sheet is provided in Figure 6.1 and Figure 6.2.

III. DEFINITION OF THE RECORDED VARIABLES

Provenience. For the surface pottery, provenience referred to the site name, the number of collection unit, and / or general surface. For the excavation pottery, it indicated the excavation unit, the number of LRF and stratigraphic level.

Temper. Temper, according to Shephard's definition, refers to the non-plastic inclusions potters deliberately

Table 6.2: Middle Assemblage. Other decorative motifs on body sherds.

Sites	Chan only	Slip+ chan	Chan+ tw	Chan+ slip + tw	Chan+ punct	Chan+ finger	Chan+ stab	Pt over. chan.	Adj. tw motifs
Goud. B	14	17	5	4	-	-	-	4	-
Toulé A	8	13	3	6	-	-	-	2	-
Toulé B	5	4	2	2	-	-	-	-	-
Akumbu A	2	7	1	2	-	1	-	1	-
Akumbu B	6	8	3	2	-	-	-	-	1
Akumbu C	7	6	2	2	-	-	-	2	-
Ndoupa	2	4	-	3	1	-	-	3	-
Bourgou A	11	14	3	2	-	-	1	2	-
BB north A	3	6	-	1	-	-	-	-	-
Boundu S.	3	9	4	3	-	1	-	3	-
Kolima A	1	5	3	2	-	-	-	2	-
Toladié	8	7	4	2	-	-	1	2	-

	Prov.	R. type	R. Angle	R. diam.	Thick.	Slip	Slip posi...	Tw.	Tw. po...	Chan.	Chan. po...	plast.	plast. po...	Paint.	Paint pos...	Ad. tw.
1	1	15	·	·	5	·	·	·	·	·	·	·	·	·	·	·
2	1	15	·	28	10	1	2	14	5	·	·	·	·	·	·	·
3	1	15	·	15	6	·	·	14	5	·	·	·	·	·	·	·
4	1	18	·	22	11	·	·	6	4	3	7	·	·	·	·	·
5	1	15	·	26	7	·	2	14	5	·	·	·	·	·	·	·
6	1	15	·	16	6	1	2	14	5	·	·	·	·	·	·	4
7	1	15	·	15	6	·	·	14	5	·	·	·	·	·	·	·
8	1	6	·	36	15	·	·	14	5	·	·	·	·	·	·	·
9	1	15	·	28	10	1	2	14	5	·	·	·	·	·	·	·
10	1	10	3	24	11	1	5	·	·	·	·	·	·	·	·	·
11	1	15	·	28	10	1	2	14	5	·	·	·	·	·	·	·
12	1	15	·	17	5	·	·	14	4	·	·	·	·	·	·	·
13	1	15	·	17	5	·	·	14	4	·	·	·	·	·	·	·
14	1	21	·	25	9	·	·	·	·	2	4	·	·	·	·	·
15	1	15	·	28	10	1	2	14	5	·	·	·	·	·	·	·
16	1	15	·	28	10	1	2	14	5	·	·	·	·	·	·	·
17	1	18	·	·	6	1	2	14	5	·	·	·	·	·	·	·
18	1	15	·	17	5	·	·	14	4	·	·	·	·	·	·	·
19	1	15	·	28	10	1	2	14	5	·	·	·	·	·	·	·
20	1	15	·	16	6	1	2	14	5	·	·	·	·	·	·	4
21	1	15	·	25	6	1	2	14	5	·	·	·	·	·	·	·
22	1	15	·	28	10	1	2	14	5	·	·	·	·	·	·	·
23	1	18	·	23	7	·	·	14	5	·	·	·	·	·	·	·
24	1	6	·	38	13	·	·	6	5	·	·	·	·	·	·	·
25	1	18	·	18	6	1	2	14	4	·	·	·	·	·	·	·
26	1	15	·	14	6	1	2	14	5	·	·	·	·	·	·	4
27	1	15	·	28	8	1	4	14	·	·	·	·	·	·	·	·
28	1	15	·	15	6	·	·	14	5	·	·	·	·	·	·	·
29	1	6	·	36	13	·	·	14	5	·	·	·	·	·	·	·
30	1	18	·	23	7	·	·	14	5	·	·	·	·	·	·	·
31	1	21	·	25	10	1	4	·	·	3	3	4	·	·	·	·
32	1	2	3	18	5	1	3	6	6	3	6	·	·	·	·	·
33	1	21	·	25	9	·	·	·	·	2	4	·	·	·	·	·
34	1	15	·	14	6	1	2	14	5	·	·	·	·	·	·	4
35	1	2	3	18	5	·	·	·	·	3	5	6	4	·	·	·
36	1	15	·	28	10	1	2	14	5	·	·	·	·	·	·	·
37	1	15	·	·	7	1	2	14	5	·	·	·	·	·	·	·
38	1	6	·	36	13	·	·	14	5	·	·	·	·	·	·	·
39	1	15	·	28	10	1	2	14	5	·	·	·	·	·	·	·
40	1	10	3	24	11	1	5	·	·	·	·	·	·	·	·	·
41	1	2	3	18	5	1	3	6	6	3	6	·	·	·	·	·
42	1	2	3	18	5	1	3	6	6	3	6	·	·	·	·	·
43	1	6	·	36	13	·	·	14	5	·	·	·	·	·	·	·
44	1	6	·	36	13	·	·	14	5	·	·	·	·	·	·	·
45	1	15	·	26	7	1	2	14	5	·	·	·	·	·	·	·
46	1	21	·	25	9	·	·	·	·	2	4	·	·	·	·	·
47	1	21	·	25	9	·	1	·	·	6	2	4	·	·	·	·
48	1	15	·	17	5	·	·	14	4	·	·	·	·	·	·	·
49	1	6	·	36	13	·	·	14	5	·	·	·	·	·	·	·
50	1	15	·	17	5	·	·	14	4	·	·	·	·	·	·	·
51	1	25	·	10	15	·	·	4	5	·	·	·	·	·	·	·
52	1	25	·	10	15	·	·	6	·	·	·	·	·	·	·	·
53	1	15	·	28	10	1	2	14	5	·	·	·	·	·	·	·
54	1	25	·	10	15	·	·	4	·	·	·	·	·	·	·	·
55	1	15	·	17	5	·	·	14	4	·	·	·	·	·	·	·
56	1	15	·	15	6	·	·	14	5	·	·	·	·	·	·	·
57	1	18	·	22	11	·	·	6	4	3	7	·	·	·	·	·
58	1	6	·	36	13	·	·	14	5	·	·	·	·	·	·	·
59	1	21	·	25	10	1	4	·	·	3	4	·	·	·	·	·
60	1	25	·	10	15	·	·	·	·	·	·	·	·	·	·	·
61	1	15	·	15	6	·	·	14	5	·	·	·	·	·	·	·
62	1	25	·	10	15	·	·	6	5	·	·	·	·	·	·	·
63	2	1	1	16	8	·	8	4	·	·	·	·	·	·	·	·
64	2	2	4	22	10	1	2	6	5	·	·	·	·	·	·	·
65	2	13	·	23	10	1	5	·	·	3	5	6	6	·	·	·
66	2	2	1	22	14	·	·	4	6	1	3	·	·	·	·	·
67	2	7	·	25	9	·	·	6	6	1	3	·	·	·	·	·
68	2	7	·	23	15	·	·	4	5	·	·	·	·	·	·	·
69	2	26	·	24	10	·	·	·	·	·	·	3	·	·	·	·
70	2	14	·	25	12	·	·	·	·	·	·	·	·	·	·	·
71	2	24	·	23	9	1	8	·	·	·	·	·	·	·	·	·
72	2	7	4	28	12	1	·	6	·	3	·	·	·	·	·	·
73	2	14	·	26	8	1	5	·	·	1	3	·	·	·	·	·
74	2	32	·	·	10	1	5	·	·	1	3	·	·	·	·	·
75	2	29	1	·	·	·	·	·	·	2	4	4	·	7	·	·
76	2	32	·	·	10	1	5	·	·	1	3	·	·	·	·	·
77	2	2	1	20	13	1	5	6	·	2	·	·	·	·	·	·
78	2	13	·	25	10	1	8	·	·	2	·	·	·	·	·	·

Figure 6.1. Survey pottery data. Coded rims

Survey and Excavation Pottery

	Prov.	Rim type	Angle	Diam.	Thick.	Dec.	slip	Slip p.	tw	tw pos.	chan.	chan pos.	plastic	plastic pos.	paint	paint posit.	ad. tw
1	1	2	3	.	10	3	1	8	.	.	3	.	.	.	.	.	.
2	1	22	.	26	12	2	1	8	.	.	.	.	.	.	.	.	.
3	1	17	.	.	8	1	.	.	.	.	.	.	.	.	.	.	.
4	1	18	.	.	10	3	1	.	.	.	3	.	.	.	.	.	.
5	1	18	.	23	8	1	.	.	.	.	.	.	.	.	.	.	.
6	1	22	.	22	10	3	1	8	.	.	2	4	.	.	.	.	.
7	1	10	.	36	18	2	1	6	.	.	.	.	.	.	.	.	.
8	1	22	.	22	8	2	1	8	.	.	.	.	.	.	.	.	.
9	2	14	3	.	13	2	1	4	.	.	.	.	.	.	.	.	.
10	2	24	.	26	8	3	1	4	.	.	2	4	.	.	.	.	.
11	2	10	3	33	18	1	.	.	.	.	.	.	.	.	.	.	.
12	2	12	1	.	12	2	1	5	.	.	.	.	.	.	.	.	.
13	2	18	.	18	10	2	1	4	.	.	.	.	.	.	.	.	.
14	2	18	.	26	12	1	2	.	.	.	.	.	.	.	.	.	.
15	2	13	3	26	.	2	1	4	.	.	.	.	.	.	.	.	.
16	2	2	1	.	5	6	.	.	6	7	1	4	.	.	.	.	.
17	2	1	3	16	12	2	1	8	.	.	.	.	.	.	.	.	.
18	2	2	3	28	10	9	1	.	.	.	2	4	.	.	1	.	.
19	2	12	1	.	2	1	.	.	.	.	.	.	.	.	.	.	.
20	2	18	.	22	10	3	1	8	.	.	2	.	.	.	.	.	.
21	2	13	.	.	.	2	1	8	.	.	.	.	.	.	.	.	.
22	2	22	.	25	8	2	1	8	.	.	.	.	.	.	.	.	.
23	2	18	.	24	10	3	1	8	.	.	.	.	.	.	.	.	.
24	2	17	.	.	6	1	.	.	.	.	.	.	.	.	.	.	.
25	2	1	2	.	7	7	1	8	6	.	1	4	.	.	.	.	.
26	3	2	3	.	6	6	.	4	1	7	4	.	.	.	.	.	.
27	3	2	3	.	7	7	1	.	6	.	4	.	.	.	.	.	.
28	3	18	.	24	11	3	1	4	.	.	.	.	.	.	.	.	.
29	3	18	.	22	10	2	1	8	.	.	.	.	.	.	.	.	.
30	3	24	.	.	.	1	.	.	.	.	.	.	.	.	.	.	.
31	3	4	4	23	11	5	.	.	6	7	.	.	.	.	.	.	.
32	4	2	3	26	10	7	1	.	6	.	.	.	.	.	.	.	.
33	4	25	.	.	10	1	.	4	.	.	.	.	.	.	.	.	.
34	4	18	.	.	8	2	1	5	.	.	.	.	.	.	.	.	.
35	4	2	1	.	11	1	.	.	.	.	.	.	.	.	.	.	.
36	5	22	.	.	11	3	.	1	.	.	3	.	.	.	.	.	.
37	5	8	3	44	20	6	.	.	1	7	3	4	.	.	.	.	.
38	5	18	.	.	.	2	1	8	.	.	.	.	.	.	.	.	.
39	5	18	.	19	7	2	1	8	.	.	.	.	.	.	.	.	.
40	5	18	.	.	8	7	1	8	14	7	.	.	.	.	.	.	.
41	5	2	2	.	.	3	1	5	.	.	2	4	.	.	.	.	.
42	5	18	.	.	8	7	1	8	14	7	.	.	.	.	.	.	.
43	5	22	.	.	.	2	.	1	.	.	.	.	.	.	.	.	.
44	5	2	1	.	11	1	.	.	.	.	.	.	.	.	.	.	.
45	5	8	3	44	20	6	.	.	1	7	3	4	.	.	.	.	.
46	5	18	.	.	.	2	1	8	.	.	.	.	.	.	.	.	.
47	5	8	3	44	20	6	.	.	1	7	3	4	.	.	.	.	.
48	5	31	.	6	10	3	1	5	.	.	3	4	.	.	.	.	.
49	5	8	3	44	20	6	.	.	1	7	3	4	.	.	.	.	.
50	5	2	3	.	15	1	.	.	.	.	.	.	.	.	.	.	.

Figure 6.2. AK1 pottery data. Coded rims

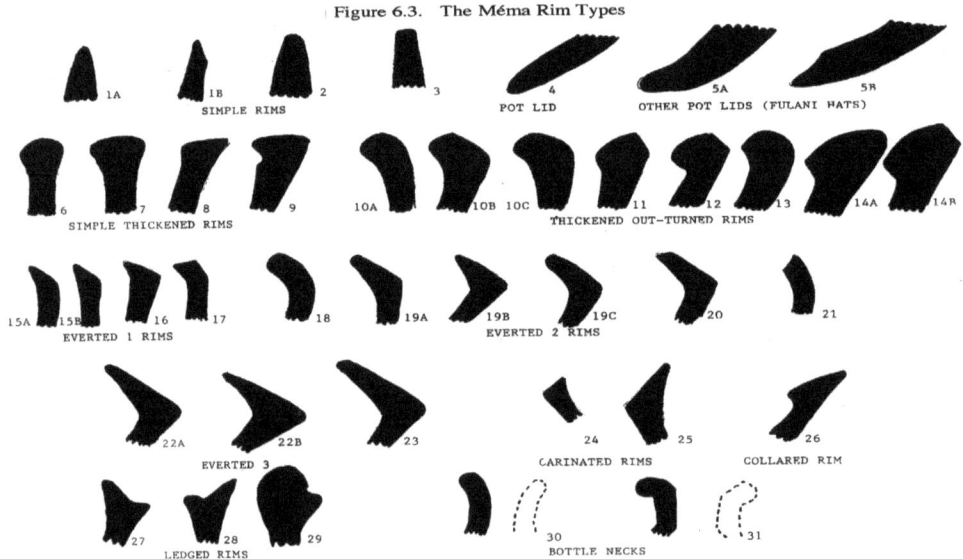

Figure 6.3. The Méma rim types

added to the clay (Shephard 1974). Its identification in the pottery of the Méma was made through visual inspection of a fresh break executed during the recording. In total, three categories of temper, grog only, grog + organic material and grog + sand, were distinguished. However, the temper, though recorded, was not included in the analysis. This was due to the fact that grog + organic tempered sherds dominated by far in the collections and did not appear to change significatly through time. The paste of these grog + organic material tempered sherds was very characteristic. The organic material (apparently chaff), had burnt away during the firing of the pots, leaving large holes in the sherd matrix.

Slip. In the Méma, slipping was a major technique for decorating pots. As it is the case today in the Inland Delta (La Violette 1987), the Méma potters may have obtained the slip for their pots from pieces of ochre whose provenience has yet to be determined. Several utilized chunks of such material were uncovered during the excavations at Akumbu A and Akumbu B. The color of the slip varied from dark orange to light orange. Its presence was detected by comparing the color of the paste of the sherd immediately below the surface with that of the sherd surface.

Twine impression. Nearly all the twine patterns present in the Méma had already been identified and described in detail by the McIntoshes during their research at Jenné jeno and Dia (SK McIntosh & RJ McIntosh 1980; Haskell et al. 1988; SK McIntosh in press). Therefore, their numeration for these twine patterns, which they have grouped into several categories of similar and related twines: braided twine roulettes (tw 1, 2, 3 and 10), Plaited twine roulettes (tw 4), twisted twine roulettes (tw 6 and 7), and cord-wrapped stick roulettes (tw 14, 15, and 17) (SK McIntosh & RJ McIntosh, 1980; Haskell et al. 1988; SK McIntosh in press), was adopted. Two other twine patterns, 'sabot' and 'counter wrapped stick', were also present. The first, 'sabot', [a roulette motif first identified at sites in the Middle Senegal Valley - Thilmans and Ravisé 1980:102] noticed only after recording was completed (we are grateful to SK McIntosh for pointing that out), was recorded as a braided twine. The second, the 'counter wrapped stick' was present only on a handful of body sherds, all recovered from the upper levels of AK1.

Plastic decoration. Plastic decoration refers to any decorative motif (aside from twine) produced by using the plastic quality of the paste. In the Méma, the most common plastic decoration technique was channelling: shallow grooves executed probably with the tip of a pointed object onto the hard and wet surface of pot. These grooves occurred singly or as a set of several parallel and generally closely spaced lines. Other plastic decoration techniques employed by the Méma potters included stabbing, punctate, stamping and fingernail impression.

Paint. Three colors of paint, black, white and red/orange, were used by the Méma potters. Paint decoration was generally applied in parallel grooves or directly onto the pot's surface. In a few cases, geometric designs (cross-hatched lines forming rough triangles or lozenges) were executed.

Rim profiles. The profile of each rim sherd was recorded by drawing the rim in its radial section. This allowed us to recognize over 30 forms or types (Figure 6.3). During the analysis, and based on morphological similarities, the various rims forms were grouped into 12 major rim classes; simple, pot lid, thickened simple, thickened out-turned, everted 1, everted 2, everted 3, carinated 1, carinated 2, collared, ledged, bottle neck.

Rim angle. Rim angle was considered only for the simple rims. For this exercise, the methodology employed by Susan K. McIntosh and described in detail in "Prehistoric investigations at Jenne, Mali" (SK McIntosh & RJ McIntosh 1980) and "Excavations at Jenne jeno, Hambarketolo and

Table 6.3: AK1 pottery collection. Other decorative motifs on body sherds.

Levels	Chanonly	Slip+chan	Chan+ tw	Chan+slip+tw	Chan+punct.	Chan+finger	Pt over chan	Pt over slip	Adj. tw motifs
1,2,3,4	2	9	3	2	-	-	1	-	-
5,6,7	3	12	5	4	-	-	2	-	-
8,10,12	4	7	4	7	1	-	-	-	-
9,11	8	17	3	2	-	-	-	1	-
13,15	10	8	7	2	-	-	1	-	-
14,16	3	5	-	2	-	-	1	-	-
17,19,21	2	8	-	4	-	1	-	-	-
18,20,23	4	9	3	2	-	-	1	-	-
25,30,31	1	3	2	3	-	-	-	-	1 (tw4 + tw14)
32,33,35	3	4	1	2	-	-	-	-	-
37,38,39	11	14	6	7	-	2	-	-	-
40,41,43	13	8	9	3	-	-	-	-	-
45,47,48	2	6	1	1	-	-	-	-	-
53,55,56	5	6	3	-	-	-	-	-	-
57,59,60	2	6	2	-	1	-	-	-	-
61,62,63	13	15	7	-	-	-	-	1	-
64,65	11	8	2	3	1	-	-	1	-
66,67,69	6	8	3	2	-	-	-	-	-

Survey and Excavation Pottery

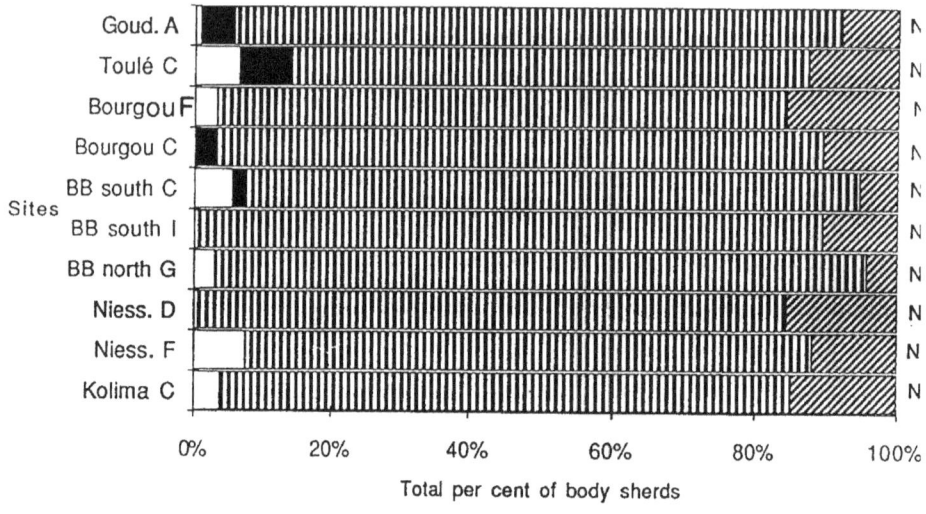

Figure 6.4. Early Assemblage. Body serd decoration by site

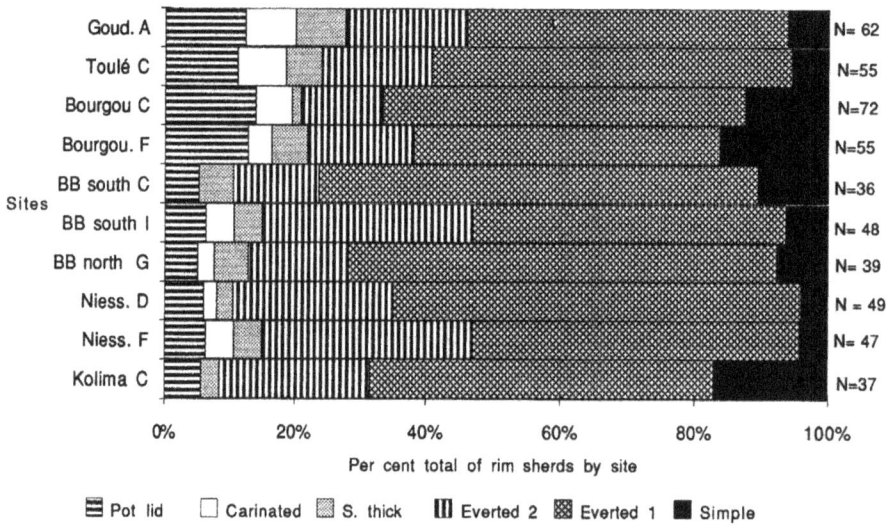

Figure 6.5. Early Assemblage. Twine decorated body sherds by site

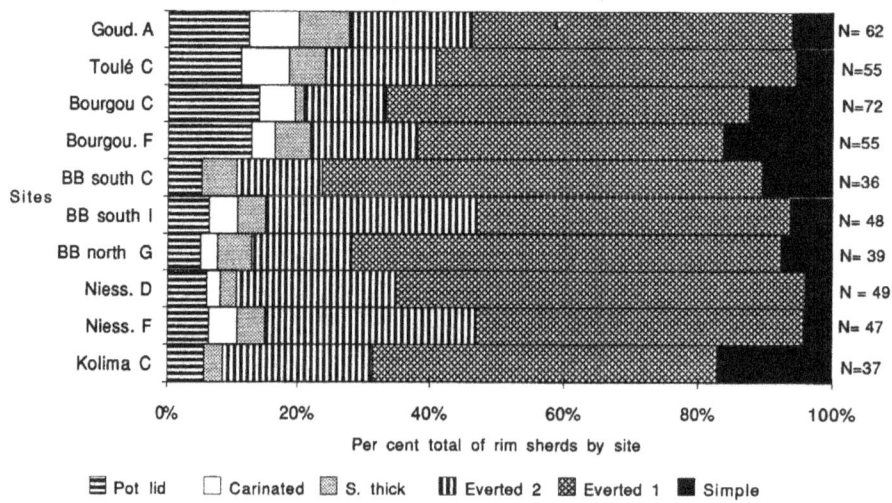

Figure 6.6. Early Assemblage. Major rim forms

48

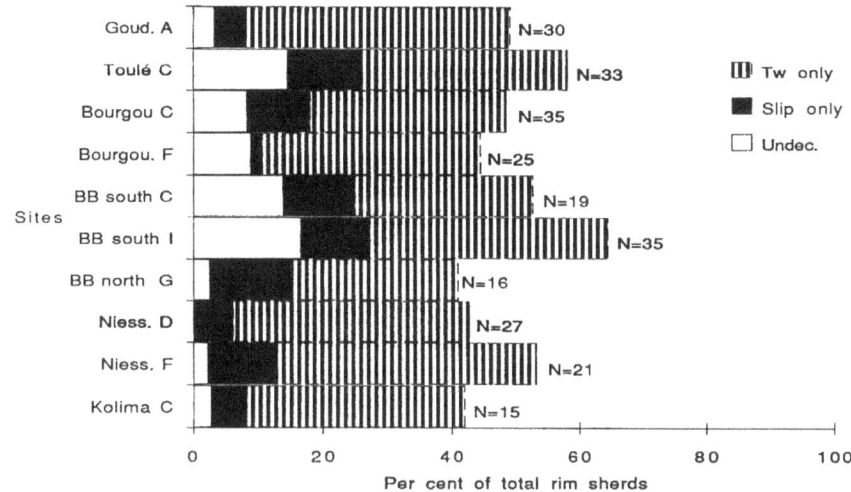

Figure 6.7. Early Assemblage. Undecorated, slipped and twine decoration

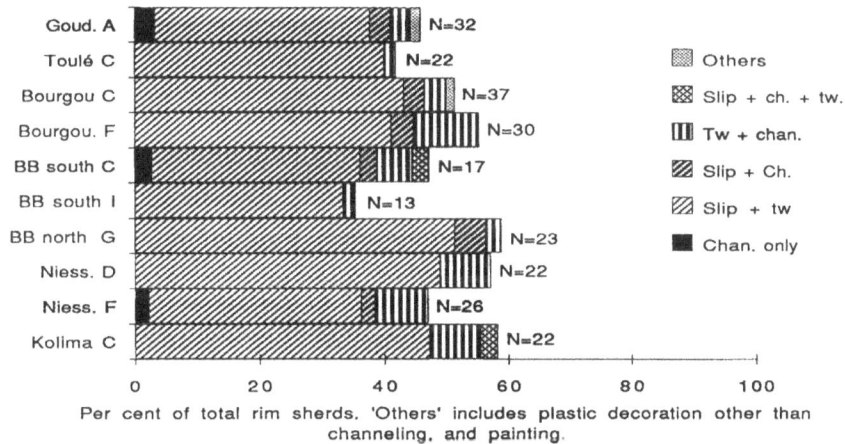

Figure 6.8. Early Assemblage. Multiple attrubute rims

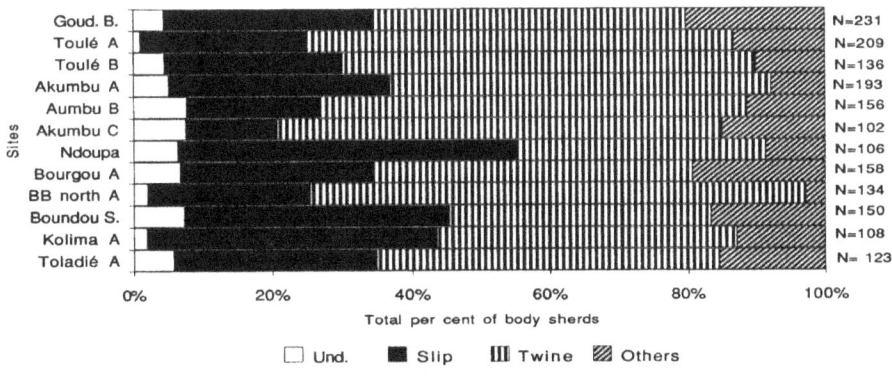

Figure 6.9. Middle Assemblage. Body sherd decoration by site

Table 6.4. Special pottery finds

Provenience	Description	Decoration
Goudourou B	Handle. Knob for pot lid	Channelled
Ndoupa	Handle. Knob for pot lid	Channelled
Ndoupa	Square base	Undecorated
Ndoupa	Square base. Pot rest?	Undecorated
Ndoupa	Fragment of bed rest	Slipped
AK1 level 10	Square base. Thick walled possible remain of a storage vessel.	Undecorated
AK1 level 10	Pottery mortar with	Undecorated and abraded surface
AK1 level 10	'Human foot' figurine	Channelled and punctuated
AK1 level 11	Fragment of pottery pestle?	Undecorated
AK1 level 13	Pottery cylinder	Twine 1 bordered with multiple channels.
AK1 level 13	Fragment of pottery pestle?	Punctuated
B.B. north A	Fragment of unidentified pottery object	Undecorated

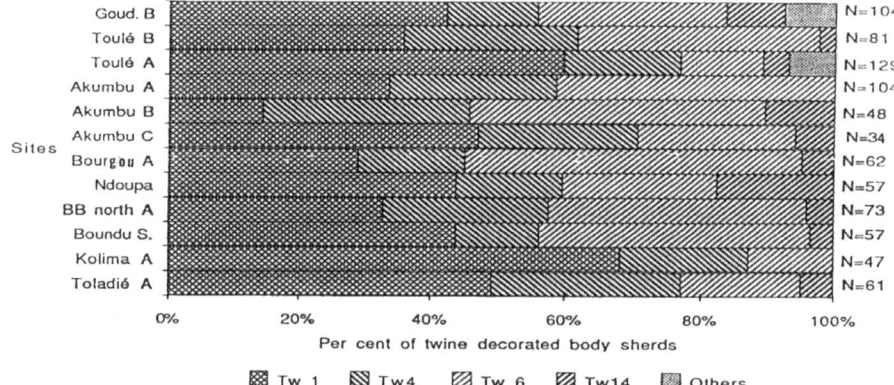

Figure 6.10. Middle Assemblage. Twine decorated body sherds by site

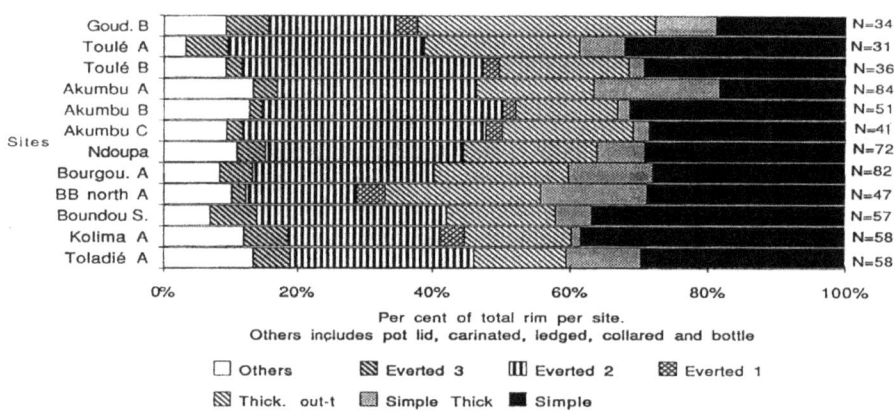

Figure 6.11. Middle Assemblage. Major rim forms

Kaniana" (SK McIntosh in press) was adopted.

Rim diameter. The diameter was estimated by placing the lip of the rim on a flat sheet of paper on which several concentric circles had been drawn. Each rim was matched against the various circles. The diameter of the circle which fitted the most closely with the arc of the rim was considered as that of the rim.

Rim thickness. The thickness was measured at the farthest point below the lip, which in many rims had deliberately been thickened or tapered.

Position of decorative motifs. For each rim, an attempt was made to record the position of the decorative motifs present. A sketch of the part of the rim present, on which the decorative motifs were illustrated, was executed.

IV. RESULTS OF THE ANALYSIS: SURVEY POTTERY

As noted above, all the three sequential pottery assemblages, Early, Middle and Late, discussed in the study, were encountered during the survey. They are presented below in chronological order.

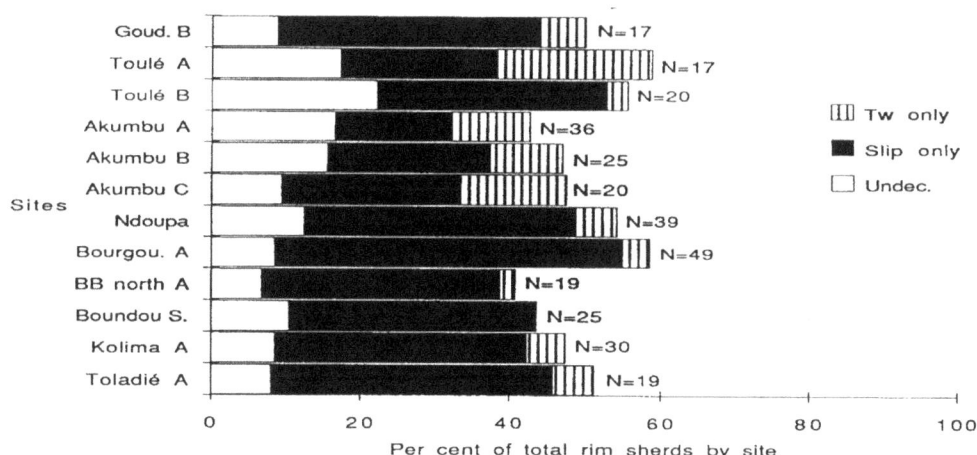

Figure 6.12. Middle Assemblage. Undecorated, slipped, and twine decorated rim sherds

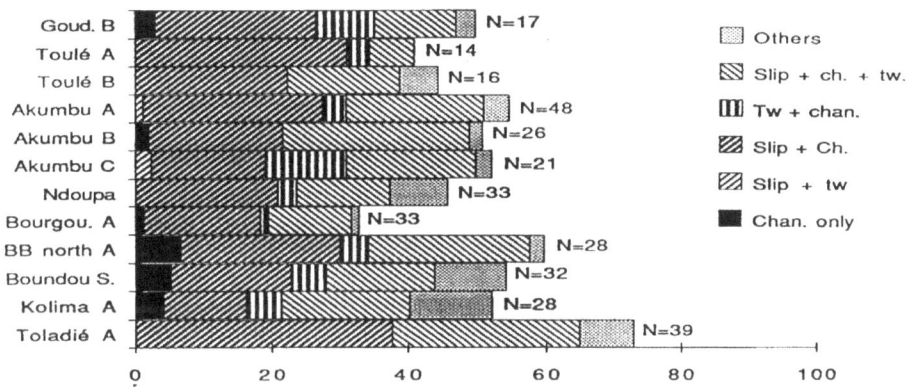

Percent of total rim sherds. 'Others' includes paint and plastic other than channeling.

Figure 6.13. Middle Assemblage. Multiple attribute rims

The Early Assemblage

The pottery collection described as Early Assemblage was characterized by the predominance of everted rims with short lip, generally decorated to the upper margin of the lip with twine impression. This assemblage was identified on the surface of 49 relatively small sized settlement mounds, extending between 0.50 ha and 3 ha in area. The majority of these sites were within the two large habitation mound clusters of Boundou Boubou and Niessouma situated on the banks of the relict water corridor of the Niakéné Maudo (see Figure 3.1). The remaining were found in the ancient floodplain and in the vicinity of large settlement mounds such as Gudourou, Kolima, Bourgou Silatigui, and Toulé. Abundant sherds with features overwhelmingly characteristic of Early Assemblage were also encountered in the thickest excavated strata of Unit AK3 (approximately 1.25m to 2.75m depth). This deposit was radiocarbon dated to the fourth/fifth century AD. Though this date can be applied to the Early Assemblage, the extent of the vertical deposit and the duration of this assemblage have yet to be determined by further investigations.

Body sherds. The majority of the body sherds of Early Assemblage were decorated. At individual sites, the percentage of decorated body sherds always exceeded 75%. Twine impression was the most important decorative technique. It was found on 75%–80% of the body sherds of the individual sites containing the Early Assemblage (Figure 6.4). Plaited twine roulette 4 was the most frequently used, as it comprised between 40% and 60% of the twine motifs present (Figure 6.5). It was followed in popularity by braided twine roulette 1, accounting for 15–30% of the twine decorated body sherds. The other twine motifs present were twisted twine roulette (tw 6), and cord wrapped-stick roulette (tw 14). Their numbers were variable, but rarely exceeded 15% of the twine patterns present. Undecorated sherds and sherds decorated only with slip were rare. At no site did their number ever constitute more than 5% of the body sherd assemblage. The other decorative motifs ["other" in Figure 6.4] are presented on Table 6.1. They include plastic decoration and multiple attributes present. Together, they were found on 10–15% of the body sherds. Channelling was the most

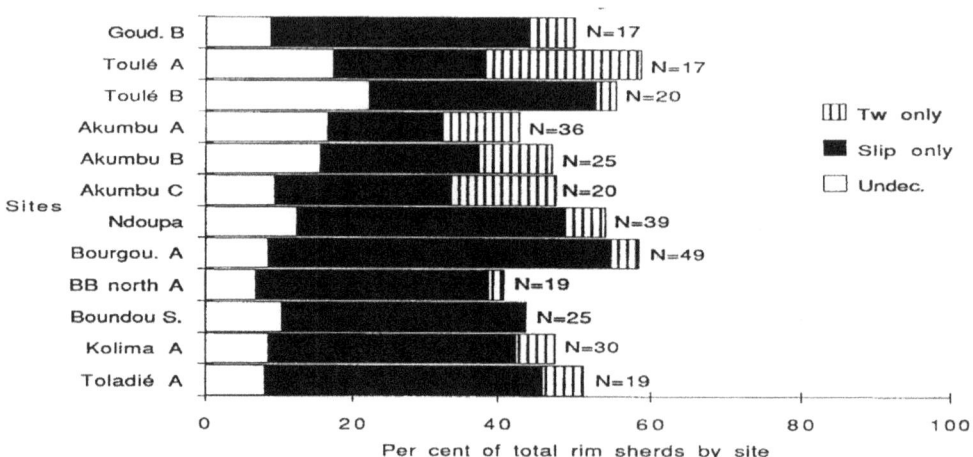

Figure 6.14. AK1 pottery. Body sherd decoration by level

important plastic decorative technique. Single or multiple channels were distinctively executed through the twine patterns (Figures 6.19 and 6.33).

Rim sherds. The Early Assemblage contained a relatively limited range of rim types (Figure 6.6). Only six (simple, everted 1, everted 2, simple thickened, carinated, and pot lid) of the 12 major rim categories were present. Among these, everted 1 rims, specially rim type **15A** and **15B** were the most frequent, and most diagnostic rim forms. They constituted 30–60% of the rim collection of individual sites containing this assemblage. They were followed in popularity by rims of category Everted 2 (especially types **18** and **21**), whose number, though variable from one site to another, constituted between 15% and 30% of the rim collection. The third rim classes were simple rims, and pot lids, (especially rim types **5A** and **5B**), equally represented by 5–10% of the ensemble. Simple thickened rims, and carinated rims were each represented by small numbers of sherds. Together, they constituted approximately 5% of the rim collection. The majority of the rims in the Early Assemblage were decorated. Twine only [commonly, plaited twine 4, and twisted cord wrapped stick twine 14], and slip + twine were the two major decorative techniques (Figures 6.7 and 6.8). Together, these two decorative techniques were recorded on more than 80% of the rims of individual Early sites. However, though associated, the slip and twine were never superimposed. The slipped zone always consisted of a narrow band along the rim inner margin, while the twine pattern was always applied onto the vessel body and often extended to the upper external margin of the rim. Plastic decoration and paint were equally rare in the Early Assemblage rim collection.

The Middle Assemblage

The pottery assemblage described as the Middle Assemblage was identified on the surface of 31 large settlement mounds primarily located along relict water corridors or within the degraded dune system. As discussed below, the pottery collection from the entire deposit of Unit AK1, dated between calibrated AD 604–681 and AD 1274–1401, as well as that of the excavated strata of AK4 and the upper levels of Unit AK3 on Akumbu B were also assigned to this assemblage.

Body sherds. As for the Early Assemblage, the majority of the body sherds of the Middle Assemblage were decorated (Figure 6.9). Undecorated body sherds constituted 5–10% of the identifiable body sherds at most of the sites containing this Assemblage. Slipping became more popular, compared to the Early Assemblage. The body sherds decorated only with slip represented 5% of the identifiable body sherds in the Early Assemblage pottery collection, jumping to 20–40% at most of the sites containing the Middle Assemblage. Twine impression, found on 40–70% of the identifiable body sherds, remained the most common decorative technique. Twine 4, very common earlier, decreased in popularity, while twisted twine 6 and braided twine 1, though variable, became more frequent (Figure 6.10). Cord wrapped stick (tw 14) was the twine motif the least frequently used. Its frequency never exceeded 5% of the twine decorated body sherds. Other types of decorative techniques (plastic decoration, multiple attributes and painting) were present, but in relatively small numbers. These 'other' decorative attributes presented on Table 6.2, represented between 5–15% of the decorated body sherds. The paint, black or white, was generally executed as horizontal lines over single or multiple channels.

Rim sherds. Virtually all the rim types and decorative techniques identified during this first season were present in this Assemblage (Figure 6.11). However, three rim classes, simple rims, everted 2 and thickened-out-turned, constituted more than 60% of the rim collection. They were followed in number by simple thickened and Everted 3 rims, wich accounted each for approximately 5–15%

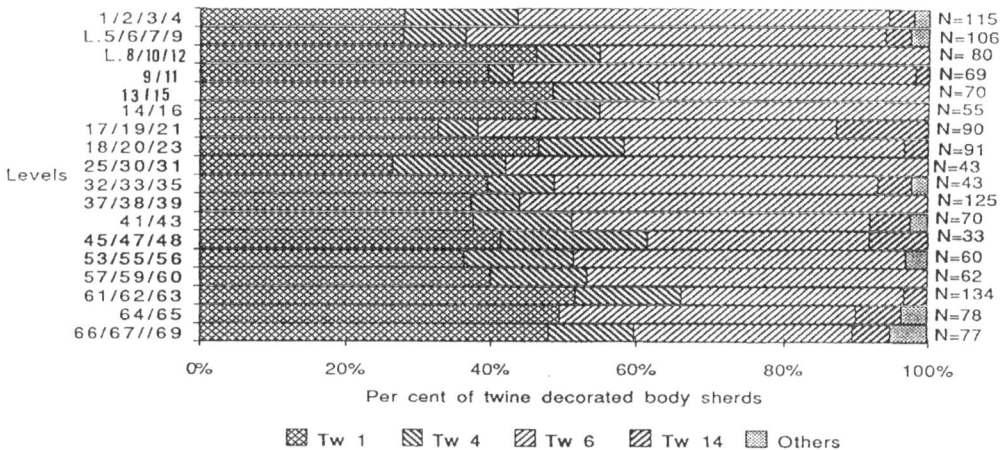

Figure 6.15. AK1 pottery. Twine decorated body sherds by level

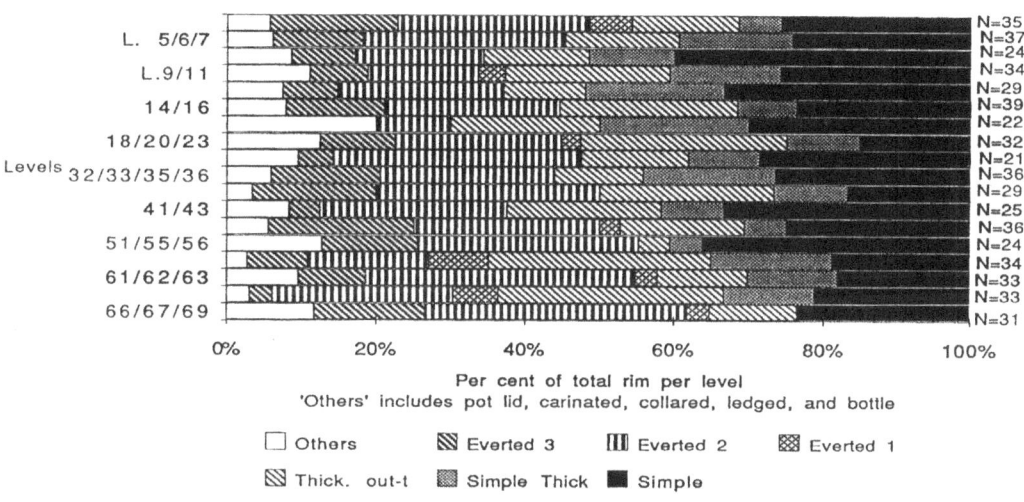

Figure 6.16. AK1 pottery. Major rim forms by level

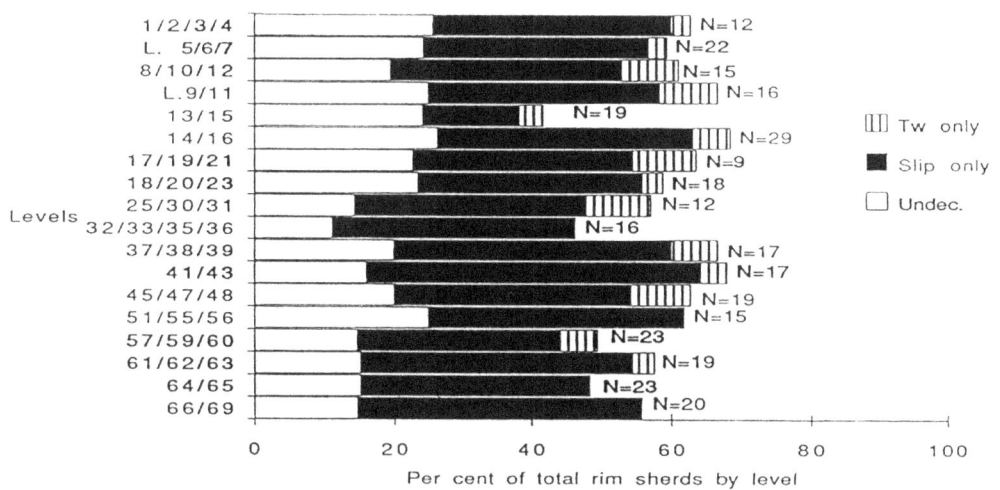

Figure 6.17. AK1 pottery. Undecorated, slipped and twine decorated

Survey and Excavation Pottery

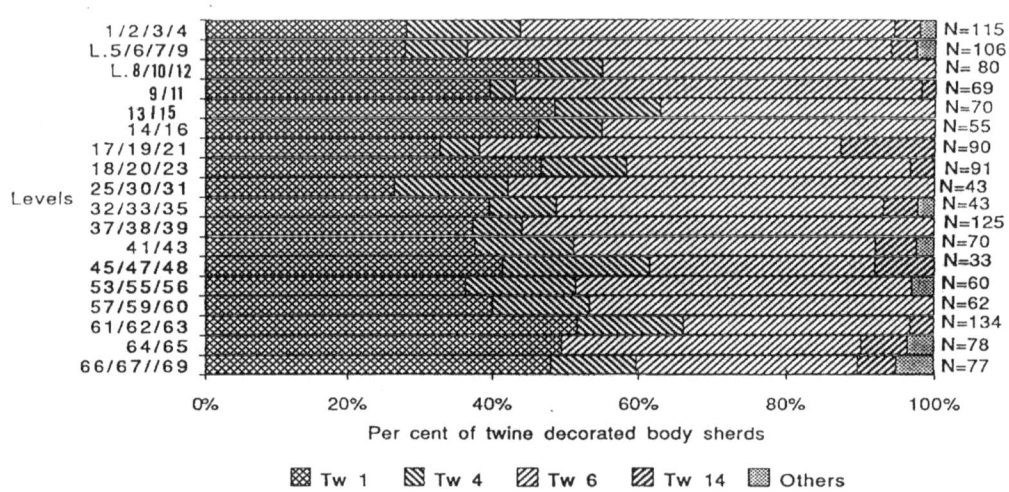

Figure 6.18. AK1 pottery. Multiple attribute rims

of the rim collection. Everted 1, the leading rim class in Early Assemblage, was represented by less than 5%. The other rim classes, carinated, collared, ledged and bottle neck, together accounted for approximately 10% of the rim assemblage. A wide variety of decorative modes and techniques, slipping only, slipping + channelling, slipping + channelling + twine impression, twine impression only, twine impression + channelling, plastic decoration (stabbing, finger impression, and punctation), and painting were encountered in the rim collection of the Middle Assemblage (Figure 6.12, 6.13). Among these, slipping only, slipping + channelling, and slipping + channelling + twine impression were the most frequent. Together, these three decorative techniques were present on 60% or more of the rims from individual Middle Assemblage sites. In this third case, slip was generally applied over channelling while the twine impressed area was commonly unslipped. The channels, in most cases, bordered the twine impressed zone. Twine impression only, found on approximately 5–20% of the rims, decreased remarkably, compared to the body sherds, where it was represented by 40–70%. This, as just noted, was certainly due to the practice of concentrating decorative motifs such as slipping and channelling on the rim and confining the twine impression to the body and shoulder. Other plastic decorations such as stabbing, punctate and finger impression were also present, but in small quantity. Painting, a decorative motif associated with channelling and slipping, was found on only approximately 5% of the rims.

The Late Assemblage

As already noted, the pottery collection identified as Late Assemblage was exclusively encountered during the survey. It was present on small and relatively low mounded habitation sites mostly located within the longitudinal dune system and always associated with numerous fragments of tobacco pipe. This placed sites containing this assemblage in the post-sixteenth century period. Tobacco pipes, a chronological marker, are said to have been introduced in the Western Sudan in 1591 by the Moroccans (Mauny, 1961). In addition, oral accounts in Nampala recall several of these sites as ancient villages founded by the Bamanan during the period of the Bamana Empire of Segu, a political authority founded in the 17th century.

Body sherds. As for the preceding assemblages, decorated body sherds made up the majority of the body sherd collection in this assemblage. Like in the other two assemblages, the number of undecorated body sherds remained small and constituted only 5–10% of the body sherds. Twine impression, generally twine 6, was the most important means of body sherd decoration. At individual sites containing Late Assemblage, it was recorded on 40–50% of the body sherds. As in the Middle Assemblage, slipping only was a popular mode of decoration and was found on 20–30% of the body sherds. Plastic decoration, confined here to channelling and multiple attributes (commonly slip + channelling) together were represented by 10-15%.

Rim sherds. Only five (collared, everted 1, everted 2, everted 3, and simple rims) of the 12 rim classes identified in 1989/90 field season were represented in the Late Assemblage. The collared rim, very rare in the Middle Assemblage, and virtually absent from the Early Assemblage, was the most frequent and most diagnostic rim of the Late Assemblage. At individual sites, it constituted 30–40% of the rim collection. Everted 1, specially rim **type16**, everted 2, and everted 3 (commonly **type 22A** and its variant type **22B,** and **23)**, were each equally represented by 20%. Simple rims and simple thickened rims, representing together approximately 5% of the assemblage, were the least important of the rim categories. Slipping + channelling (30–40%) was the most frequent decorative motif. Twine 6 impression, recorded on 25% of the rim collection, was commonly associated with other decorative motifs such as slipping and channelling. The other decorative techniques encountered included slipping only (15%), channelling with no slip (less than 5%) and painting over channelling, found only on four specimens.

V. RESULTS OF THE ANALYSIS: EXCAVATION POTTERY

As already noted, only the pottery from Unit AK1 was recorded and included in the analysis. This was attributed to the limited number of personnel available for the recording.

Body sherds. With respect to several ceramic atttributes, the body sherd collection showed little change through the deposits of AK1, and a great deal of similarity to the Middle Assemblage defined on surface material. Undecorated body sherds constituted 10–20% of the identifiable body sherds (Figure 6.14). Like in the Middle Assemblage, slipping, encountered on 20–50% of the body sherds, remained the most common decorative mode in most stratigraphic levels. It was followed in frequency by twine impression, found on 30–60% of the body sherd collection. Among the various twine motifs present, twisted twine 6 and braided twine 1 were the most frequent. These twine motifs, though variable in relative frequency, dominated in most of the excavated levels. Plaited twine 4, the third twine, was represented by 5–10% (Figure 6.15). Cord wrapped stick roulette (tw 14), fish vertebra roulette, and a new twine motif 'the counter wrapped stick' were also present, but in insignificant numbers. Together, they represented <5% of collection. Other decorative motifs, plastic decoration (mostly channelling), painting, and multiple attributes, though present, were relatively rare. Together, they characterized 5–20% of AK1 body sherds. These other decorative motifs, lumped together under the category 'other' are presented on Table 6.3.

Rim sherds. The rim collection from AK1 displayed many of the ceramic attributes of the Middle Assemblage. Simple rims, everted 2 rims and thickened out-turned rims dominated, and together constituted more than 60% of the rim collection of most stratigraphic levels (Figure 6.16). They were followed in frequency by simple thickened and everted 3 rims, each represented by approximately 5–15% of the rim assemblage. Carinated rims, ledged rims, and bottle necks were consistently present in small number in the he deposits. They are lumped together in the 'others' category in Figure 6.15. Everted 1 rims (especially rim **types 15A** and **15B**, the most common and diagnostic rim forms of Early Assemblage), appeared sporadically in the lower levels, especially between level 61 and level 69. However, they were still mixed with other rim classes, particularly thickened out-turned rims and everted 2 rims, all characteristic of the Middle Assemblage. As for the Middle Assemblage, slipping only (20–40%) and slipping + channelling (15–30%), remained the two most popular decorative techniques found in AK1 rim collection (Figures 6.17 and 6.18). They were followed in frequency by slip + channelling + twine, represented by 5–20%. Twine impression only was found on only 5–10% of AK1 rims. As previously observed, this low frequency of twine impression alone was certainly due to the practice of decorating the body and shoulder of the vessels with twine, and the rim with slipping and channelling. Other decorative techniques encountered included stabbing, finger impression, punctuated, and painting. These, together found on 5% of the rims, were almost always concentrated within the slipped area and commonly associated with channelling.

Interpretation of the excavation pottery

The fact that only the pottery from AK1 was recorded and included in the analysis obviously represents a shortcoming that the reader will easily appreciate. As a consequence, the presence of Early Assemblage pottery in the lower excavated levels of unit AK3 is based on the identification and co-occurrence of same ceramic attributes observed in the survey pottery assigned to this assemblage. This conclusion, based on observation during both the excavation and daily inspection of the ceramic after it was washed and left to dry, has yet to be supported by quantitative data. The same remark applies to the excavated strata of Unit AK4, and the upper excavated levels of Unit AK3, which produced pottery collections with characteristic features of the Middle Assemblage. The pottery collection from AK1 clearly represents the same ceramic horizons as the Middle Assemblage. Not only does the composition of the rim forms from AK1 (Figure 6.16) evoke that of the Middle Assemblage (see Figure 6.11), but the decoration techniques (slipping only, slipping + channelling, and slipping + channelling + twine impression (especially twine 6), were not only frequently used but characteristic of the Middle Assemblage. As already noted, the little variability through time within the pottery collection of AK1 is certainly attributable to the relatively short period of occupation the unit, which extended a minimum of seven centuries. Sherds with characteristic features of Early Assemblage appeared in the lower levels of the unit. However, their number remained too small to mark a real change in the general character of the pottery collection of the unit.

VI. DESCRIPTION OF THE DIAGNOSTIC RIM FORMS BY ASSEMBLAGE

This section is a brief description of the most common and diagnostic rim forms encountered in each assemblage and in the pottery collection from AK1. Representative samples of these common and diagnostic rim types are illustrated in Figures 6.19 through 6.29 (at the end of this chapter). Rim forms are summarized in Figure 6.3.

Early Assemblage diagnostic rims
Rim types 15A and **15B**. Everted rim with short lip, only slightly outward from the body. The wall thickness ranged from 5mm to 10mm and the diameter was generally distributed between 15cm and 25cm. The great majority were decorated with twine impression, commonly tw

14 and tw 4, applied on the outer surface and either up to the outer upper margin of the lip, or leaving a narrow undecorated zone at the lip. Most of the twine decorated rims were also slipped; but the slip was always limited to a band along the rim's upper inner margin. A small number (<10%) were decorated with two twine motifs. In these cases, tw 14, along the upper outer margin is adjacent to tw 4, commonly applied on the shoulder and body.

Rim type 18. The lip, though longer than in the two preceding types, is also only slightly everted outward from the body. Decorative technique, similar to that on types 15A and 15B, consists commonly of twine impression, generally tw 14, or tw 4, and slipping along the inner upper margin of the rim. The rim diameter of more than 3/4 of these rims was distributed between 15cm and 25cm. The wall thickness ranged from 6mm to 12mm.

Rim types 5A and **5B.** Thick-walled pot lids nicknamed Fulani Hats. Wall thickness was always >15mm, sometimes reaching 25mm and the diameter distribution was 30cm–40cm (1/4 approximately), 41cm–50cm (1/2 approximately) or >50cm (1/4 approximately). They were also present in the Middle Assemblage. However, the decorative techniques were different. In the Early Assemblage, they were consistently decorated with twine impression, commonly twines 4, 14 or 6. Slipping may be present, but was always restricted to a narrow strip along the upper inner margin of the rim. In the Middle Assemblage, by contrast, they were generally undecorated or simply slipped.

Rim type 24. Carinated rims. In the Early Assemblage, they are distinctively decorated with twine impression above the carination, and in few cases, with multiple channels on the inner surface. Rim diameter was relatively small and generally distributed between 15 and 20cm. Wall thickness ranged from 8mm to 14mm.

Middle Assemblage diagnostic rims
Rim types 1A, 1B, 2, and 3. Simple rims for closed or open vessels. Generally lavishly decorated on the rim with slip, channelling (one or more channels), and sometimes with white or black painting. Twine impression, commonly twisted and braided twines (tw 6 or tw 1), may be present, but is generally applied far below the rim and always on the unslipped area. Single or multiple channels may also border the twine decorated zone. Painting, if present, is applied as horizontal lines on the channels. Wall thickness was generally small and ranged between 4mm to 12mm. Rim diameter was distributed between 15cm and 25m.
Rim types 19A and its variants **19B, 19C, and 20.** Everted rims, with medium lip, significantly outward from the body, giving these rims a larger rim diameter, compared to types **15A**, **15B**, and **18**. Generally slipped (usually in both outer and inner surfaces) and channelled with a single or multiple channels, generally executed on the rim, or bordering the twine decoration, if present. Twine impression (commonly twine 6 or twine 1) may occur on the body and on the unslipped zone. Wall thickness ranged from 9mm to 13mm the rim diameter was distributed between 15cm–18cm, (1/4, approximately) 20–24cm (1/2 approximately), 25cm -30cm (1/4 approximately).

Rim types 10A, 10B, and their variants **10C through 14B.** Thickened rims with a more or less pronounced out-turned flange, and relatively thickened wall below the rim. These rims, morphologically diverse and accounting for 20% of the Middle Assemblage, were virtually absent from both the Early Assemblage and the Late Assemblage. Usually, they were decorated with a series of decorative motifs, slipping only, slipping + channelling , and sometimes painting, all generally concentrated on the rim area. A twine impressed zone (tw6 or tw1) may be present, but is located far down below the rim, on an unslipped area. More than 60% of these rims had a wall thickness distributed 10 and 15mm. The rim diameter ranged between 17cm and 34 cm; 17cm–24cm (1/3 approximately), 25cm -34 cm (2/3 approximately).

Everted 3: Rim type 22A, and its variants **types 22B** and **23.** Everted rims with long lip, significantly everted outward from the body. Slipping (on both outer and inner surface) + channelling on the rim is the dominant decorative modes. Rim diameter on 3/4 of these rims fall distributed between 20–25cm.

Rim type 30, and **31.** Bottle neck defined by their restricted rim diameter (>10cm). These rims, like the simple rims, were commonly lavished with multiple decorative motifs, including slipping, multiple channels, and painting, and more rarely twine impression, on the body.

Rim type 25. Carinated rims. The lip above the carination is much longer than in the carinated rims seen in the Early Assemblage. Frequently decorated only with slip on the outer surface, and sometimes channelled on the lip. Wall thickness ranged from 7mm to 12mm, and diameter was generally distributed between 15m and 25cm.

Late Assemblage diagnostic rims
Rim type 26. Collared rim always distinctively decorated on the collar with multiple channelling . Twine 6 impression may be present, but is applied farther below the rim and bordered with chaneling. Rim diameter distribution was generally distributed between 18cm and 26cm and thickeness ranged from 7mm to 15mm.

Rim type 16. Everted rim with short lip above the inversion point. Generally decorated with twine 6, applied on the outer surface far below the rim. The rim inner surface is generally slipped. One or two channels may also be found along the lip inner margin. Thickness ranged 7mm to 15mm from and diameter was generally distributed between 15cm and 25cm.

Rim type 22A, 22B, and 23. Everted rims with long lip and frequently a rim diameter of 25cm or more. These types were also present in the Middle Assemblage, but with different decoration techniques. Here, in addition to slipping, they were distinctively decorated with multiple channels on both outer and inner surfaces of the lip. Usually, twine 6 impression was applied on the body.

VII. SPECIAL POTTERY FINDS (Table 6.4)

In total, two handles, three bases, one pottery cylinder, and six curious and unusual baked clay objects (including a pottery mortar with an abraded surface, a fragment of bed rest, two possible pottery pestles and an unidentified fired clay object) were encountered. These special pottery finds (Table 6.4) are illustrated in Figures 6.30 and 6.31.

VIII. CONCLUSIONS AND DISCUSSION

The three pottery assemblages identified in the survey pottery display some fundamental differences in ceramic features, especially in the patterning of rim forms and decorative techniques. Their sequence was demonstrated by both radiocarbon dates obtained during the excavations at Akumbu A and Akumbu B, and the presence of time marker artifacts such as fragments of tobacco pipes. The Middle Assemblage, the best represented in the excavations, can be said with confidence to date between the seventh and fourteenth century AD. The duration of both the Early and the Late Assemblages has yet to be determined. As already noted, abundant sherds with characteristic features of the Early Assemblage were present in the lower excavated levels of AK3, and in a deposit dated to the fourth/fifth century AD. As this assemblage was collected on the surface of small, but deeply stratified mounds, it is possible that its duration extends back in time several centuries. Since the Late Assemblage was associated with numerous fragments of tobacco pipe, it likely is no earlier than the end of the sixteenth century AD. This was supported by the oral traditions, which attributes the founding of several of the sites containing Late Assemblage pottery to the Bamanan during the political hegemony of the Bamanan kingdom of Segou.

Though a few IA sites [Kolima in the eastern sector of our survey area, Péhé on the bank of the Fala de Molodo, and sites B–E] were previously investigated by Christoforoff (Mauny 1961), Szumowski (1956), and Haaland (1980)] respectively, no quantitative data on the pottery from those sites were available. However, the complete vessels from Kolima and Péhé, described and photographed respectively by Pascale Schmit (1985), and Szumowski (1956) display the same decorative attributes in particular the braided twine (Szumowski 'Barakalé'), the plaited twine, the channelling and black painting over channelling , found in abundance in the Middle Assemblage. These same decorative motifs are also present on the handful of pot sherds from sites B–E photographed by Haaland (1980). The presence of the Middle Assemblage pottery attributes at those sites is not surprising, specially for Kolima, and site B–E which have been radiocarbon dated to the fourteenth century AD and

eighth AD respectively Fontes et al. (1980; 1991; Haaland 1980). Péhé, recorded again during our regional site survey, was assigned to the Middle Assemblage, based on its surface material, especially the pottery. The relatively high number of painted wares in the pottery from Kolima (20 or more than 20% of the 99 vessels described by Schmit) (1986: 51) might be attributable to biased sampling. As was the practice during colonial time, the prime objective of Christoforoff, the excavator of the site (Mauny 1961: 97), was the quest of museum objects. Therefore, he likely selected only nicely decorated vessels.

Of the three assemblages, the Middle Assemblage is by far the most varied, in terms of both rim forms and decoration techniques. It is not known yet whether this broad variability of the Middle Assemblage is attributable to its relatively larger sample, or to the presence of a possibly more heterogeneous population at Middle Assemblage sites. Most of these sites averaged 10–20 ha in area, compared to less than 5ha for most early sites.

The presence in the Middle Assemblage of 'luxury' painted wares, especially pottery bottles, always lavishly decorated with a wide array of decorative motifs including slipping, channelling , plastic decoration, and black or white painting, is noticeable. As discussed further below, these 'luxury' painted wares have been found in the Upper Niger Delta (SK McIntosh & RJ McIntosh 1980; SK McIntosh in press), and the Lakes (Desplagnes 1951; Mauny 1961; Lebeuf & Paques 1970), all situated farther along the Niger River.

In the Upper Inland Delta, the Jenné-jeno's Phase III (AD 400 to AD 900) and Phase IV (AD 900 to 1400) pottery (SK McIntosh & RJ McIntosh, 1980; SK McIntosh in press) are partly covered by the period of AK1 pottery collection assigned to Middle Assemblage and dated to AD 604–681 and AD 1274–1401. A similar range of decorative motifs, [slipping, twine impression (braided twine, twisted twine and cord wrapped stick twine), plastic decoration and painting] observed in the pottery of the Inland Niger Delta during Phase III and Phase IV (SK McIntosh & RJ McIntosh 1980; Haskell et al. 1988; SK McIntosh in press) is also present in the Middle Assemblage of the Méma. In addition, thickened rims with an out-turned flange, which appeared in the Upper Inland Delta in Phase III, and became very popular in Phase IV (SK McIntosh & RJ McIntosh, 1980; Haskell et al. 1988; SK McIntosh in press) are very common in the Méma and in the Middle Assemblage. Carinated rims, very common in the pottery collection of the Jenné and Dia, especially in Phase III (SK McIntosh & RJ McIntosh 1980; Haskell et al. 1988; SK McIntosh in press), are also present in both the Méma Early and Middle Assemblages, but in low frequencies. In addition, pottery cylinders, present in the Jenné Jeno collection (SK McIntosh in press) are also present in Méma Middle Assemblage, but represented by only one example. This pottery cylinder, open at both ends, and decorated with braided twine bordered with multiple channels (see Figure

6.30) was found in a disposal pit dated to the thirteenth century AD.

Despite these affinities, the pottery collections of the two regions during the mid-first to early second millennium AD show some radical differences. With the exception of channelling, plastic decoration, so prolific and diversified [e.g., stabbing, stamping, comb impression, comb dragging] in the Jenné and Dia regions during Phase IV to include stabbing, stamping and comb dragging (SK McIntosh & RJ McIntosh1980; Haskell et al. 1988; SK McIntosh in press) was relatively rare in the Méma Middle Assemblage. The most striking difference between the pottery collections of the two regions is the paste. Organic material (probably chaff), the most common temper in the Méma, is virtually absent from the Inland Delta (SK McIntosh & RJ McIntosh, 1980; Haskell et al. 1988; SK McIntosh in press). The miscellaneous pottery with appliqué decoration (generally anthropomorphic and zoomorphic relief), found at Jenné Jeno, is also absent from the Méma collections.

Apart from the presence of twine impression, the Early Assemblage, present in the fourth/fifth century but of unknown duration, is different from the pottery of the Upper Inland Delta. It consisted of a pottery with coarse paste tempered with organic material, generally unslipped (at least on the outer surface), and decorated with plaited twine or twisted cord-wrapped stick. This, however, needs to be investigated further, as no Early Assemblage material from the excavation has yet been analysed.

Similarly, the situation for the Late Assemblage is not yet clear. This Assemblage, also known only from the survey, and dated to after the sisteenth century AD, seems to be stylistically different from the McIntoshes Phase V, dated to AD 1500–1900 (SK McIntosh and RJ McIntosh 1980; Haskell et al. 1988), and from the pottery collection from the historical site of Hamdallahi, dated to the nineteenth century AD (Gallay et al. 1991). The plastic decoration (especially comb dragging) and applied red painting in the McIntosh's Phase V and the pottery collection from Hamdallahi are absent from the Méma Late Assemblage, dominated by collared and everted rims, generally decorated with twisted twine 6 and multiple channels on the rims. These differences also need to be substantiated by more data, especially larger samples from excavations.

In the Lakes Region, acomplete excavated sequence is available only from the site of Mouyssam, near Sumpi. Interestingly, the pottery from the nine meters of cultural deposits from Mouyssam (KNT 2), deposited between the third and seventh century AD, (Raimbault 1991: 369) showed little change through time. This pattern, also observed at Akumbu A, is certainly also attributable to rapid accumulation. Of the three assemblages recognized thus far in the Méma, the Middle Assemblage appears to present the clearest affinities with the last phase of the pottery collection from Mouyssam, dated between AD 400 and AD 680. Both collections contain similar rim forms, including a wide variety of everted rims [which account for 30-50% of the pottery collection from Mouyssam (Raimbault 1991: 369) and approximately 20–40% of the Méma Middle Assemblage], the thickened rims with an out-turned flange, the carinated rims for small and shallow bowls mostly left undecorated or only slipped, the pottery bottles, and the large pot lids, the Fulani Hats. Other ceramic attributes, in particular the organic material temper, the heavy use of red slip, the twine impression (twisted twine and braided twine) channelling and white and black painting are also present in the two collections. These same pottery attributes have been documented at the nearby mounds of Kawinza and Toubel, occupied respectively between AD 340–605, and AD 655-1015 (Raimbault 1991; Raimabault & Togola 1991). Despite these affinities, the pottery from these sites near Sumpi displays some striking differences with the Méma Middle Assemblage. Painting, found on more nearly 50% of the pottery collection of Mouyssam, is rare in the Méma Middle Assemblage. In addition, some pottery forms, especially the elongated pottery painted pottery bottles, found in funerary context at Kawinza (Raimbault 1991 & Togola 1991: 293) are significally different by their height from those of the Méma.

Farther downstream, around Diré and Goundam, the bulk of the documented pottery collection comes from the funerary tumuli of Kouga (excavated by Mauny in 1054 and dated to cal AD 900–1250), Killi and El Oualaji, both excavated by Desplagnes (1903; 1951) at the turn this century. All these funerary tumuli have produced a number of pottery elements, in particular the small carinated bowls and the pottery bottles, present in the Méma Middle Assemblage. Again, potteries painted with distinctive white crossed-hatched geometric designs on deep red slip abundant in the collection of Kouga (Mauny 1961: 111), and the nearby habitation site also excavated by Mauny (1961), are rare in the Méma. Also worthy to note in passing is the fact that the use of pottery bottles in funerary rituals documented at many sites of the Lakes Region (Sidibé & Raimabult 1991; Mauny 1961; Desplagnes 1903; 1951), has not thus far been observed in the Méma.

Outside the Middle Niger, comparison between the pottery of the Méma and other collections is difficult, due to the paucity of pottery studies. However, the presence of one example of footed vessel (uncovered in level 39, just above a small hearth dated to the seventh century AD) is interesting. The 'Tellem' footed vessels, generally linked to funerary rituals (Bedaux 1980; de Grunne 1983), have been found in a narrow band extending over some 1,000 km along the Niger River, from Niani (the presumed capital of the Empire of Mali), to Timbuktu. Bedaux (1980), who has studied the geographical distribution of these footed vessels, links their large diffusion to population movements.

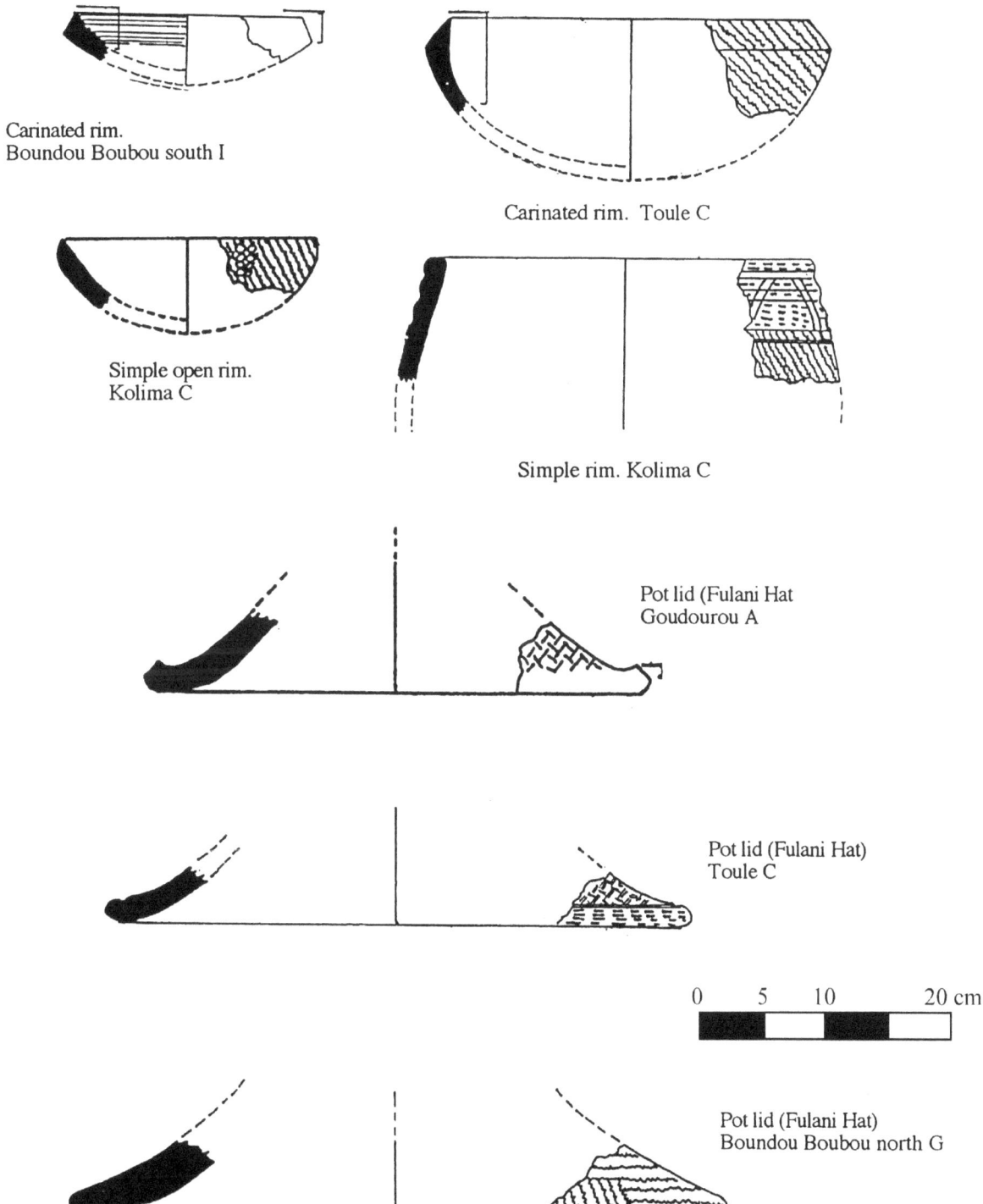

Figure 6.19. Early Assemblage. Examples of simple, carinated rims and pot lids (Fulani hats)

Survey and Excavation Pottery

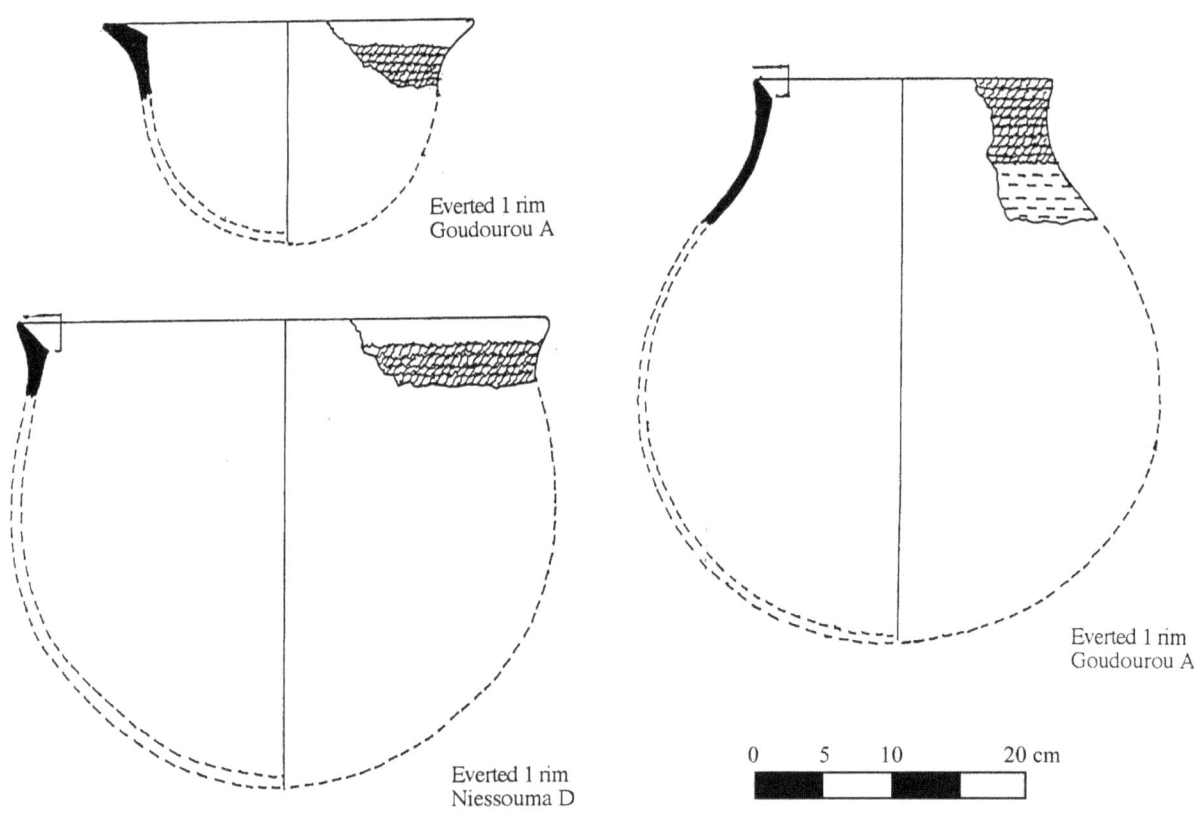

Figure 6.20. Early Assemblage. Examples of everted rims

Archaeological Investigations of Iron Age Sites in the Mema Region, Mali (West Africa)

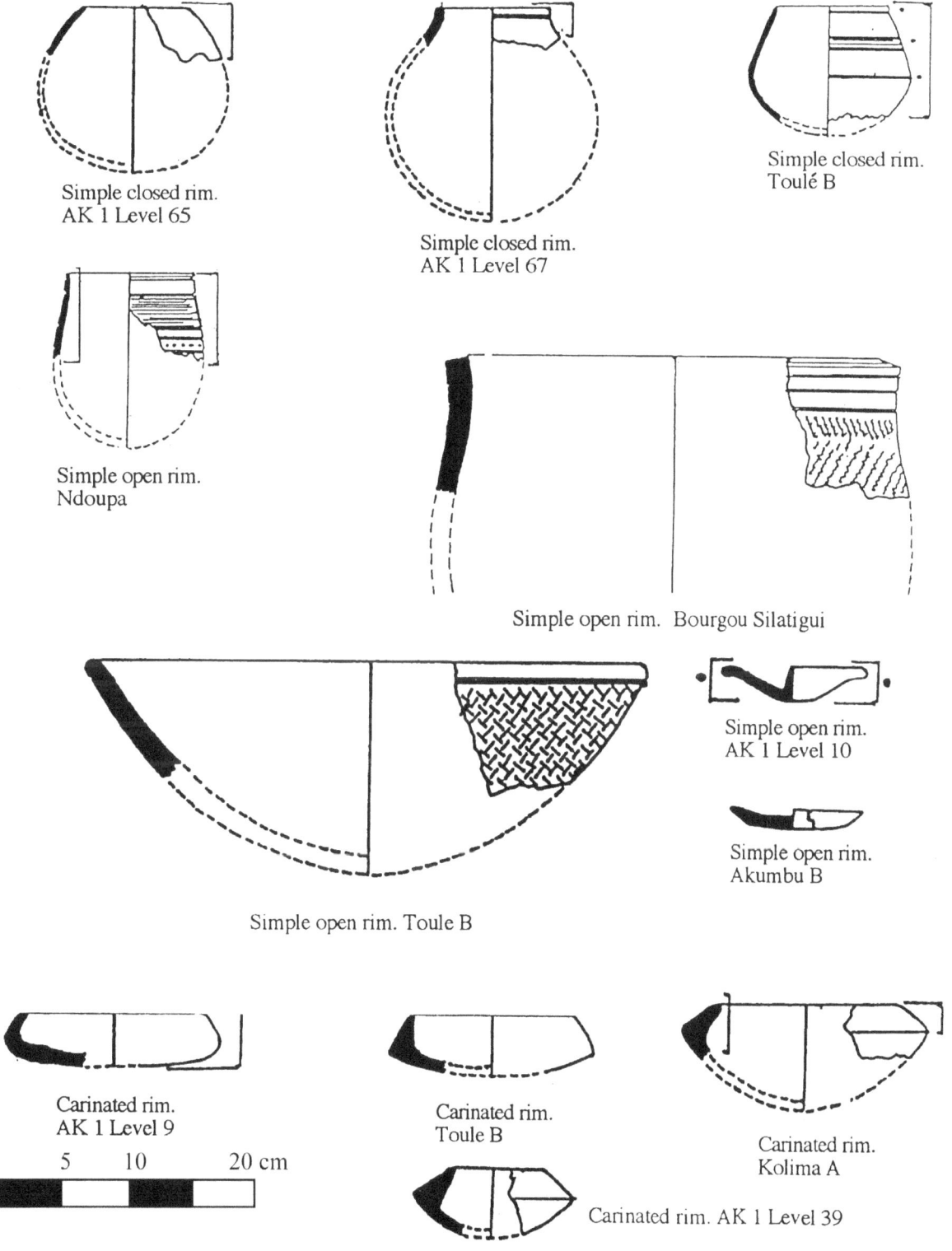

Figure 6.21. Middle Assemblage and AK1 pottery collections. Examples of simple and carinated rims

Survey and Excavation Pottery

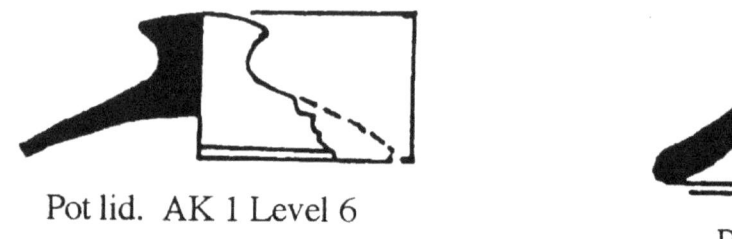

Pot lid. AK 1 Level 6

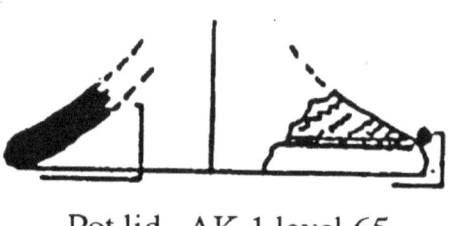

Pot lid. AK 1 level 65

Pot lid (Fulani Hat) Bourgou Silatigui A

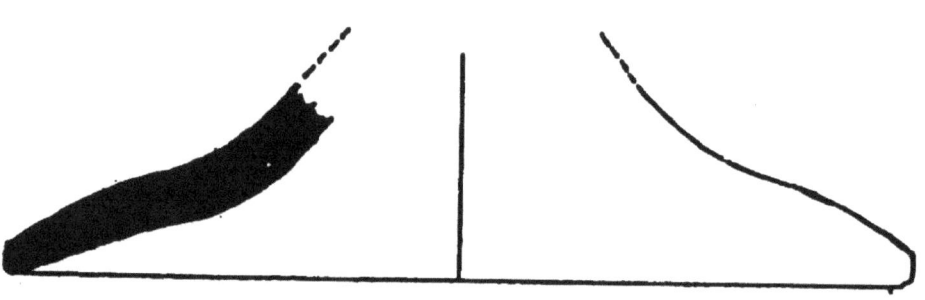

Pot lid (Fulani Hat) AK 1 Level 10

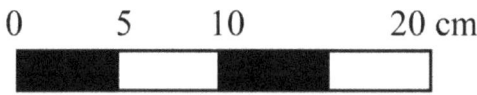

Figure 6.22. Middle Assemblage and AK1 pottery collections. Examples of pot lids

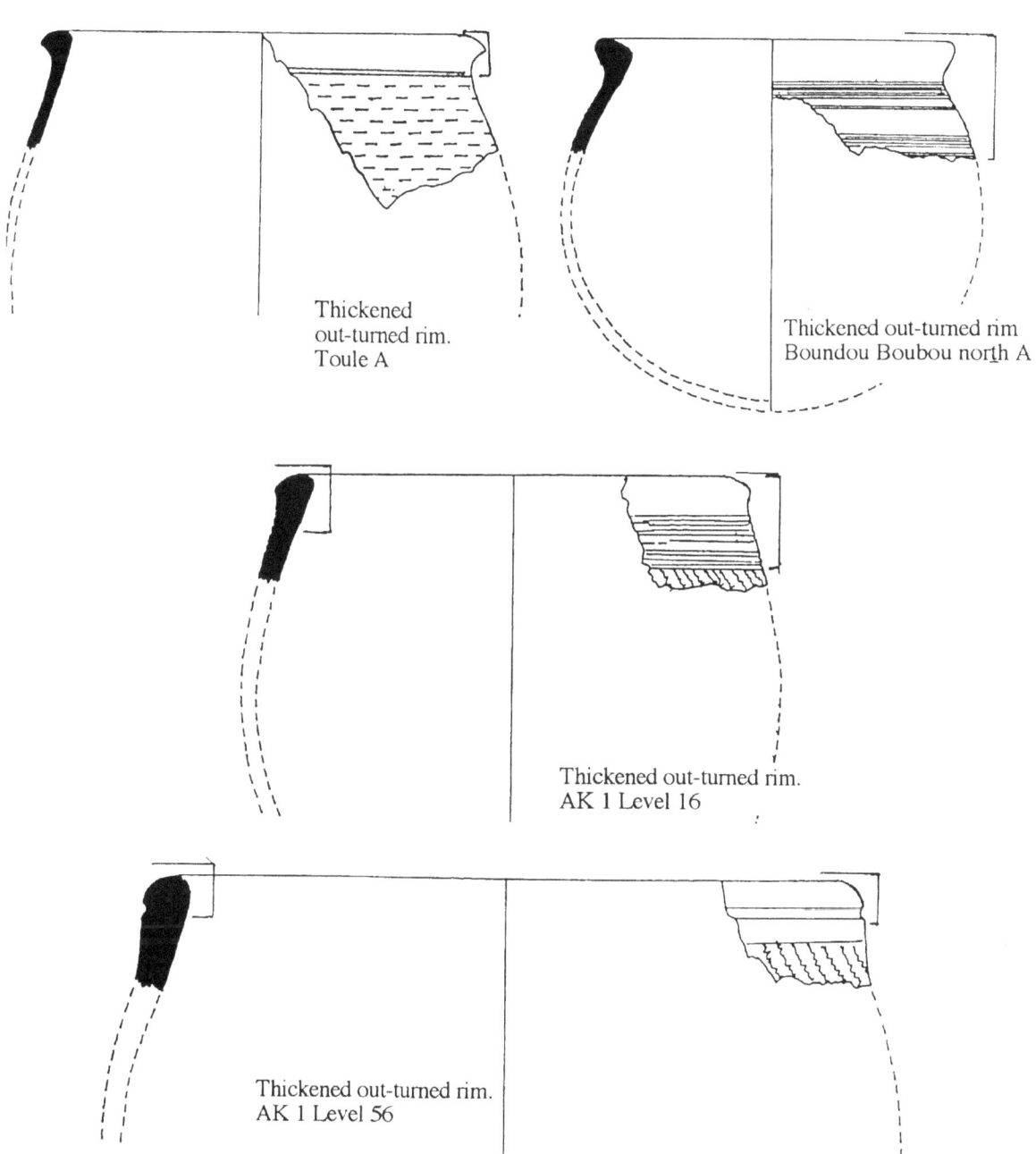

Figure 6.23. Middle Assemblage and AK1 pottery collections. Examples of thickened out-turned rims

Survey and Excavation Pottery

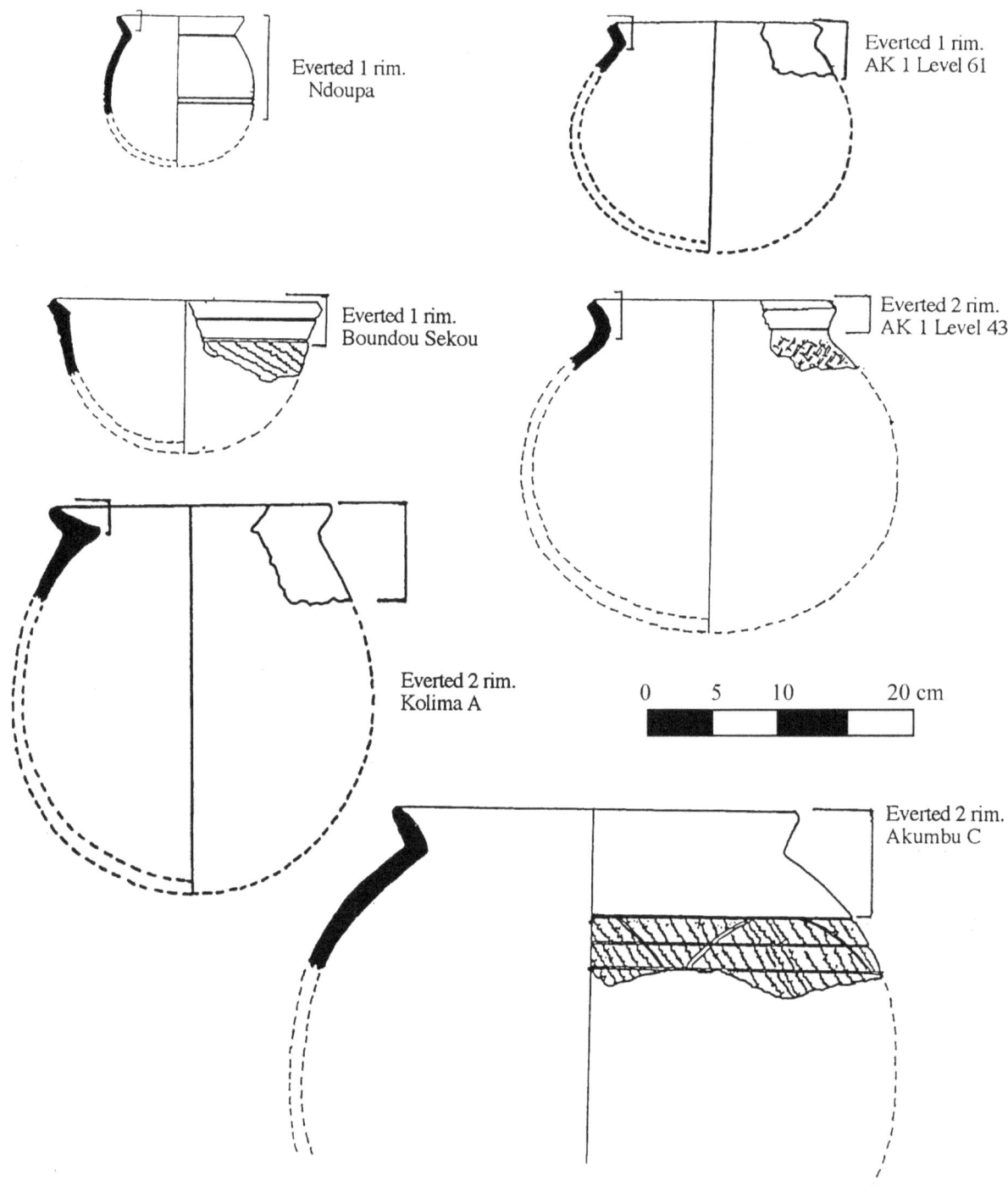

Figure 6.24a. Middle Assemblage amd AK1 pottery collections. Examples of everted rims

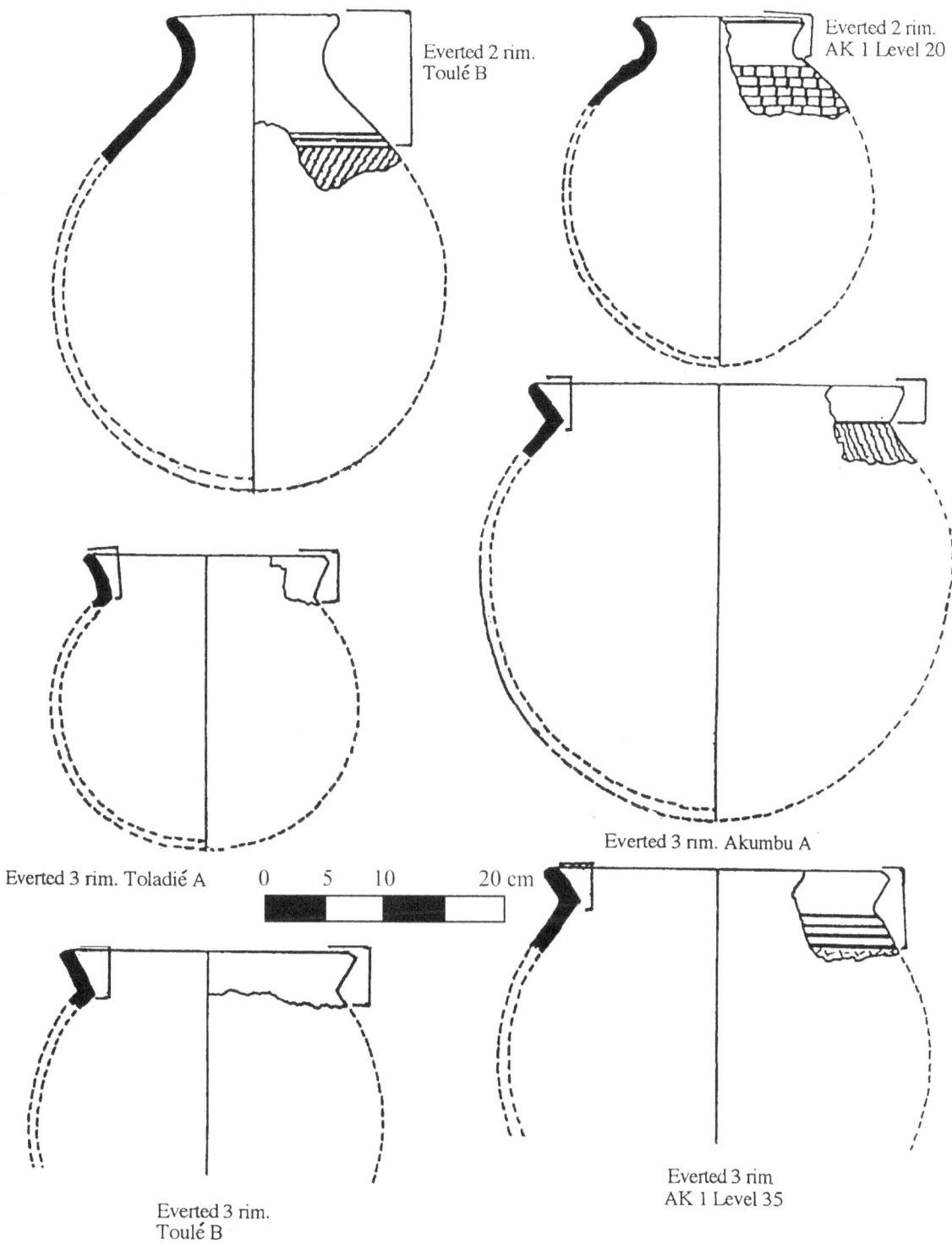

Figure 6.24b. Middle Assemblage amd AK1 pottery collections. Examples of everted rims.

Survey and Excavation Pottery

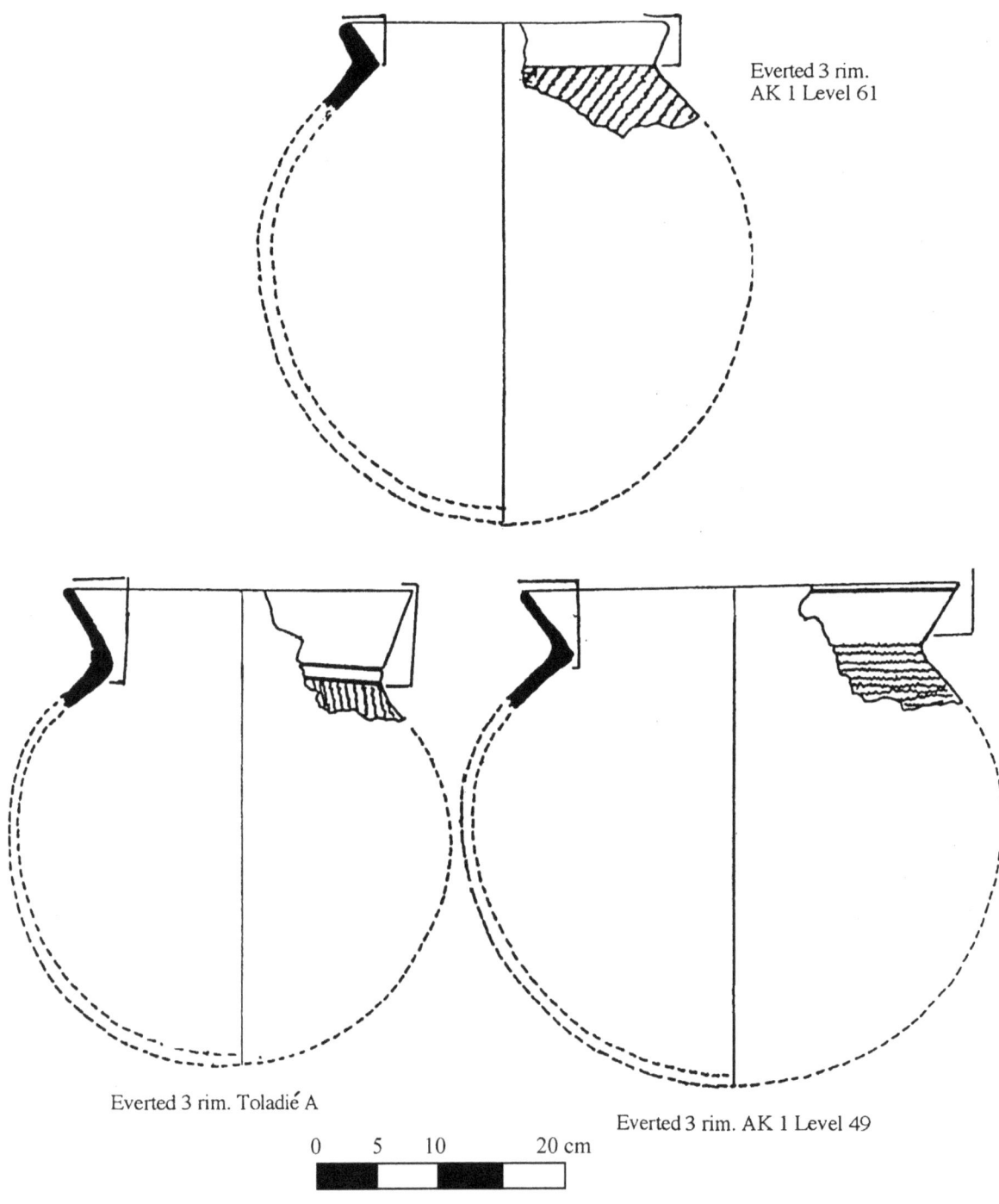

Figure 6.24c. Middle Assemblage amd AK1 pottery collections. Examples of everted rims

Archaeological Investigations of Iron Age Sites in the Mema Region, Mali (West Africa)

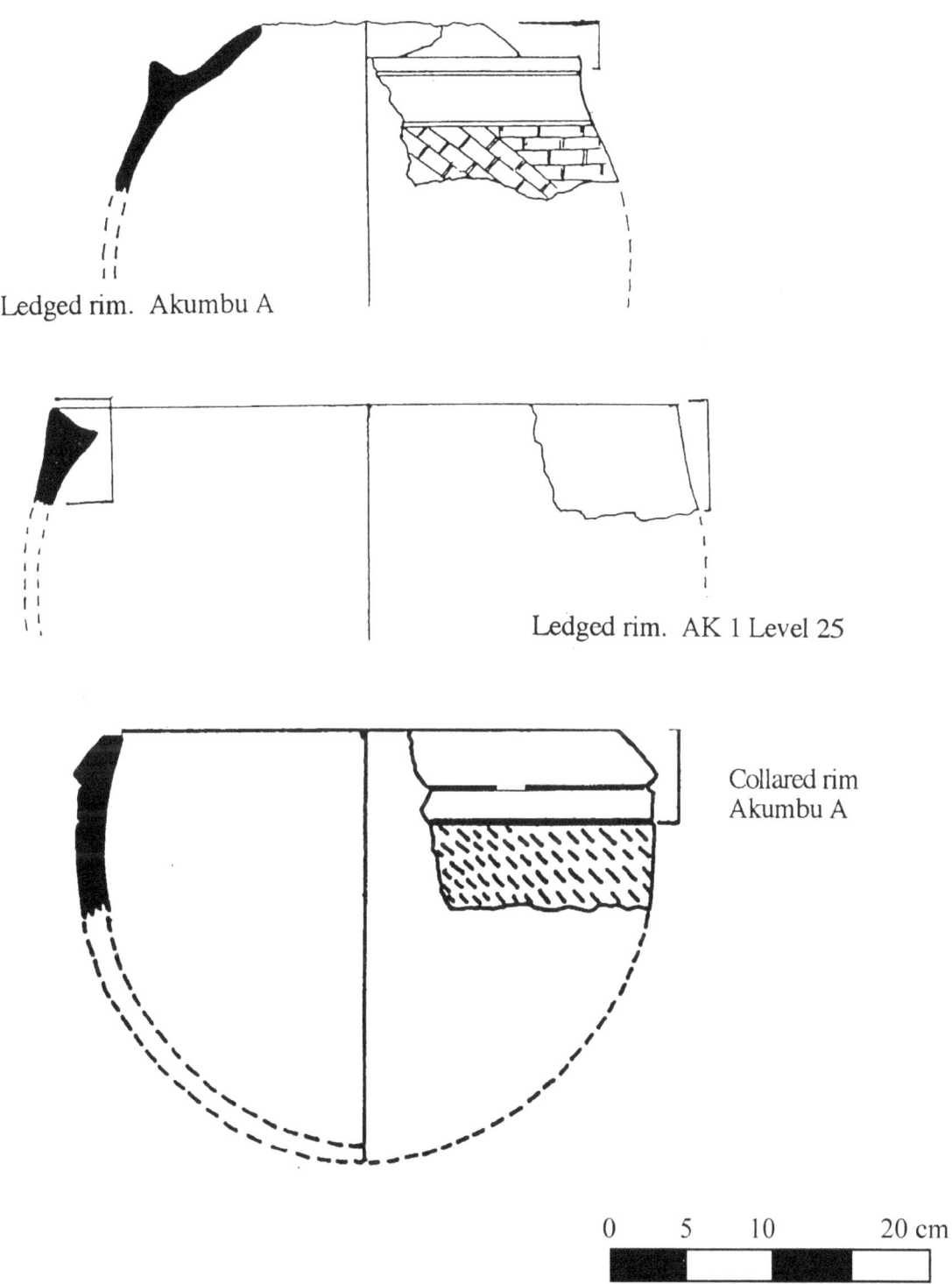

Figure 6.25. Middle Assemblage. Examples of everted rims

Survey and Excavation Pottery

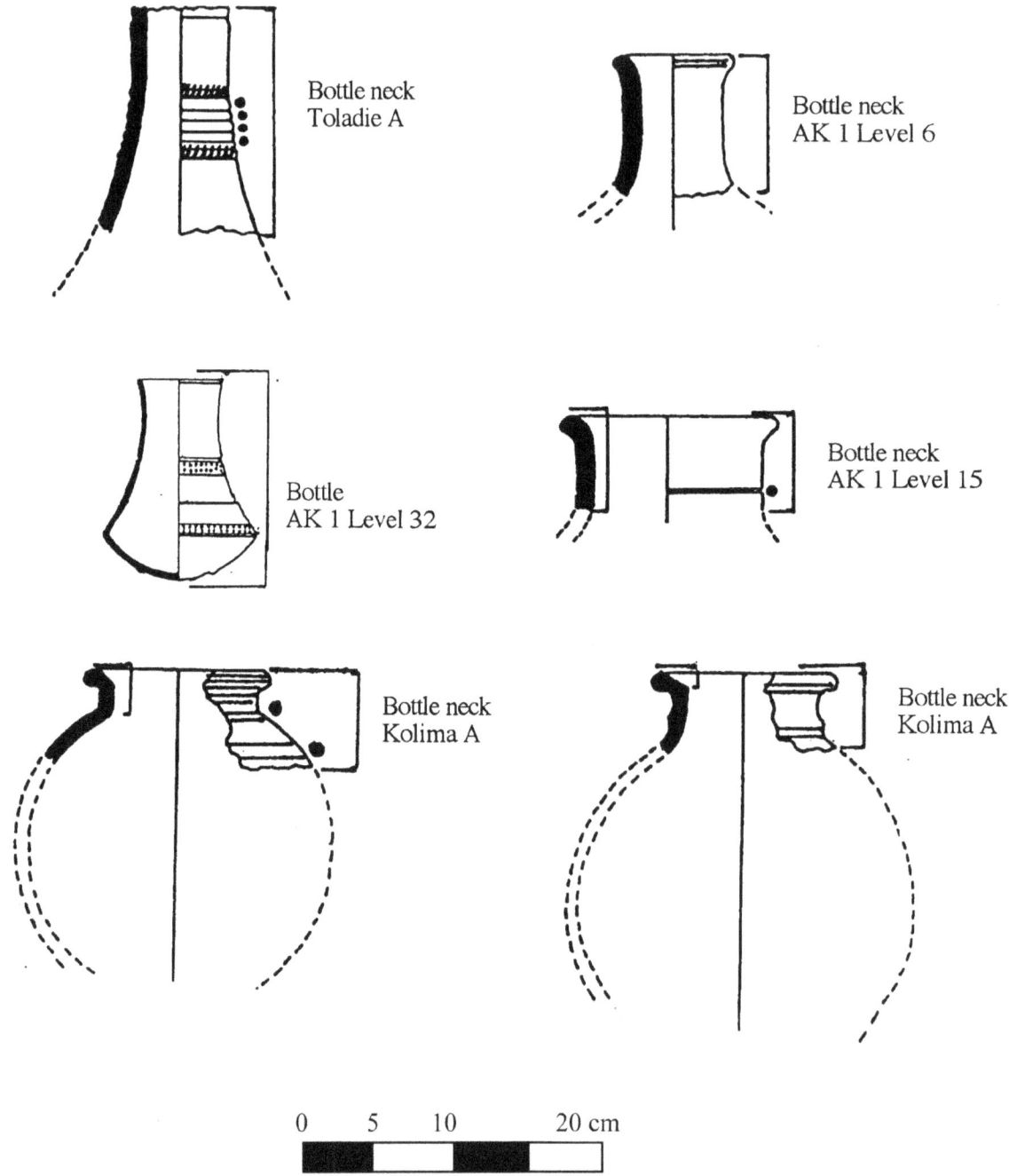

Figure 6.26. Middle Assemblage amd AK1 pottery collections. Examples of bottle necks

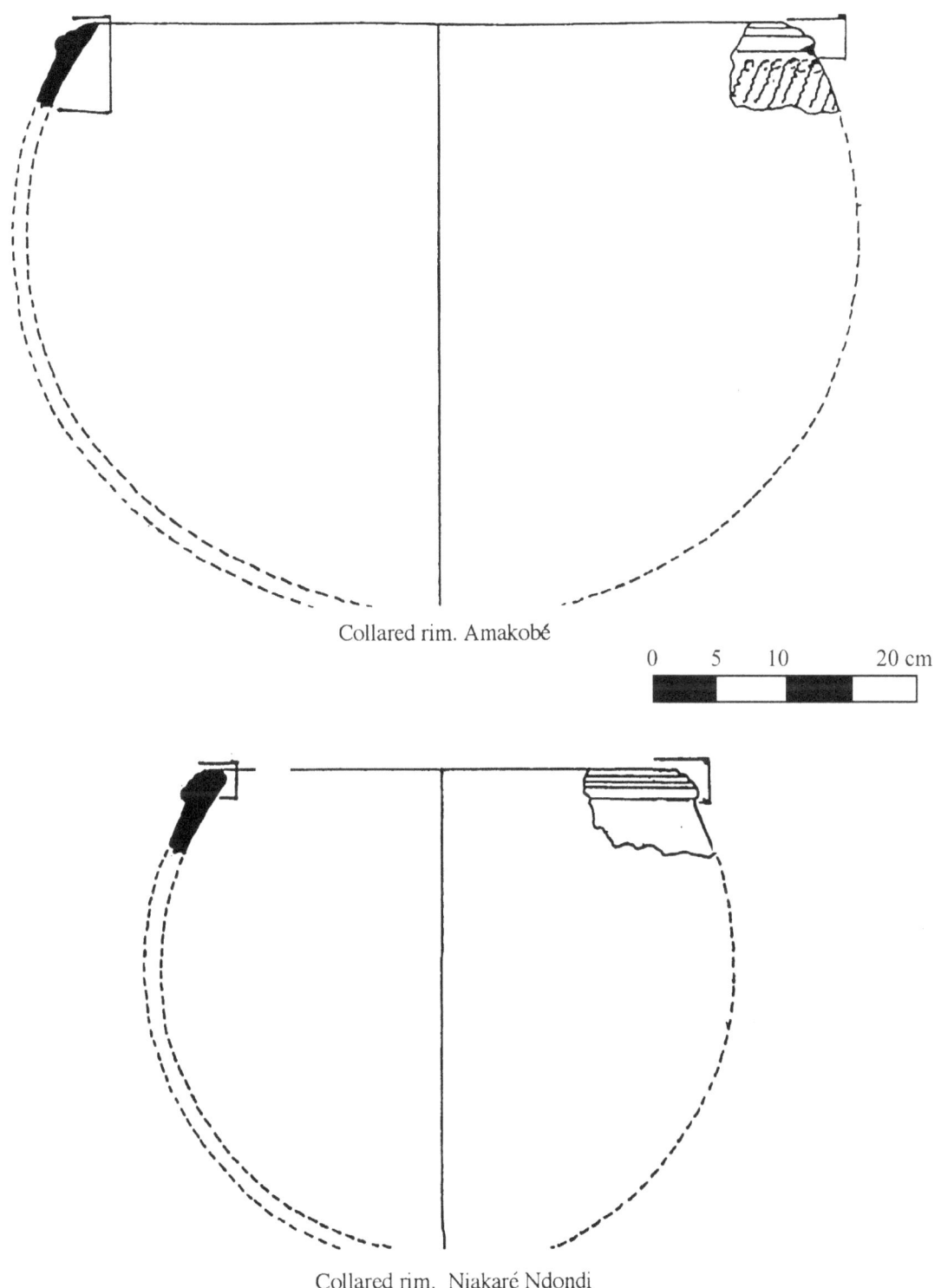

Figure 6.27. Late Assemblage. Examples of collared rims

Survey and Excavation Pottery

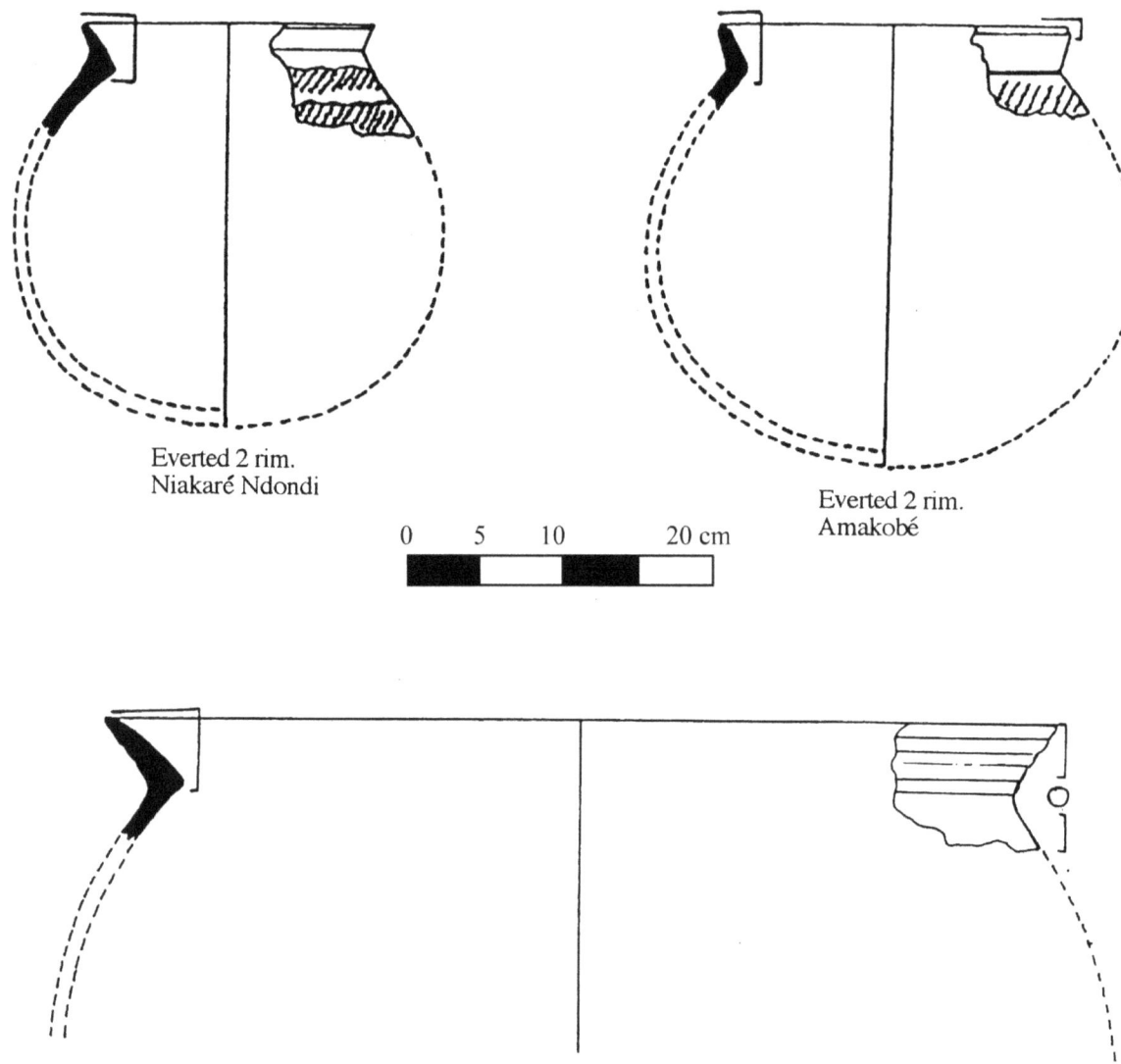

Figure 6.28. Late Assemblage. Examples of everted rims

Archaeological Investigations of Iron Age Sites in the Mema Region, Mali (West Africa)

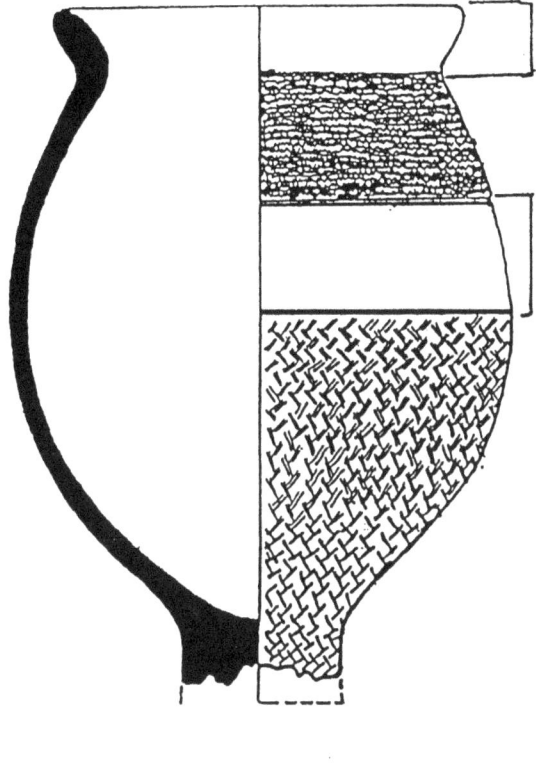

Complete vessl (Jidaga)
AK 3 Burial

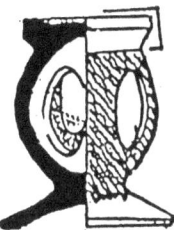

'Tellem' tripod
AK 1 Level 39

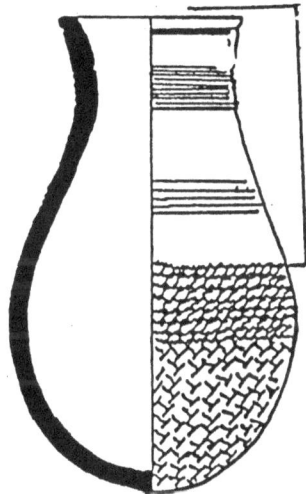

Complete vessel with everted rim
AK 1 Level 7.

Figure 6.29. Complete vessels from AK1 and AK3

Survey and Excavation Pottery

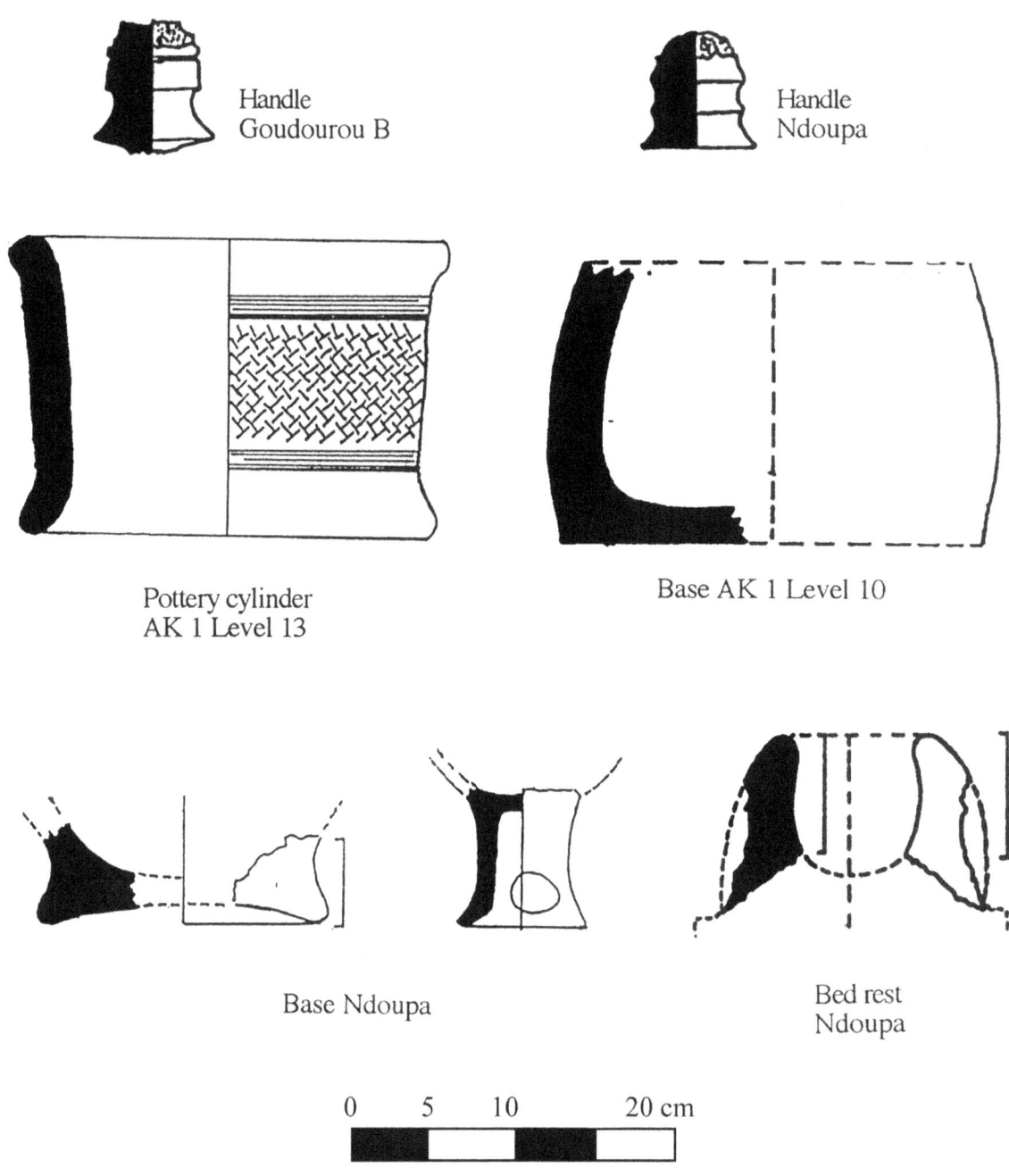

Figure 6.30. Special pottery finds. Handles, bases, pottery cylinder, and bed rest

Archaeological Investigations of Iron Age Sites in the Mema Region, Mali (West Africa)

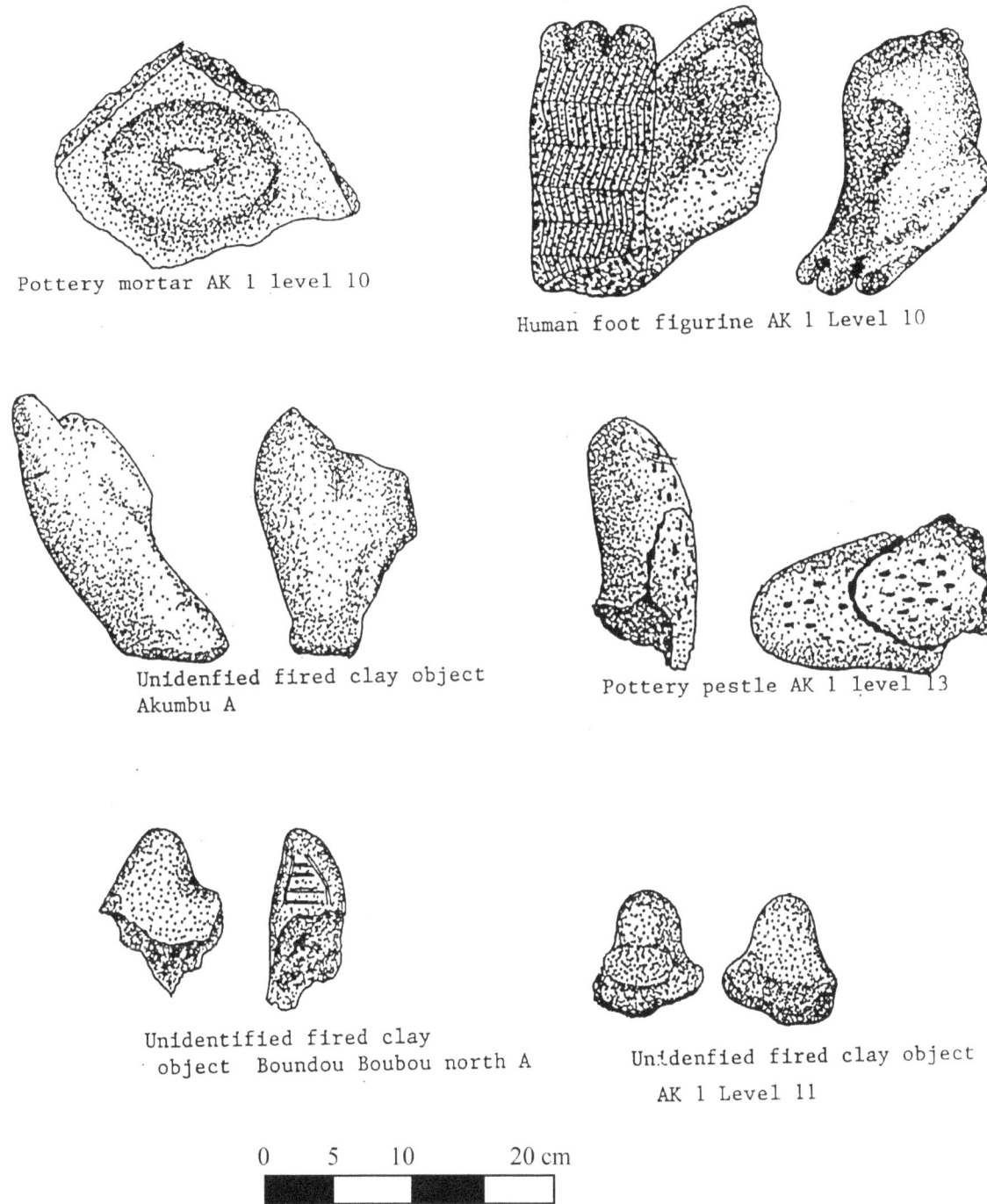

Figure 6.31. Special pottery finds. Pottery mortar, pottery pestle, and human foot figurine

Survey and Excavation Pottery

Figure 6.32. Early Assemblage. Twine decorated rims

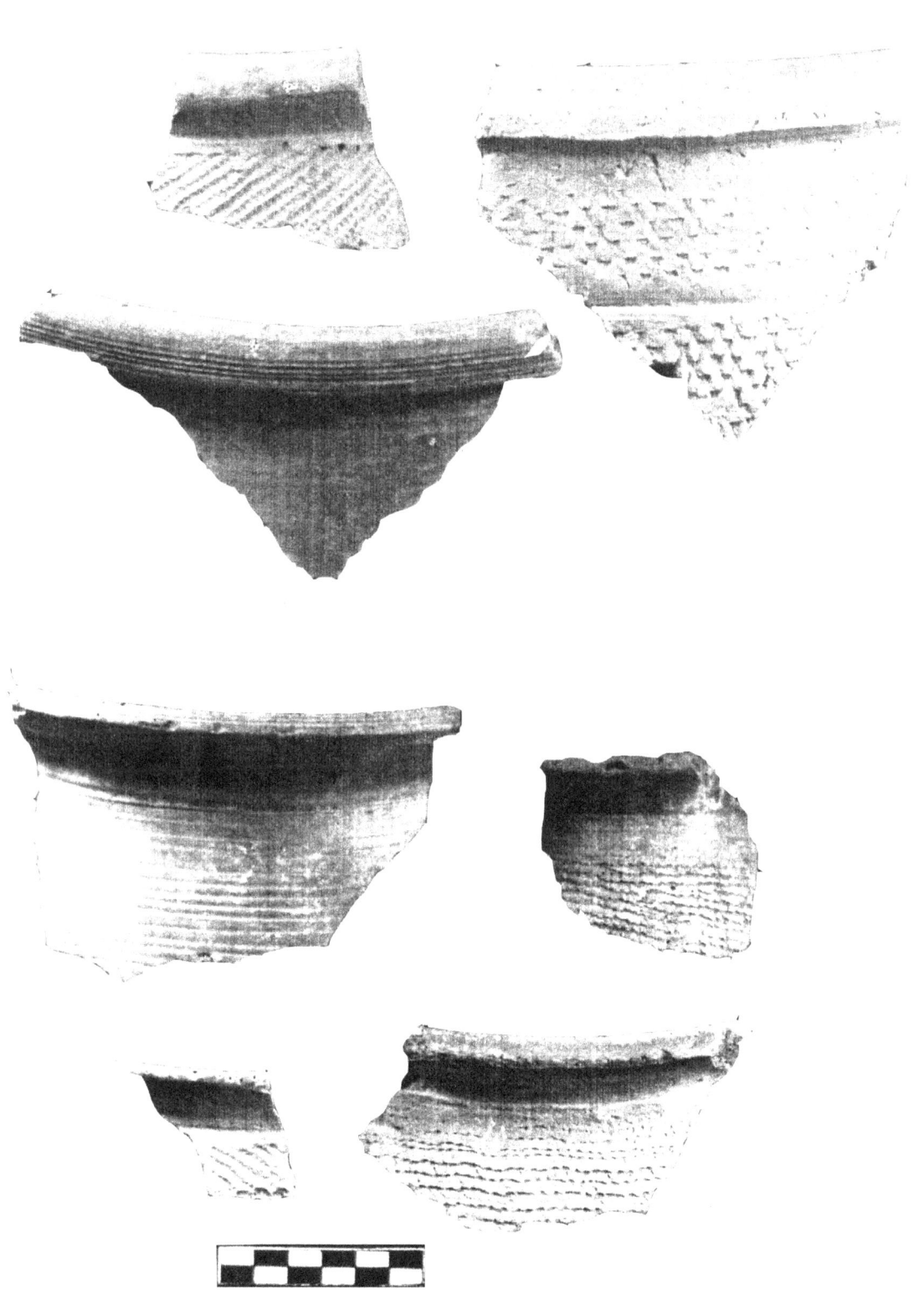

Figure 6.33. Middle Assemblage. Channeled and twine decorated rims

Survey and Excavation Pottery

Figure 6.34. Middle Assemblage. Channeled and twine decorated rims

Figure 6.35. Middle Assemblage. Examples of channeled, twine decorated and painted body sherds

Survey and Excavation Pottery

Figure 6.36. Late Assemblage. channeled and twine decorated rims

CHAPTER 7
CONCLUSIONS

ORIGIN OF IRON AGE OCCUPATION IN THE MÉMA

Overall, the results of this first integrated program of regional site survey and excavations constitute a first step toward filling in the gap in our knowledge of the archaeology of the Méma. The 137 sites (28 LSA sites, 109 IA sites) identified during the regional survey suggest an intense occupation of the region during both the LSA and the IA. This potential of the Méma (currently a sparsely populated Sahelian zone) to attract both the herding/hunting/gathering peoples of the LSA and IA populations was clearly associated with a period of climatic amelioration.

The earliest dates available for human occupation documented at the LSA site of Kobadi in the Méma range between 4000 and 3000 BP (Raimbault et al. 1987, 1991). Both the human osteological remains and artifacts (bone harpoons, groundstone implements, and ceramics) uncovered at this site are of Saharan affinity (Raimbault et al. 1987, 1991). This indicates that the Méma may have constituted a passageway for LSA populations moving out of the desiccating Sahara. These southerly manifestations and adaptations of LSA populations have been documented elsewhere in other better-watered regions such as the Tilemsi Valley in north eastern Mali (Smith 1979), Dhar Tichitt in southern Mauritania (Munson 1976; Holl 1985), and the basin of the Baoulé river in western Mali (Huysecom 1991). Unfortunately, issues like the chronology and nature of the transition from stone to iron in the Méma could not be answered by this field season. The earliest date for IA deposits is a fourth to fifth century AD date obtained from the lower excavated levels of Akumbu B. Akumbu A, the largest mound, at which two excavation units were opened, appears to be a relatively late site, occupied between the seventh and early fourteenth century AD. However, the presence in the region of numerous LSA sites and of deeply stratified IA sites with Early Assemblage material on their surface (to which a fourth/fifth century AD date applies at Akumbu), permit the hypothesis that the Méma IA culture developed out of the LSA culture represented at the many LSA sites identified during the regional site survey. We believe that many of these deeply stratified Early Assemblage sites rest upon terminal LSA deposits. This makes the Méma a prime and interesting region to investigate some of the most pressing issues of West African prehistory such as the beginning of agriculture and iron technology.

The earliest IA occupation yet recorded in the whole Middle Niger is documented at Jenné jeno, founded c.250 BC by populations already acquainted with iron (McIntosh & McIntosh 1980; SK McIntosh in press). As no LSA sites has yet been found anywhere in the alluvial floodplain of the Inland Delta, the McIntoshes (1980) believe that Jenné-jeno's first settlers probably migrated from the western fringe of the Inland Delta (probably the Méma) after the introduction of iron technology. This hypothesis is supported by a tradition collected at Dia by Cheik Tidiane Hayidara (personnal communication Septembre 1992) which identifies the Méma as the origin of the Nono, the first settlers of Dia in the Upper Niger Delta.

Evolution of Iron Age occupation in the Méma
The Méma IA occupation resulted in the formation of habitation mounds, found throughout the study area. Many of these habitation mounds appear to have been permanently occupied for several centuries, as demonstrated by the nearly one millenium-long excavated sequence (fifth century AD to early 14th century AD) at Akumbu mound complex.

The preliminary relative chronology for sites identified during regional survey shows that IA settlement patterns and landform preferences underwent dramatic changes through time. Sites relatively and preliminarily dated to the early to mid-first millenium AD overwhelmingly consisted of small sized settlements, packed together in clusters. These compacted clusters of small sites were preferentially situated close to the banks of now relict water corridors. Though the evidence is still lacking, the flood regime in those water corridors may have been active during the period of occupation of the early sites, allowing a reliance on aquatic or floodplain resources. As already noted, both the depth of the deposits (estimated to be on average 3–5m), and the single fourth/fifth century AD date for those sites, suggest that LSA deposits possibly rest beneath the IA deposits at some of them.

During the period encompassed by the Middle Assemblage (seventh to early fourteenth century AD), site areas exploded to an average of 10–20 ha, reaching nearly 80 ha at Toladié A, the largest site within the survey area. This spectrum of site sizes during the period of the Middle Assemblage clearly implies a population explosion, and a possible trend toward aggregation on fewer, but larger and centralized settlements. The onset of improved climatic conditions, especially adequate rainfall, between 700 AD and 1100 AD (McIntosh 1983; Brooks 1986) may have been favourable to the growth of these large Middle Assemblage settlements. Though many of the settlements during the Middle Assemblage lined the banks of ancient water corridors, as during the preceding period, other ecological zones, such as the degraded dune system, also became occupied.

Late Assemblage sites which displayed fragments of tobacco pipes (believed to have been introduced only in late sixteenth century) were, according to local informants, the result of a penetration of the region by the Bamana after the abandonment of the large and urban size site of the Middle Assemblage. These Bamana, probably millet farmers, settled preferentially on the light sandy soil of

Conclusions

the longitudinal dunes, or at its contact with the degraded dunes.

Speculation on site clustering in the Méma
As already noted, the phenomenon of site clustering in the Méma is present as early as the LSA. It became prevalent during the period of the Early Assemblage. A network of small and contemporaneously occupied sites are packed together in the Boundou Boubou, Niessouma and Bougou Silatigui areas(to cite only a few examples). This prevalence of site clustering can be interpreted as the embryo of urbanism in the Méma. As argued by RJ McIntosh (1991), who has studied the same phenomenon elsewhere in the Middle Niger, each of these small sites may have housed one ethnic or corporate group which interacted with each other without the sacrifice of their own linguistic identity, material culture and economic specialization (RJ McIntosh & SK McIntosh 1988; RJ McIntosh 1991). During the period of the the Middle Assemblage, relatively fewer but larger and more centralized settlements such as Toladié, Akumbu, and Bourgou Silatigui, were surrounded by smaller satellite sites. Possibly, like their counterparts in the better-studied Upper Inland Niger Delta (SK McIntosh & RJ McIntosh 1980; Haskell et al. 1988; SK McIntosh in press; RJ McIntosh 1991), these aggregated large urban entities were home to a larger and more heterogeneous population and provided services to the surrounding satellite sites. The situation of site clustering is favoured by the unique ecological conditions of the Middle Niger, where most regions comprise many geomorphological zones or soil types. Indeed, Gallais (1967) in an ethnographic study stresses how these mosaic geomorphologic zones or soil types can be appealing to many ethnic groups. This ethnic crowding, instead of leading to violent confrontation, leads to economic specialisation and interaction between the various groups (Gallais 1967). This interaction between ethnic or specialist groups is reflected in mythologies which relate mythical inter-ethnic food aid (for example a Bozo feeding a hungry Dogon with his own flesh) in times of economic stress (RJ McIntosh & SK McIntosh 1988).

Speculation on the economy at Akumbu
Large amounts of flotation samples were collected during the excavations at Akumbu. The processed samples are currently deposited at Korofina, the storage facility of the ISH, awaiting analysis. Therefore, the only evidence of plant exploitation we possess for now are the casts of *Pennisetum* millet stalks uncovered throughout the deposits at AK1, AK3 and AK4. This crop was present at Dhar Tichitt in southern Mauritania by 900 BC (Munson 1976). It was possibly present in the Méma during the same period, given the fact that both regions were occupied by terminal LSA populations. Surprisingly, fish and other aquatic animal remains were more abundant and more diversified at Unit AK3 on Akumbu B (especially in its lower excavated levels) than at both Unit AK1 and Unit AK4 on Akumbu A (see Appendix 1). This implies that aquatic and also probably floodplain resources played an important role in the economy of Akumbu mound complex during the earliest phase of its occupation. However, given the erratic occurrence of fish and other aquatic animals at both AK1 and AK4 on Akumbu A, the importance of such resources later declined. The exact reasons for this decline are not yet known. But it is possible that Akumbu A was not occupied at all by fishermen. Also possibly, the water corridor of the Niakéné Maoudo (at the western end of which the site complex is located) had shrunk considerably when Akumbu was founded or was not flowing at all due to strangulation. Terrestrial animals, including antelopes, elephant, warthogs, and hares were heavily exploited. Not surprising for a West African IA site of Akumbu's antiquity, domesticated animals, such as goats, cattle, sheep, chicken, and more spectacularly, horse and domesticated ass found in a deposit dated to the seventh century AD, were very well represented (see Appendix 1).

Another important economic activity was iron production. Several major Middle Assemblage sites, including Akumbu, Kolima, Bourgou Silatigui, Goudourou, and Boundou Boubou, revealed on their outskirts evidence of iron smelting in the the form of clustered furnace remains associated with slag concentrations. Both, the number of the furnaces, and the size of the slag heaps uncovered near in the southern part of the Méma, testify that smelting was done at an industrial scale, or over a long period of time, or both. This industrial iron production, also documented by Randi Haaland (1980) on the bank of the Fala de Molodo in the southern part of the Méma, highly suggests that the demand for iron for local consumption, or for trade with neighbouring regions, such as the Wagadu and the Inland Niger Delta, was great. Suitable conditions for this kind of iron production included the presence of the ferruginous lateritic crust of the Boulel Ridge, and possibly the existence of abundant accacia trees for large amounts of wood fuel. This implies the existence in the Méma of more humid conditions than today.

It should also be reiterated here that long distance trade played an important role in Akumbu's economy. Evidence for such economic activity is provided by the presence of copper objects, stone beads, cowrie shells, and spindle whorls. The copper at Akumbu occurred between the eighth century AD and early fourteenth century. This is a relatively late date compared to Jenne-jeno where copper objects appeared around the fifth century AD (SK McIntosh & RJ McIntosh 1980; SK McIntosh in press). Though the precise sources of the copper objects found at Akumbu are unknown, they probably originated from Akjoujt (in Mauritania) or Nioro du Sahel (in northwesten part of Mali). These two sites are the closest known sources for coppers (Mauny 1961; Lambert 1971). The stone beads, though also from unknown sources, were probably brought in to the site from outside. The significance of the cowrie shells and the spindle whorls uncovered at Akumbu has already been discussed. These two commodities constitute the most striking evidence for Akumbu's involvement in trans-Saharan trade and Islamic influence on the site. The cowries (yet to be identified to species) are likely the shells of *Cypraea moneta,* which, along with *Cypraea annulus* are said to have been exclusively the cowrie shells traded in West Africa (Johnson 1970: 17). The shells of the species of *Cypraea Moneta*, are said to be the earliest species to penetrate Sub-Saharan West Africa through the trans-Saharan trade (Mauny1961; Johnson 1970). Relevant to this question is the finding by Monod (1969) at Ma' den Ijafen of a lost caravan with neary 3000 rods of copper and thousands of cowrie shells. Both Mauny (1961) and Johnson (1970) attest that El Bekri noted their use as currency at least in the eleventh century AD in many parts of the Middle Niger. However, the bulk (13 specimens), were found in a funerary context and were certainly used to adorn the corpse before burial.

Affinities and differences between the Méma and other regions of the Middle Niger
In their studies around Jenne and Dia, the McIntoshes suggested that the entire Upper Niger Delta constituted in the terminal first millennium AD and mid-second millennium AD a "culture area" characterized by the presence of same artefact attributes (in particular the pottery), and other cultural elements, including architectural techniques and burial practices. As affinities of the material culture of the Upper Delta were uncovered in the Lakes Region and in the Niger Bend, the McIntoshes concluded that the entire Middle Niger might have constituted in the terminal first millennium AD and early second millennium AD a vast region of cultural interaction and integration (SK McIntosh & RJ McIntosh 1980; Haskell et al. 1988; SK McIntosh in press).

In the light of the results of the 1989/90 field season, it is now possible to assess, at least preliminarily, to what extent the Méma was integrated in this cultural interaction along the Middle Niger.

In this comparison, I will first consider the Jenné and Dia regions in the Upper Niger Delta. In Chapter 6, I pointed out the affinities of the Méma Middle Assemblage (dated between the seventh century and the fourteenth century AD) with the Jenne-jeno and Dia Phase III and Phase IV pottery collections. These affinities included the same decorative techniques [slipping, channelling, twine (braided twine, twisted twine, and plaited twine) impression, and black and white painting], and similar pottery forms such as long necked water flasks (pottery bottles), pottery cylinders, bicornuate bed rests, and pottery pestles. In addition to these pottery attributes, other elements of the Méma culture appear to be similar to that of the Upper Niger. For instance, clustered and simultaneously occupied sites, a prevalent model of occupation in the Méma during in the mid-first millenium AD and early second millenium AD, is reported from the Jenné and Dia regions during the same period (SK McIntosh & RJ McIntosh 1980; Haskell et al. 1988; SK McIntosh in press).

The 1989/90 field season also pointed out some striking differences between the material culture of the Méma and that of the Upper Niger Delta. Plastic decoration, very diversified in Jenne-jeno Phase IV pottery, is limited almost exclusively to channelling in the Méma Middle Assemblage. Some motifs, comb dragging and stamping, common at Jenne-jeno and Dia, seem not to have attracted the fancy of the Méma potters. Painted wares, abundant in Jenne-jeno and Dia pottery collections, are represented by less than 10% in the Méma Middle Assemblage. Organic temper is prevalent in the Méma while grog is most frequently at both Jenne-jeno and Dia. Morever the miscellaneous potteries with raised motifs numerous at Jenne-jeno appear to be absent from the Méma. Furthermore, a significant difference between the two regions is found in architectural elements and techniques. The rounded clay bricks, *djenné -ferey*, used in building mud walls at many Upper Niger sites, including Jenne-jeno (SK McIntosh & RJ McIntosh 1980; SK McIntosh in press), Shoma, Mara (Haskell et al.1988), Toguéré Galia and Toguéré Doupwil (Bedaux et al.1978) appear to be absent from the Méma. Mud walls detected during the excavations at Akumbu were constructed with a single or two rows of crude irregular rectangular mud bricks. Also, the archaeological evidence shows that typical to the period of the Méma Middle Assemblage was intense mound occupation which resulted in rapid and sometimes extremely rapid accumulation. This situation, well illustrated at Akumbu A (with 7.5m of cultural deposits accumulated in a maximum of seven centuries), has not thus far been documented in the Jenné and Dia regions.

Moving farther downstream in the lakes Region, affinities of the Méma material culture during the first millennium AD and early second millennium AD are reported from many sites. As already noted, the same decorative techniques [slipping, channelling, black and white painting, and twine (twisted twine, plaited twine, and braided twine) impression] of the Méma Middle Assemblage have been identified at Mouyssam, Toubel, and Kawinza, all near Sumpi and respectively dated to AD 300-680, AD 340-605, AD 655-1055 (Raimbault 1991; Raimbault & Togola 1991). In addition to these decorative elements, characteristic rim forms (everted rims, thickened rims with an out-turned flange, carinated rims for small and shallow bowls mostly left undecorated or only slipped, pottery bottles, and large pot lids, a.k.a. Fulani Hats) of the Méma Middle Assemblage are reported from Mouyssam, Toubel, and Kawinza. It is also relevant to note here that some of these aforementioned pottery forms, in particular the small carinated bowls and the pottery bottles, are present around Goundam and Diré at the funerary tumuli of Kouga (dated to calAD 900-1250) Killi, and El Oualaji (Mauny 1961; Desplagnes 1903; 1951). Kouga and Killi also contain white and black painted wares (Desplagnes 1903; Mauny 1961). Beyond pottery features, artifact attributes and surface features indicate the presence of affinities with the Méma material culture at many Lakes Region sites. Burnt features for example, present at nearly 30% of the Middle assemblage sites, are reported from both habitation and funerary tumuli. However, it should be noted that, the

Conclusions

nature and function of these burnt features (common to the two regions), are as yet insufficiently investigated. As noted earlier, two burnt features excavated at Akumbu A revealed use as an oven. Those in the Lakes Regions have been differently interpreted as sacrificial places (Desplagnes 1907), or an attempt to harden the surface of the funerary tumuli at the surface of which they were found (Mauny 1961; Fontes et al. 1980; 1991). The intense mound occupation which resulted in extremely rapid accumulation in the Méma is also observed at Mouyssam, near Sumpi. The 9.5m of cultural deposits at this site were accumulated in less than four centuries, between AD 300 and AD 680 (Raimbault 1991: 322). Interestingly, the pottery of Akumbu A, like that of Mouyssam, showed little change through time, possibly due to the rapidity of accumulation. One last affinity of the Méma and the Lakes Region appears to be the presence of clustered sites. This phenomenon, well underway in the Méma by the first mid-millennium AD, is also reported from the Lakes Region (Desplagnes 1907; Dembélé 1986, 1991; Fontes et al. 1991). At this point, however, a full comparison of the phenomenon of site clustering in the two regions is not possible due to the fact that the chronological and functional relationship between clustered sites in the Lakes Region have not yet been examined.

As for the Upper Inland Niger Delta, the above outlined affinities of the Méma material culture in the Lakes Regions do not preclude differences between the two regions. Painted wares, for instance, appear to be more abundant in the Lakes Regions than in the Méma. This situation is well illustrated at Mouyssam whose pottery collection contains more than 50% painted wares (Raimbault 1991: 369). Other elements of differences between the two regions seem to be present in burial practices. The popular use of pottery bottles in funeral context documented at the habitation site of Kawinza (Raimabult & Sidibé 1991) and at the funerary tumuli near Goundam and Diré (Desplagnes 1903; 1951; Mauny 1961) appear to be pratically unknown in the Méma. In addition, the impressive tumuli, with affluent burials, as well as the elaborate megalithic monuments of the Lakes Region appear not to have extended to the Méma.

In the Niger Bend and Gao region, the scarcity of data on excavated artifacts precludes comparison of the material from those regions and that from the Méma. However, in their survey around Timbuktu and Gourma Rharous in 1984, the McIntoshes (SK McIntosh & RJ McIntosh 1986) report twine (twisted twine, plaited twine and braided twine) impression, channelling, black and white painting, and organic material temper, (all identified in the Méma Middle Assemblage) at the surface of sites relatively dated between 500-1500 AD.

In summary, the available archaeological evidence suggests that the Méma was, to some extent, related to at least to two regions (the Upper Inland Niger Delta, and the Lake Regions) of the Middle Niger during the terminal first millennium AD and early second millennium AD. Interaction between the Méma and those regions may have taken the form of transmission of cultural elements from one region the other through population movements, or exchange of goods, or both. Some of the industrial iron production of the Méma, for example, may have been traded to the Upper Niger Delta which lacks good iron ore. Relevant here is the current economic symbiosis between the Méma and the Inland Niger Delta. Transhumant Fulani from the Inland Niger Delta move into the Méma during the rainy season to exploit the rich flora of grass. In the dry season, when ponds in the Méma are dry, they return to the Inland Delta where water is available and to exploit the lush *burgu* pastureland (Gallais 1967).

The aforementioned differences between the Méma and regions of the Middle Upper Niger (namely the Upper Niger Delta and the Lakes regions) appear to indicate that the Méma was a separate 'cultural province' which was marginal in many aspects to the cultural interaction and integration that appear to have characterized the Middle Niger during the terminal first millenium and early second millennium AD. This marginal role is possibly attributable to the Méma's location, some 100km north of the Niger River, which, undoubtedly, served as the major axis of communication and transmission of cultural elements.

Affinities of the Méma material culture outside the Middle Niger

Comparison between the Méma and regions outside the Middle Niger (e.g. the Wagadu and regions of southern Mali) is difficult because very little has been reported on the material culture of those regions. I explained in Chapter 1 that both the oral traditions and the local chronicles such as the *Tarikh Es Soudan* (Es Sa' di 1900) and the *Tarikh El Fetach* (Kati 1964) allude to the movements of iron-using Soninké across the Méma from the Wagadu. In addition, the Soninké empire of Wagadu, assumed to correspond to the Empire of Ghana, is said to have vassalised the Méma at several occasions. Unfortunately, the 1989/90 archaeological program does not offer enough evidence to sustain these claims and to illuminate the nature of the relationship between the Méma and the Wagadu. As already noted most archaeological programs executed in the Wagadu have focused on the ruins of the stone buildings of Kumbi Saleh and on the traded goods found at the site. All of these denote North African and Islamic influence on the site, and thus do not provide enough insight into the initial culture present at the site.

Similarly, the situation of the Soninké empire of the Méma, said to have been founded after the dislocation of the Soninké Empire of Wagadu, remains unclear. The excavations at Akumbu, as well as the regional site survey did not reveal the existence or presence of a centralized political authority in the form of a monument, palatial edifice, or any other artefact of power. This situation, it should be noted, appears to be common in the Western Sudan. During the extensive archaeological work executed in the Upper Niger Delta in the 1970s and 1980s (Bedaux et al. 1978; SK McIntosh & RJ McIntosh 1980; Haskell et al. 1988; SK McIntosh in press), only two city walls were encountered: at Jenne-jeno (SK McIntosh & RJ McIntosh 1980) and at Shoma (Haskell et al. 1988). In the Manden, the only public building or artefacts of power known so far are the putative conference room encountered at the site of Niani by Filopowiak (1979), the sacred vestibule of Kangaba, the *Kaama bolon*, and the xylophone of Sumaoro, said to have been taken by Sunjata, and still jealousely kept at Niagassola (Camara 1990:82).

As for the Wagadu, the nature of the relationship between the Méma and the Manden (the crucible of the medieval empire of Mali) is not elucidated by the results of this field season. Sunjata, the founder of the Empire of Mali, is, however, said to have exiled in the Méma and annexed it after the battle of Krina which marks the beginning of the empire of Mali (Niane 1960; Ly Tall1970; Cissé 1988).

These types of disagreement between oral traditions and archaeology, not uncommon in African history, stem from the nature of oral tradions which may exaggerate the role of a small group linked to the ruling clan. According to Seydou Camara, Sunjata's exile in the Méma is too exaggerated in many variants of Sunjata's epic. This exile should be regarded as part of Sunjata's initiation which, necessarily, had to include confronting the hero with difficulties in a far away land (S. Camara personnal communication August 1992).

One last affinity of the Méma material culture outside the Middle Niger should be mentioned. A small footed vessel, similar to the "Tellem" tripod bowl was uncovered in a deposit dated to the seventh century AD. The "Tellem" footed vessels, generally linked to funerary rituals (Bedaux 1980; de Grunne 1983), appear to have had a wide distribution. Bedaux (1980) reports their presence at many sites, including Niani, Dogo, Tiebala, Jenne, Galia, Fatoma, Kumbi Saleh, and Sanga. Bedaux (1980) links the large diffusion of these footed vessels to population movements.

This preliminary research in the Méma has clearly raised a number of interesting questions concerning the chronology and evolution of IA occupation. From the available archaeological evidence, the early urbanism documented elsewhere in the Middle Niger, appears to have extended to the Méma. This is justified by the presence of early and extreme site clustering found in many parts of the Méma. The premature abandonment of some of these extreme site clusters lends support to oral accounts that identify the Méma as a passageway or centre of dispersion of populations during the IA. This phenomenon of premature abandonment, presumably accountable to early strangulation of water corridors, however, needs further investigation. In addition, the issues of chronology and transition between the IA and LSA cannot be answered without further excavations.

BIBLIOGRAPHY

BACHMANN, H-G., 1982. The Identification of Slags from Archaeological Sites. *Occasional Publication*. Number 6. Institute of Archaeology. University of London.

BATHILY, A., 1975. Discussion of the Traditions of Wagadu with Some Reference to Ancient Ghana Including a Review of Oral Accounts, Arabic Sources and Archaeological Evidence. *Bulletin de l'Institut Fondamental d'Afrique Noire* (B) 1:3–93.

BEDAUX, R., 1980. The Geographical Distribution of Footed Bowls in the Upper Niger Delta Region. In B.K. Dumett (ed.) *West African culture Dynamics: Archaeological and Historical Perspectives*. World Anthropology, The Hague. pp 247–258.

BEDAUX, R.; CONSTANDSE-WESTERMANN, T.; HACQUEBORD, L.; LANGE, A.; and J. VAN DER WAALS 1978. Recherches archéologiques dans le Delta intérieur du Niger. *Palaeohistoria*. 20:92–220.

BERTHIER, S., 1981. *Fouilles d'un ensemble d'habitations, quartier de la mosquée, site de Koumbi Saleh*. Presented at the 3è colloque des archéologues de l'Afrique de l'Ouest, Dakar.

BESSAC, H., 1951. A propos des ruines de Teghaza (Sahara occidental). *Notes Africaines* 51:69–70.

BLATT. A., 1980. *Origin of Sedementary Rocks*. Prentice Hall. Englewood, New Jersey.

BINFORD, L., 1964. Consideration of Archaeological Sampling Design. *American Antiquity* 29:425–441.

BROOKS, G., 1986A Provisional Historical Shema for Western Africa Based on Seven Climatic Periods (c. 9000 BC to the 19th century). *Cahiers d'Etudes Africaines* 26:43–62.

CAMARA, S., 1990. *La tradition orale en question: Conservation et transmissions des traditionshistoriques au manden: le centre de Kéla et de Minijan*. Thèse pour le Doctorat de l'Ecole des Hautes Etudes en Sciences Sociales, Paris. I.

CHAVANE, B. et FELLER, C., 1986. Construction de l'habitat et activité métallurgique dans un site protohistorique de la moyenne vallée du Sénégal. Effets sur l'environnement actuel. *Cahier des Sciences Humaines*. 22:49–56.

CHIEZE, V., 1991. La métallurgie du fer dans la Zone lacustre: archéologie et archéométrie. In Raimbault, M. et Sanogo K. (ed.). *Recherches archéologoiques au Mali*. Editions Karthala, 22–24, Boulevard Arago, Paris. pp. 449–472.

CIPEA (Centre International pour l'Élevage en Afrique)., 1981. *Evolution de l'utilisation des terres et de la vegetation dans la zone soudano-sahelienne du projet C.I.P.E.A. au Mali*. Document de Travail 3. CIPEA, Addis Ababa.

CISSE, Y.T., 1988. *La grande geste du Mali: des origines à la foundation de l'Empire: Les tradions de Krina au colloques de Bamako*. Karthala, 22–24 Boulevard Arago, Paris.

CUOQ, J.M., 1975. *Recueil des sources arabes concernant l'Afrique Occidentale du VIIIe au XIVe siècles*. C.N.R.S., Paris.

DELAFOSSE, M., 1912. *Haut-Sénégal-Niger*. 3 vols, Paris.

DEMBELE, M., 1986. *Entre Debo et Faguibine, étude sur la morphologie et la typologie des sites archéologiques d'une région lacustre au Mali*. Thèse de troisième cycle, Ecole des Hautes Etudes en Sciences Sociales, Paris.

DEMBELE, M., 1991a. Les missions Léré–Faguibine (1981-1983). In Raimbault, M. et Sanogo K, (ed.). *Recherches archéologiques au Mali*. Karthala 22-24, Boulevard Arago, Paris. pp. 63–80.

DEMBELE, M., 1991b. La prospection en zone lacustre. In Raimbault, M. et Sanogo K, (ed.). *Recherches archéologiques au Mali*. Karthala 22-24, Boulevard Arago, Paris. pp. 174-184.

DESPLAGNES, L., 1903. Etude sur le tumulus de Killi. *L'Anthropologie* 14:151–172.

DESPLAGNES, L., 1907. *Le Plateau Central Nigérien: Une mission archéologique et ethnographique au Soudan français*. Paris.

DESPLAGNES, L., 1951. Fouilles du tumulus d'El Oualadji (Soudan). *Bulletin de l'I.F.A.N.*, 13:1159–1173.

DPC (Division du Patrimoine Culturel), 1985. *Mission inventaire des sites archéologiques du Méma: Rapport de mission*. D. P. C., Bamako.

DEVISSE, J. and S. ROBERT (eds.), 1983. *Tegdaoust III: Recherches sur Aoudaghost, campagnes 1960-1965*. Mémoire No. 25, Editions Recherche sur les Civilisations, Paris.

FILIPOWIAK, W., 1979. *Etudes Archéologiques sur la Capitale Médièvale du Mali*. Szczecin: Museum Narodowe.

FILIPOWIAK, W., JASOSZ, S, and WOLAGIEWCZ, R., 1968. Les recherches archéologiques Plono-guinéennes à Niani an 1968. *Materialy Zachodnioporskie*, 14:621–648.

FISH, S. and S. KOWALEWSKI (eds.), 1990. *The Archaeology of Regions*. Washington D. C.: Smithsonian.

FONTES, P.; PERSON, A.; and J.F. SALIEGE, 1980. *Prospection et études analytiques des sites archéologiques dans le delta intérieur du Niger (Mali)*. Institut des Sciences Humaines, Bamako.

FONTES, P., DEMBELÉ, A., RAIMBAULT, M. 1991. Prospection de sites archéologiques de la région des Lacs et du Delta intérieur du Niger (1980). In Raimbault, M. et Sanogo K. (ed.). *Recherches archéologoiques au Mali*. Editions Karthala, 22–24, boulevard Arago, Paris. pp. 27–62.

FURON, R., 1929. L'ancien delta du Niger. Contribution a l'étude de l'hydrologie ancienne du Sahel soudanais et du sud saharien. *Revue de Géographie Physique et Géologie Dynamique* 2:265–274.

GALLAIS, J., 1967. *Le Delta Intérieur du Niger*. Mémoire de l'IFAN No. 79, 2 vols. Institut fondamental d'Afrique Noire, Dakar.

GALLAY, A., HUYSECOM, E., HONEGGER, M., MAYOR, A., 1990. *Hamdalllahi, capitale de l'empire peul du Massina, Mali.–Première fouille archéologique, études historiques et ethnoarchéologiques*–Franz Steiner Verlag Stuttgart GMBH.

GRUNNE, B. de, 1983. *La poterie ancienne du Mali. Quelques remarques préliminaires*. Munchen, Galerie Biedermann.

GUITAT, R. 1972. Carte et repertoire des sites neolithiques du Mali et de la Haute-Volta. *Bulletin de l'Institut Fraçais d'Afrique Noire B* 34:896–925.

HAALAND, R., 1980. Man's Role in the Changing Habitat of the Mema During the Old Kingdom of Ghana. *Norwegian Archaeological Review* 13:31–46.

HASKELL, H. (in prep.) Report on the 1989–90 Excavations at AK2.

HASKELL, H.W.; McINTOSH, S.K.; and R.J. McINTOSH, 1988. *Archaeological reconnaissance in the region of Dia (Mali). Final report to the National*

Geographic Society. Submitted to National Geographic Society, Washington.

HOLL, A., 1985. Subsistence Patterns of the Dhar Tichitt Neolithic, Mauritania. *African Archaeological Review* 3:151–162.

HOPKINS, J.E.P. AND N. LETVZION, 1981. *Corpus of Early Arabic Sources for West African History*. Cambridge University Press, Cambridge.

HUYSECOM, E., 1990. *Fanfannyégèné 1. Un abri sous roche à occupation néolithique au Mali. _ La fouille, le matériel archéologique, l'art rupestre–* Franz Steiner Verlag Wiesbaden.

JOHNSON, M., 1970. The Cowrie Currencies of West Africa. *Journal of African History*, 11:17–49.

KATI, M., 1964. *Tarikh el Fetach* (trans. O. Houdas). Paris.

LAMBERT, N., 1971. Les industries sur cuivre dans dans l'Ouest Saharien. *West African Journal of Archaeology* 1:9–21.

LaVIOLETTE, A.J., 1987. *An Archaeological Ethnography of Blacksmiths, Potters, and Masons in Jenne, Mali (West Africa)* Ph. D. dissertation, Department of Anthropology, Washington University.

LeBEUF, A. and PAQUES, V., 1970. Archéologie Malienne. *Objets et Mondes*. Supplément 10/3.

LEVTZION, N., 1973. *Ancient Ghana and Mali*. Methuen, London.

LEWICKI, T., 1974. *Arabic External Sources for the History of Africa to the South of the Sahara*. London.

LY TALL, M., 1977. *Contribution a l'histoire de l'empire du Mali*. Nouvelles Editions Africaines, Dakar.

MAES, E., 1924. Notes sur les pierres taillées et gravées, sur les pierres alignées et sur les murailles de pierres en ruines situées près du village de Tondidarou (Soudan Français). *Bulletin Historiques et Scientifiques de l'Afrique Occidentale Française*, pp. 31–48.

McINTOSH, R.J., 1983. Floodplain Geomorphology and Human Occupation in the Upper Inland Delta of the Niger. *Geographical Journal* 149:182–202.

McINTOSH, R.J., 1991. Early Urban Clusters in China and Africa: The Arbitration of Social Ambiguity. *Journal of Field Archaeology* 5:199–212.

McINTOSH, R.J. and S.K. MCINTOSH, 1983. Forgotten Tells of Mali: New Evidence of Urban Beginnings in West Africa. *Expedition*, 25, 35–46.,

McINTOSH, R.J. and S.K. MCINTOSH, 1988. From "siècles obscurs" to Revolutionary Centuries on the Middle Niger. *World Archaeology* 20:141–165.

McINTOSH, S.K., 1981. A Reconsideration of Wangara/Palolus, Island of Gold. *Journal of African History* 2:89-158.

McINTOSH, S.K., 1984. *Blacksmiths and the Evolution of Political Complexity in the Mande Society: An Hypothesis.* Paper read at the School of American Research Advanced Seminar on Complex Societies in Africa, Santa Fe, NM., October.

McINTOSH, S.K., 1985. *Excavations at Jenne-jeno, Hambarketolo and Kaniana (Inland Niger Delta)*. The 1981 Season. Berkeley: University of California Press

McINTOSH, S.K. and R.J. MCINTOSH, 1980. *Prehistoric Investigations at Jenne, Mali*. Cambridge Monographs in African Archaeology, 2. B.A.R., Oxford., 1984. The Early City in West Africa: Towards an Understanding. *African Archaeological Review* 2. pp 73–98.

McINTOSH, S.K. and R.J. MCINTOSH, 1986. Archeological reconnaissance in the region of Timbuktu, Mali. *National Geographic Research* 2:302–320.

McINTOSH, S.K. and R.J. MCINTOSH, 1988. From Stone to Metal: New Perspective on the Later Prehistory of West Africa. *Journal of World Prehistory* 2:89–133.

MAUNY, R., 1952. Un age de cuivre au Sahara occidental? BIFAN 1952., pp. 168–180.

MAUNY, R., 1961. *Tableau géographique de l'ouest africain au moyen age d'après les sources écrites, la tradition et l'archéologie.* Mémoire de l'Institut Français d'Afrique Noire 61, 2 vols. Dakar.

MONOD, T., 1969. Le "Ma'den Ijafen": une épave caravanière ancienne dans le Majabat al-Kroubra. *Acts of the First International Colloquium of African Archaeology*. Fort Lamy. pp 115–124.

MONOD, T. and MAUNY, R., 1957. Decouverte de nouveaux instruments en os dans l'Ouest Africain, in *Acts of the Third Pan African Congress on Prehistory*. Livingstone, 1955 pp. 242–247

MONTEIL, C., 1929. *Les empires du Mali. Études d'histoire et de sociologie soudanaises.* Maisonneuve et Larose, Paris.,

MONTEIL, C., 1953. La légende du Ouagadou et l'orgine des Soninké. *In Mélanges ethnographiques.* Mémoire de l'Institut Fondamental d'Afrique Noire, Dakar. no 23 p. 359–408.

MUELLER, J.W. (ed.), 1975. *Sampling in Archaeology*. Tuscon: University of Arizona Press.

MUNSON, P., 1976. Archaeological Data on the Origins of Cultivation in the Southwestern Sahara and Their Implications for West Africa. In Harlan. J., de Wet, J., and A. Stemler (eds.), *Origins of African Plant Domestication:* pp. 187–209. Mouton, The Hague.

NIANE, D.T., 1960. *Soundiata ou l'épopée mandingue.* Présence Africaine, Paris.

RAIMBAULT, M., 1986. *Le gisement néolithique de Kobadi (Sahel malien) et ses implications paléohydrologiques.* Proceedings of the 1986 I.N.Q.U.A. Symposium: 393–397. Dakar.

RAIMBAULT, M., 1991. La céramique de la fouille de la butte de KNT 2. In Raimbault, M. et Sanogo K, (ed.). *Recherches archéologiques au Mali.* Karthala 22 -24, Boulevard Arago, Paris. pp. 324 -371.

RAIMBAULT, M. and DUTOUR, O., 1990. Découverte de populations mechtoïdes dans la le néolithique du Sahel malien (gisement lacustre de Kobadi); implications paléoclimatiques et paléanthroplogiques. *Anthropologie* C.R. Acad. Sci. Paris, t. 310, Série III, pp. 631–638.

RAIMBAULT, M.; GUERIN, C.; and M. FAURE, 1987. Les vertébrés du gisement néolithique de Kobadi (Mali). *Archaeozoologia* 12:219–238.

RAIMBAULT, M. and SANOGO, K., 1991. Les résultats stratigraphiques. In Raimbault, M. et Sanogo K, (ed.). *Recherches archéologiques au Mali.* Karthala 22 -24, Boulevard Arago, Paris. pp. 301–323.

RAIMBAULT, M. and SIDIBE, S., 1984. Premiers resultats de la Mission d'Inventaire des Sites dans la Zone Lacustre du Mali, du 5 au 30 janvier 1984. . Report on file, ISH, Bamako

RAIMBAULT, M. and TOGOLA, T., 1991. Les missions d'Inventaire dans le Méma, Kareri et Farimaké (1984 et 1985). In Raimbault, M. et Sanogo K, (ed.). *Recherches archéologiques au Mali.* Karthala Boulevard Arago, Paris. pp. 81–90.

REDMAN, C.L., 1974. *Archaeological sampling strategies.* Addison-Wesley Module 55. Reading, Massachussets.

ROBERT-CHALEIX, D., 1983. Fusaioles decorées du site de Tegdaoust. In DEVISSE, J. and S. ROBERT (eds.) *Tegdaoust III: Recherches sur*

Aoudaghost, campagnes 1960-1965. Mémoire No. 25, Editions Recherche sur les Civilisations, Paris, pp. 447–513.

ES'SADI, 1900. *Tarikh es-Sudan* (trans. O. Houdas). Paris.

SANOGO, K., 1991. Approche méthodologique. In Raimbault, M. et Sanogo K, (ed.). *Recherches archéologiques au Mali.* Karthala, Boulevard Arago, Paris. pp. 165 -173.

SARR, M. 1972. Les civilisations des toguérés de la plaine de Sévaré. Etudes Maliennes (May 1972) pp. 2–16.

SCHMIT, P., 1985. *Les sites de buttes de la région de Diré (Mali). Premiers résultats de l'inventaire des sites archéologiques du nord de la zone lacustre (mission d'avril 1986).* Mémoire de DEA. Universitée de Paris I, Panthéon Sorbonne, Faculté des Lettres et des Sciences Humaines. p. 49.

SHEPARD, A., 1964. *Ceramics for the Archaeologist.* Carnegie Institue of Washington.

SIDIBE, S. and RAIMBAULT, M., 1991. Les recherches sur le terrain. In Raimbault, M. et Sanogo K, (ed.). *Recherches archéologiques au Mali.* Karthala 22 -24, Boulevard Arago, Paris. pp. 273 -280.

SMITH, A.B., 1979. Bieogeographical considerations of colonization of the lower Tilemsi Valley in the second millenium BC. *Journal of Arid Environments* 2:355–258.

STUIVER, M., & PEARSON, G. W., 1986. High-precision calibration of the radiocarbon time scale, AD 1950–500 BC. Trondheim, Norway: *Radiocarbon,* 805–838.

SZUMOWSKI, G., 1954. Fouilles à Fatoma (Région de Mopti, Soudan). *Notes Africaines,* 64, 102–108., 1956 Fouilles à Nantaka et kélébéré (région de Mopti, Soudan). *Notes Africaines* 70, pp. 33–38., 1957. Fouilles au nord du Macina et dans la region de Ségou. *Bulletin de l'Institut Français d'Afrique Noire* (B)19:224–58.

THILMANS, G., & RAVISE, A., 1980.). *Protohistoire du Sénégal II: Sintiou Bara et les Sites du Fleuve.* Dakar: I.F.A.N.

THOMASSEY, P., & MAUNY, R, 1951. Campagne de fouilles à Koumbi Saleh. *Bulletin de l'Institut Français d'Afrique Noire,* 13:438–462.

TRICART, J., 1965. *Rapport de la mission de reconnaissance géomorphologique de la vallée moyenne du Niger.* Mémoire de l'Institut Fondamental d'Afrique Noire No. 72. Dakar.

URVOY, Y. 1942. *Les Bassins du Niger.* Mémoire de l'Institut Français d'Afrique Noire. No. 4. Dakar.

VIELLARD, G. 1940. Sur quelques objets en terre cuite de Djenné. *Bulletin de l'Institut Fondamentale d'Afrique Noire* (B) 3:347–350.

Appendix I: Preliminary Analysis of the Faunal Remains

APPENDIX 1

AN INITIAL REPORT ON THE FAUNA OF AKUMBU (MALI)

Kevin C. MacDonald
Department of Archaeology
Cambridge University
Cambridge, UK

Wim Van Neer
Department of Zoology
Musée Royal de l'Afrique Centrale
Tervuren, Belgium

INTRODUCTION

The Akumbu faunal assemblage, though small in size, promises to answer many questions on late Holocene environmental and economic change in the Ancient Inland Niger Delta of Mali (the Dead Delta or Mema region). It will be shown from the fauna of the earliest excavated occupations at Akumbu (c.400-600 AD), that the environment at this time was not very dissimilar from the lacustrine/swamp biotype recorded at nearby Late Stone Age sites such as Kobadi and Kolima-Sud (cf. Raimbault et. al. 1987, MacDonald et. al. in prep.). By the time of the sites abandonment (c.1400 AD) it can be demonstrated that the environment around Akumbu was much like the dry Sahelian scrubland that surrounds the site today. How and when perennial waters departed from the vicinity of the site between these two periods is a more difficult question, and can only be a matter for conjecture with the data we have at hand.

This report is termed "initial" as the recent completion of identifications and its production in isolation from fauna recovered from the near by Late Stone Age sites of Kolima-Sud, 1251-1, and Tiabel Goudiodié does not allow as full an exposition of data as would be desirable in a final report. Such a report will appear in due course. Additionally, it should be noted that the analysis of the fish fauna from Akumbu has just been completed and so only the most basic details of this analysis are available here. Furthermore, additional excavations at Akumbu planned for 1993 so as to reach the basal levels of AK3, are necessary to better define faunal change at the site. For the moment, presented here are identifications made on the materials available, and my (KCM's) observations on the meaning of these identifications. The quantity of the faunal sample does not safely allow us to speculate on quantitative change in the fauna or even spatial economic distribution on the site. Fauna present should be treated to some extent as "on/off" values with some speculative emphasis given to taxa present in greater numbers. The fauna of Jenne-jeno is a good lesson in this regard, with numerous spatially distributed excavation units yielding dissimilar faunal ratios for coeval time periods. In a best case scenario, with larger exposures, such data may be taken to represent the horizontal distribution of human activities or different "group" areas (cf. MacDonald 1991, Crabtree 1990). In this case, too many pieces of the puzzle are absent to make all but cautious statements.

CONTEXTS

The Akumbu assemblage dates from approximately 400 AD to 1400 AD and comes from three excavation units (AK1, AK3 and AK 4) excavated in the Spring of 1990. AK1 supplied the bulk of the animal bones, which is not surprising since it was the largest of the units (though it was reduced to a similar size in the lower levels), and the only one to reach sterile soil (though not the pre-600 AD earlier occupation). AK3 supplies the earliest animal remains (those dating between 400 and 600 AD). Excavations in AK4 (uppermost levels dated securely to c. 1200 AD) did not reach Early Iron Age (EIA) ceramics, and thus the deepest excavated levels should not date to before 600 AD. For a detailing of chronological aggregations used in the faunal analysis see Tables 1 and 2.

In all 345 identifiable fragments of mammalian bone, 1 identifiable fragment of Amphibian bone, 23 identifiable fragments of reptilian bone, 68 identifiable fragments of bird bone and 768 identifiable fragments of fish bone were recovered from Akumbu in 1990, a total of 1205 identifiable fragments. By way of comparison, this is almost half the number recovered from the 1981 field season at Jenne-jeno (MacDonald in press-a.). The size of the Akumbu assemblage despite the small number and size of its excavations is testament to the efficiency of screening (1cm and 2mm mesh) carried out at Akumbu.

METHODOLOGY

The faunal material from the 1990 excavations at Akumbu was studied with the aid of extensive comparative collections housed at The Field Museum of Natural History (Chicago), The Museum of Comparative Zoology (Harvard University), the U.S. National Museum of Natural History (Washington, D.C.) and the British Museum [Natural History] (London and Tring). In each of these cases the Mammals collections were utilised, only in one case (the BM[NH]) were avian and reptile collections consulted. Subsequent recording and measuring of these remains was carried out at the Faunal Remains Unit (Cambridge University). Fish remains were identified by Dr. Wim Van Neer at the Musée Royal de l'Afrique Centrale (Tervuren).

It has been emphasized previously (cf. MacDonald in press-a.) that the precise taxonomic identification of African bovid remains on the basis post-cranial morphology is essential in African archaeozoology. Only through the consultation of relatively comprehensive collections (such as those utilised) and the compilation of morphological and metrical differentiations between osteologically similar taxa (e.g. the work of Peters 1986a and 1986b) can we proceed.

In the analysis, all bone fragments of all taxa which were identifiable to part (with the exceptions of ribs and -- in the case of mammals -- sesamoids) were identified to the most precise possible level and treated quantitatively. Any elements of Bovidae that could not confidently be taken to sub-family, genus, or species on the basis of morphology- -in most cases fragments of the vertebral column and long bone shaft fragments--were identified only to size class. Following Brain (1974), I utilise a size class system based on the categories "small," "small-medium," "large-medium," and "large." However, as Brain originally devised his system only for wild South African species, I use a different definition of boundaries relevant to the wild and domestic bovids of West Africa (as presented in MacDonald in press-a.).

Problematic differentiations, particularly that between the African buffalo *(Syncerus)* and cattle *(Bos* sp.), were aided by morphological criteria supplied in Peters (1986a), Gentry (1978), and Guerin and Faure (1983). It should be noted that after extensive comparison with modern comparative specimens that I am not in agreement with all of Peters criteria, although for the most part they are very good. I have added a few of my own which will be discussed in a future publication.

For all taxa, "non-diagnostic" fragments were taken to precise taxon only when they were clearly associated with diagnostic elements such as separated tooth rows.The assemblage is presented both in terms of minimum number of individuals (MNI) and number of individual specimens present (NISP) (see Table 1). MNI is aggregated by clusters of depositionally coeval levels within the same unit to form an extreme "Minimal Number of Individuals." NISP may be considered to be at another extreme the "Maximum Number of Individuals" as some researchers have asserted, stating the statistical improbability that more than one bone from any one animal would survive to be identified (Hesse and Wapnish 1985). It should be noted, however, that I am not in accord with this argument -- far too many partially articulated carcasses are recovered archaeozoologically for this to be true.

MNI was calculated as follows: All elements attributable to species, or in some cases to osteologically similar genera (e.g. *Ovis/Capra*), were checked for the duplication of element zones of the same side (if relevant), by unit level (it should be noted that I utilise a zone system for the description of fragmentary skeletal elements to calculate a more accurate MNI). The number of such duplications were treated as MNIs. (Elements which are not determined to side [e.g. phalanges], or which are not 'sided' [e.g. vertebrae], were simply divided by their maximum total number per taxon). MNIs were further augmented by instances of significant size differences between elements of opposite sides, and by the presence of immature individuals versus mature specimens.

NISP was calculated as follows: All remains determinate as to element, and attributable to species or other taxonomic grouping by morphology or association, were counted. Separated fragments of a single element possessing fresh breaks were treated as one fragment. Separated fragments without fresh breaks were counted as the number of fragments which could have been taxonomically identified, or associated, individually.

No metric data is presented here. Measurements of domestic and wild taxa will be available in a later report.

BONE CONDITION, MODIFICATION AND BUTCHERY

The condition of the bone recovered from Akumbu was variable. Material from rapidly sealed contexts, such as trash pits, were of course better preserved. But all remains, however deposited, were subject to post-depositional stresses. Post-depositional damage to bone structure had at least five agents at the site: calcium leaching, surface weathering, crystal growth (Gypsum ?), rodent gnawing and dog-sized carnivore gnawing.

The most frequently occuring of these was calcium leaching (46 incidents amongst the identifiable mammalian bone). Calcium leaching can of course only be detected in bones whose structure, while becoming powdery and friable (usually through rain water percolation), are still sound enough to be recovered and analysed. From the data at hand it would seem that damage from leaching was probably heaviest at AK4 (32% of identified elements effected) than in AK1 (9% of identified elements effected) and AK3 (13% of identified elements effected). This is most probably due to different soil types. Leaching occured throughout the sequence in all units.

Surface weathered bone (showing diagnostic surface cracking) was recovered almost exclusively from AK4 (8 incidences, 14% of identified elements), indicating fewer sealed depositional contexts in that unit. Surface weathered bone occured at AK4 in levels 12, 14, 17, 22, 25 and 27. Only a single incident of surface weathered bone was identified from AK1 (level 18), and none from AK3. It should be noted that leaching would obscure surface weathering.

Internal crystalline growth. leading to the splitting of bone, was uncommonly frequent at Akumbu. Only units AK1 and AK3 were effected, with incidences in AK 1 levels 17, 19 and 64, and AK3 levels 11 and 37.

Appendix I: Preliminary Analysis of the Faunal Remains

Rodent gnawing of bone occured at AK1 in levels 9, 21 and 47; at AK3 in levels 10 and 37; and at AK4 in level 22. It is intersting to note that dog-sized carnivore gnawing of bones was only detected in contexts dating to between 600 and 1400 AD (AK1 level 14 and AK4 level 22).

In four incidences bone recovered from Akumbu was seen to have been made into ornaments. In three of these instances they were the first phalanges of antelopes, pierced at the distal end to form a pendant. It is perhaps a poignant testimony to continuous cultural tradition, despite environmental change, that the first of these (from AK1 lv.41, c.600-1000 AD) was of a riverine species (*Redunca redunca*), while the latter two (from AK1 lvs. 18 and 22, c.1000-1200 AD) were of a sahelian species (*Gazella rufifrons*). In one other incident, a centimetre wide fragment of unidentifiable long bone shaft (perhaps once part of a finger-ring) had been incised with two horizontal bands and polished at the edges (AK1 level 21, c.1000-1200 AD).

The butchery and roasting study of the Akumbu assemblage provides us with striking details on the manner of food preparation at the site. In tandem, filetting cutmarks on meat bearing elements are completely absent and charring of bone is very rare (15 occurences in total on mammals and 8 on birds). Skinning cutmarks (on lower leg bones, cf. Binford 1981) had 8 eight occurences on Bovids only. The chopping on bone with a metal cleaver was also rare (11 occurences on mammals only, usually of large size). Interestingly it is certain that at least 3 fragments bare saw marks (unmistakable striations on evenly and smoothly cut bone fragments). Sawed bone occurs in the following contexts : AK1 lvs 45, 20 and 9. Thus, it would appear that "saw technology" was present at Akumbu from between 600 and 1000 AD onwards. To conclude, from the available evidence it would appear that while some roasting occured (partculary of terrestrial fowl and ovicaprines) the primary means of meat preparation at Akumbu was boiling or "stewing." This is in agreement with the modern cooking techniques of Malian sedentists such as the Bambara (pers. observ. and S.K. McIntosh pers.comm.). Lack of filleting marks would suggest that for the most part carcasses were skinned and then divided by the cracking, cleaving and/or sawing, and subsequently fragmentary meat bearing elements cooked by boiling. It will be interesting to see if future Iron Age bone materials from the Mema support these observations.

MAMMALIAN REMAINS

As would be expected from a West African Iron Age or "Protohistorique" context, the Akumbu assemblage contains both domesticated and wild mammals. Domesticated animals dominate the assemblage. Domestic Cattle of an uncertain variety and non-dwarf "Savanna" Sheep and Goats make up almost half of the identified mammal bones. More spectacularly, horse (and perhaps also the domesticated ass) as well as domestic dog are both well represented at Akumbu. In the case of the domestic horse the finds from Akumbu represent the earliest precisely dated (c. 600-1000 AD) and indisputably identified remains of such animals from West African archaeological contexts (cf. Law 1980). Some of the wild mammals present include small quantities of riverine/lacustrine antelope species early in the sequence (the Common Reedbuck [*Redunca redunca*] and the Kob [*Kobus kob*]) and larger quantities of Sahelian antelopes later in the sequence (the Red-Fronted Gazelle [*Gazella rufifrons*] and the Dama Gazelle [*Gazella dama*]). Other wild mammals present which are of particular interest include Elephant (*Loxodonta africana*), Warthog (*Phacochoerus aethiopicus*), Libyan Striped Weasel (*Poecelictis libyca*), African Civet (*Viverra civetta*) and Patas Monkey (*Erythrocebus patas*). Notes on the most important of these identifications and their significance are presented below.

a. Wild Bovidae

Of all antelopes present the Red-Fronted Gazelle (*Gazella rufifrons*) was the most numerous. Not present in any of the Mema LSA faunal assemblages studied, the Red-Fronted Gazelle is an inhabitant of dry sahelian woodland although it may occur in more well-watered areas if they abut such terrain (Spinage 1986, also cf. VanNeer and Bocoum 1991 for an identification of *rufifrons* at the Iron Age site of Tulel Fobo in the Sénégal River Valley). More riverine/lacustrine species (the Kob and the Common Reedbuck) occur only fleetingly early in the sequence. It should be noted that these taxa cannot live farther than a few kilometres from a permanent water source (Spinage 1986).

b. Domestic Bovidae

Both cattle and ovicaprines were present at Akumbu throughout the sequence. With the data at hand it is impossible to state whether the cattle were humped (*indicus*) or humpless (*taurus*). No morphologically diagnostic elements such as orbital rims or thoracic vertebral spines were recovered. Metric data is sparse, but it would suggest that from 600 AD *indicus* could have been present on the basis of size. It is also possible, however, that such elements could simply represent a large (longhorn?) humpless breed.

The Ovicaprines of Akumbu were of a size similar to those modern sheep and goat breeds described by Epstein (1971) as "Savanna types" (that is to say, non-dwarf). All measurable elements recovered were well within the size range (withers height 60+ cm) of such breeds, which are preferred by modern migratory pastoralists. Utilising the morphological criteria of Boessneck (1969) it was possible to differentiate sheep from goat in several instances on the basis of post-cranial remains. Also, in one instance, a distinctive goat (*Capra hircus*) straight horncore was present (AK1 level 41). Other definitive goat remains were recovered from the early and late Middle Iron Age (MIA) levels of AK1, the early MIA levels of AK3 and from the Early-Mid MIA levels of AK4. Remains attributable to

Ovis aries were recovered from the Middle and Late MIA levels of AK1 and the Early-Mid MIA levels of AK4.

c. The Akumbu Equids

Horse (*Equus caballus*) was identified at Akumbu on the basis of dental morphology (on a maxillary 3rd premolar) and post-cranial metric criteria (on a first phalanx), both from AK1 level 63 (c. 600-1000 AD) (criteria supplied by Eisenmann 1986). To the authors knowledge these are the earliest confirmed dates for domestic horse available in West Africa. Other Equid remains were recovered from numerous contexts at Akumbu, including other early contexts such as AK1 levels 62, 64 and 67. All of the Equid remains recovered from Akumbu are of a size comparable to that of horse remains that have been available for study, and in most cases larger than specimens of *Equus asinus* (Ass) which have been available for study. As there remains a degree of incertitude, these remains are listed as "*Equus caballus/asinus*." It should be noted that in one case (a scapula from AK1 level 67) charring was present on an equid bone. Additionally the disarticulated nature of these finds would suggest the consumption of these equids when their days of use had come to an end.

d. The Akumbu Dog

Domestic dog (*Canis familiaris*) has been identified at Akumbu from AK1 levels 67, 55 and 10 as well as from AK3 level 29. The earliest of these is the occurrence of a proximal tibia at unit AK3 level 29 (c. 400-600 AD). These remains were separated from the indigenous jackals on the basis of newly derived metric criteria based on all comparative specimens available at the US National Museum of Natural History and the Harvard Museum of Comparative Zoology (cf MacDonald and MacDonald in. prep.). Metric comparison of the Akumbu specimens with modern comparatives will be available in this forthcoming publication. Remains which were not measurable or not clearly differentiable from the West African jackals (*Canis aureus* and *adustus*) were simply identified as "*Canis sp.*". No canid bones were charred or bear cutmarks, but there presence disarticulated and near living areas may indicate their use as a foodstuff.

f. Other Mammals

Several other mammals of note were identified from the Akumbu assemblage. Elephant (*Loxodonta africana*) was represented by a cleaved distal radius from AK1 level 39 (it should be noted that Elephant has also been identified from the Mema LSA site of Kolima-Sud). The African Civet (*Viverra civetta*) was identified from AK3 level 18. In "Medieval" West Africa civet skins and musk were valued as trade items (Lovejoy 1985), although it is fully possible that this individual was obtained locally. A calcaneus of the Patas Monkey (*Erythrocebus patas*) was also identified from AK3 level 18. Patas monkeys are today associated with open and wooded savanna habitats (Haltenorth and Diller 1980). As the temporal provenance of AK3 level 18 is not secure, the monkey could conceivably been obtained locally or traded in as a "pet."

AVIAN, REPTILIAN, AND AVIAN REMAINS

a. The Avian Remains

The Avian assemblage at the site was dominated by terrestrial fowl. These fowl were osteologically differentiated using metric and morphological material supplied in MacDonald (in press-b). Verifiable chicken remains at Akumbu date to as early as 1000 to 1200 AD. The Guineafowl is present from earlier in the sequence but no criteria exist at present (if such criteria do exist) to differentiate wild and domesticated Guineafowl. The presence of chicken at Akumbu is not surprising in light of a growing corpus of identifications of the bird in contexts dating to before 1000 AD (cf. MacDonald 1992). It is interesting to note that thin brown eggshell (of a size comparable with chicken or guineafowl eggs) occur in numerous contexts at Akumbu (AK1 levels 8 and 10 and AK3 levels 18, 20 and 45). The presence of this eggshell may be early evidence for the consumption of domesticated fowl eggs in West Africa.

Other Birds present of note include: a duck from AK3 level 18 (probably *Anas crecca* or *querquedula* on the basis of size), a Vulture (*Aegypius/Gyps sp.*) from AK3 level 6 represented by charred talons and a distal femur, and Ostrich (*Struthio camelus*) represented by undecorated eggshell from AK1 levels 6 and 9.

b. The Reptilian and Amphibian Remains

The Reptilian and Amphibian assemblage of Akumbu is very small and only remarkable in a few aspects. First is the environmental significance of *Crocodylus sp.* attested to by a distal fibula from AK1 level 66, and second are small serpent remains which are the only fauna potentially associated with the burials of AK3 (levels 22 and 28). While some fragments of large mammal bone appear in these contexts, they would appear from cutmarks and their low utility value (fragmentary bones of the lower limb) to be food refuse from abutting trash pits. These small serpent vertebrae are, however, almost unique to these burials at the site and may have some symbolic significance. Eight small serpent vertebrae were recovered from AK3 level 28 and two from AK3 level 22. The present state of comparative collections to which I have access does not allow the more precise identification of these remains. Suffice to say, the small serpent remains are from a snake the size of an American garter snake, whereas those termed "medium" (from other contexts) are from a snake the size of an American rattlesnake or larger.

Also worthy of note is a single skull roof identifiable to *Varanus exanthematicus* (the Savanna Monitor) from AK1, level 15 (c.1200-1400 AD). This is the only specifically diagnostic element for Monitor lizard recovered from Akumbu, and it is significant that at this stage in the sequence it is represented by the Sahelian species *V. exanthematicus* rather than the riverine/lacustrine species *V. niloticus*.

Appendix I: Preliminary Analysis of the Faunal Remains

The only remains of turtle recovered from the site in 1990 was a plastron fragment assignable to the semi-aquatic species of *Pelomedusa subrufa* (AK1, lv.1; c.1200-1400 AD). This species is indideneous to the African Sahel today, where it is adapted to living beside seasonal water bodies or ponds during the brief rainy season and estivating during the Spring/Summer dry season (Ernst and Barbour 1989).

CONCLUSIONS

From the earliest excavated occupation of Akumbu (c.400-600 AD) domestic cattle and ovicaprines were present. Cattle are of an uncertain type (*indicus* - humped, or *taurus* -- humpless). What little metric evidence is available does not rule out the presence of humped breeds, in all but the earliest phase (c.400-600 AD) of known occupation. No evidence was recovered which would indicate the presence of dwarf ovicaprines which were the predominant type of ovicaprine at the Inland Niger Delta site of Jenne-jeno (MacDonald in press). Instead, less-tropical "Savanna" type ovicaprines (as utilised today by nomadic pastoralists such as the Fulani) dominate the assemblage. Horse (possibly ass as well) and domestic dog were present at the site by between 600 and 1000 AD and conceivably earlier. Chicken is present from between 1000 and 1200 AD and it would appear, from eggshell recovered in surprising frequency from the site, that eggs of *Gallus* (potentially including other birds such as *Numida*) as well as meat were consumed. Until larger exposures are excavated at Iron Age sites such as Akumbu in the Mema (to reveal corral or animal pen areas) it will be difficult to say to what extent peoples settled at such sites were domestic stock-keepers and to what degree they may have traded for their stock with nomadic pastoral visitors.

The wild fauna of the site indicate a significant terrestrial prey component including antelopes, warthog, elephant, terrestrial fowl and hares. There is comparatively sparse evidence for aquatic resource exploitation: single fragments of duck and crocodile, no hippopotamus or soft-shelled turtle, and very little fish. It is possible that from the earliest excavated levels that Akumbu was at some distance from permanent water sources. It is also possible that the peoples who left there refuse in the areas encompassed by the units excavated were not fishers. The small quantity of fish present could perhaps be accounted for as trade with neighbouring fishing groups or even long distance trade of dried fish. Such activities are attested to be Arabic documentary evidence from the "Medieval" era of West Africa (c.1200-1400 AD; cf.Lovejoy 1985).

What does the faunal evidence tell us in terms of the environment? From the limited evidence we have for the earlier known occupation of Akumbu (including remains from the period 600-1000 AD) it would appear that resources similar to those available to the first Late Stone Age inhabitants of the Mema region were also available to the early inhabitants of Akumbu. Riverine/Lacustrine antelopes (*Kobus* and *Redunca*) which require a permanent source of water in the vicinity were present as well as crocodile. Vegetation was still plentiful enough to support elephants. More Sahelian species such as the Red-Fronted Gazelle (*Gazella rufifrons*) were perhaps hunted in less well-watered ground to the west of Akumbu. By the time period of 1000 to 1200 AD however all fauna having strong associations with permanent waters had disappeared. Other arid Sahelo-Saharan species such as the Libyan Striped Weasel (*Poecelictis libyca*) and the Dama Gazelle (*Gazella dama*) appear, and *Gazella rufifrons* becomes the dominant wild game species. By the end of the occupation (c.1200-1400 AD) domestic animals, which were capable of surviving in number the increasingly dry conditions, make up the bulk of the assemblage. It is possible that environmental detirioration at Akumbu occurred earlier or later than at other parts of the floodplain, such as near Kalifa Gallou the putative ancient exile of Sunjata in the Thirteenth century.. Floodwaters could simply have ceased to reach the site, which was located on the edge of the ancient dead delta's floodplain. In any case it is almost certain that permanent waters connected with a major basin were not present near Akumbu after 1000 AD; this on the basis of a disappearance of all animal types relevant to such fluvial networks. Future fieldwork in the Mema may wish to investigate sites on the eastern half of the ancient floodplain to study the retreat of the Dead Delta over space and time.

BIBLIOGRAPHY

Binford, L.R. 1981 *Bones: Ancient Men and Modern Myths*. New York: Academic Press.

Boessneck, J. 1969 Osteological Differencves between Sheep (*Ovis aries* Linné) and Goat (*Capra hircus* Linné)," in Brothwell and Higgs Eds. *Science in Archaeology (2nd Edition)* Bristol: Thames and Hudson, pp. 331-358.

Crabtree, P.J. 1990 Zooarchaeology and Complex Societies: Some Uses of Faunal Analysis for the Study of Trade, Socila Status and Ethnicity. in Schiffer Ed. *Archaeological Method and Theory*. (Volume 2). Tucson: University of Arizona Press. pp.155-205.

Eisenmann, V. 1986 Comparative Osteology of Modern and Fossil Horses, Half-asses and Asses. in Meadow and Uerpmann Eds. *Equids in the Ancient World (Volume 1)*. Wiesbaden: L. Reichert Verlag. pp.67-116.

Epstein, H. 1971 *The Origin of the Domestic Animals of Africa*. New York: Africana Publishing.

Ernst, C.H. and Barbour, R.W. 1989 *Turtles of the World* Washington, D.C.: Smithsonian Press.

Haltenorth, T. and Diller, H. 1980 *A Field Guide to the Mammals of Africa*. London: Collins.

Law, R. 1980 *The Horse in West African History*. Oxford: OUP.

Lovejoy, P.E. 1985 The Internal Trade of West Africa to 1800. in Ajayi and Crowder Eds. *History of West Africa (Volume 1)*. New York: Longman. pp.648-690.

MacDonald, K.C. 1989 *The Identification and Analysis of Animal Bones from West African Archaeological Sites*. BA Honors Thesis, Rice University.

MacDonald, K.C. (in press - a.) Analysis of the Faunal Remains. In S.K. McIntosh and R.J. McIntosh Eds. *Jenne-jeno: A Report on the 1981 Excavations and Survey*. University of California Publications in Archaeology, Berkeley: University of California Press.

MacDonald, K.C. 1992 The Domestic Chicken (*Gallus gallus*) in Sub-Saharan Africa: A Background to its Introduction and its Osteological Differentiation from Indigenous Fowls (Numidinae and *Francolinus sp.*), *Journal of Archaeological Science* 19:303-318.

MacDonald, K.C., VanNeer, W., and Togola, T. (in prep) Fish Remains, Environmental Change and Iron Age Economy in the Méma Region (Mali).

MacDonald, R.H. and MacDonald, K.C. (in prep) The Domestic Dog (*Canis familiaris*) in Sub-Saharan Africa: A Background to its introduction and its Osteometric Differentiation from African Jackals and the Hunting Dog (*Lyacon pictus*), *Journal of Archaeological Science*.

Raimbault, M., Guérin, C. and Faure, M. 1987 Les Vertébrés du gisement néolithique de Kobadi. *Archaeozoologia* 1: 219-238.

Spinage, C.A. 1986 *The Natural History of Anteopes*. London: Croom Helm.

Van Neer and Bocoum 1991 Etude archéologique de Tulel-Fobo, site protohistorique (IVe-Xe siècle) de la moyenne vallée du Fleuve Sénégal (République du Sénégal). *Archaeozoologia* 4: 93-113.

von den Driesch, A. and Boessneck, J. 1974 Kritische Anmerkungen zue Widerristhohenbere-chnung aus Langenmassen vor-und frühgeschichtlicher Tierknochen. *Saugetierkundliche Mitteilungen*. 22:325-348 (Translation by Barbara West)

Appendix I: Preliminary Analysis of the Faunal Remains

Table 1. Mammalian remains by Unit and Phase
(MNI/NISP)

TAXA	AK1			AK3			AK4		TOTAL
	MIA / Early	MIA / Middle	MIA / Late	EIA	MIA / Early	MIA / Mid-Late	MIA / Early-Mid	MIA / Middle	
Date (AD)	600-1000	1000-1200	1200-1400	400-600	ca. 600-1000	ca. 1000-1400	ca. 600-1200	1000-1200	
lvs.	39-67	18-38	1-17	29-40	8-28	1-7	11+	1-10	
Phacochoerus aethiopicus	--	--	--	--	1 / 1	--	--	--	x / 1
(Warthog)									
Sylvicapra grimmia	--	--	--	1 / 2	1 / 1	--	--	--	x / 3
(Common Duiker)									
Kobus kob	1 / 1	--	--	--	--	--	--	--	x / 1
(Kob)									
Redunca redunca	1 / 3	--	--	--	--	--	--	--	x / 3
(Common Reedbuck)									
Alcelaphus buselaphus	--	--	--	1 / 1	--	--	--	--	x / 1
(Hartebeeste)									
Gazella dama	--	1 / 1	--	--	--	--	1 / 1	--	x / 2
(Dama Gazelle)									
Gazella rufifrons	1 / 1	1 / 8	1 / 3	1 / 3	1 / 3	--	1 / 3	1 / 2	x / 23
(Red-Fronted Gazelle)									
Ovis/Capra -- Savanna Var.	3 / 11	3 / 19	4 / 29	1 / 2	3 / 9	1 / 2	3 / 32	1 / 1	x / 105
(Savanna Sheep and Goat)									
Bos sp.	2 / 9	2 / 3	3 / 22	1 / 2	2 / 5	--	1 / 3	--	x / 44
(Domestic Cattle)									
Small Bovid	x / 1	--	x / 1	--	x / 1	--	--	--	x / 3
Small Medium Bovid	x / 7	x / 13	x / 30	x / 5	x / 8	x / 2	x / 8	x / 3	x / 76
Large Medium Bovid	x / 5	--	x / 1	x / 1	x / 1	--	--	--	x / 8
Large Bovid	x / 8	x / 3	x / 6	--	x / 1	--	x / 1	--	x / 19
Equus caballus	1 / 2	--	--	--	--	--	--	--	x / 2
(Domestic Horse)									
Equus caballus/asinus	1 / 4	1 / 4	1 / 6	--	1 / 2	--	--	--	x / 16
(Domestic Horse or Ass)									
Loxodonta africana	1 / 1	--	--	--	--	--	--	--	x / 1
(African Elephant)									
Cricetomys gambianus	--	2 / 4	1 / 1	--	--	1 / 1	1 / 1	--	x / 7
(Giant Gambian Rat)									
cf. *Acomys cahirinus*	--	--	--	--	1 / 1	--	--	--	x / 1
(Common Spiny Mouse)									
Rodentia gen. et. sp. indet.	--	--	--	--	x / 6	x / 1	--	--	x / 7
(Indeterminate Rodents)									
Lepus sp.	--	--	1 / 1	--	1 / 2	--	1 / 2	--	x / 5
(Hare)									
Canis familiaris	1 / 2	--	1 / 1	1 / 1	--	--	--	--	x / 4
(Domestic Dog)									
Canis sp.	1 / 2	1 / 1	1 / 6	--	1 / 1	--	--	--	x / 10

(Jackal or Domestic Dog)								
Poecilictis libyca	--	--	--	--	--	1 / 1	--	--	x / 1
(Libyan Striped Weasel)								
Viverra civetta	--	--	--	--	1 / 1	--	--	--	x / 1
(African Civet)								
Erythrocebus patas	--	--	--	--	1 / 1	--	--	--	x / 1
(Patas Monkey)								
TOTAL	x / 57	x / 56	x / 107	x / 17	x / 44	x / 7	x / 51	x / 6	345

Table 2. Avian, reptile and Amphibian Remains by Unit and Phase (MNI/NISP)

TAXA	AK1			AK3			AK4		TOTAL
	MIA / Early	MIA / Middle	MIA / Late	EIA	MIA / Early	MIA / Mid-Late	MIA / Early-Mid	MIA / Middle	
Date (AD)	600-1000	1000-1200	1200-1400	400-600	ca. 600-1000	ca. 1000-1400	ca. 600-1200	1000-1200	
lvs.	39-67	18-38	1-17	29-38	8-28	1-7	11+	1-10	
AVES									
Struthio camelus	--	--	X	--	--	--	--	--	X
(Ostrich)									
Bubulcis ibis	--	--	1 / 1	--	--	--	--	--	x / 1
(Cattle Egret)									
Anas sp. [medium]	--	--	--	--	1 / 1	--	--	--	x / 1
(Medium-sized Duck)									
Aegypius/Gyps sp.	--	--	--	--	--	1 / 4	--	--	x / 4
(Vulture)									
Gallus gallus	--	1 / 2	3 / 18	--	--	--	--	--	x / 20
(Chicken)									
Francolinus cf. bicalcaratus	1 / 1	--	--	--	--	--	1 / 1	--	x / 2
(Double-Spurred Francolin)									
Francolinus sp. (small)	--	--	--	--	1 / 1	--	--	--	x / 1
(Small Francolin Species)									
Numida meleagris	1 / 1	--	1 / 1	--	--	--	1 / 1	--	x / 3
(Guineafowl)									
Gallus/Francolinus	x / 2	--	x / 6	--	x / 1	--	--	x / 2	x / 11
(Chicken or Francolin)									
Gallus/Numida	x / 1	--	x / 11	--	--	--	x / 1	--	x / 13
(Chicken or Guineafowl)									
Corvus albus	--	--	1 / 1	--	--	--	--	--	x / 1
(Pied Crow)									
Aves indet.	--	--	x / 7	--	x / 3	x / 1	--	--	x / 11
(Indeterminate Bird)									
TOTAL	x / 5	x / 2	x / 45	--	x / 6	x / 5	x / 3	x / 2	x / 68
REPTILIA									
Pelomedusa subrufa	--	--	1 / 1	--	--	--	--	--	x / 1
(African Helmeted Turtle)									
Varanus exanthematicus	--	--	1 / 1	--	--	--	--	--	x / 1

Appendix I: Preliminary Analysis of the Faunal Remains

(Savanna Monitor)									
Varanus sp.	--	--	2 / 4	--	1 / 1	1 / 1	--	--	x / 6
(Indet. Monitor Lizard)									
Sauria gen. et sp. indet.	--	--	--	--	1 / 1	--	--	--	x / 1
(Indeterminate Lizard)									
Crocodylus sp.	1 / 1	--	--	--	--	--	--	--	x / 1
(Crocodile)									
Serpentes indet. (small)	--	--	--	--	2 / 10	--	--	--	x / 10
(Small Snake)									
Serpentes indet. (medium)	--	--	1 / 1	--	1 / 2	--	--	--	x / 3
(Medium-sized Snake)									
TOTAL	x / 1	--	x / 7	--	x / 14	x / 1	--	--	x / 23
AMPHIBIA									
Salientia gen. et. sp. indet.	--	--	--	--	1 / 1	--	--	--	x / 1
(Indeterminate Frog or To)									
TOTAL	--	--	--	--	x / 1	--	--	--	x / 1

Table 3. Fish Remains from Akumbu by Unit and Phase
(MNI/NISP)

TAXA	AK1			AK3			AK4		TOTAL
	MIA / Early	MIA / Middle	MIA / Late	EIA	MIA / Early	MIA / Mid-Late	MIA / Early	MIA / Middle	
Date (AD)	600-1000	1000-1200	1200-1400	400-600	ca. 600-1000	ca. 1000-1400	ca. 600-1000	1000-1200	
lvs.	39-67	18-38	1-17	29-38	8-28	1-7	11+	1-10	
Heterotis niloticus	--	--	--	--	3 / 4	1 / 1	--	--	3 / 5
Gymnarchus niloticus	--	1 / 1	--	--	1 / 1	1 / 1	--	--	3 / 3
Alestes / Brycinus sp.	--	--	--	--	1 / 1	--	--	--	1 / 1
Hydrocynus sp.	--	--	--	--	1 / 1	--	--	--	1 / 1
Distichodus sp.	--	--	--	--	1 / 2	--	--	--	1 / 2
Citharinus sp.	--	--	--	--	1 / 1	--	--	--	1 / 1
Cyprinidae	--	--	--	--	1 / 1	1 / 1	--	--	2 / 2
Bagrus sp.	--	--	--	--	--	--	1 / 1	--	1 / 1
Auchenoglanis sp.	1 / 1	--	--	--	1 / 2	--	--	--	2 / 3
Clariidae	3 / 7	2 / 5	3 / 6	1 / 1	14 / 214	1 / 2	3 / 5	--	27 / 240
Synodontis sp.	4 / 11	--	1 / 1	--	16 / 66	1 / 1	--	--	22 / 79
Lates niloticus	6 / 19	5 / 7	3 / 9	--	6 / 35	1 / 1	4 / 20	--	25 / 91
Tilapiini	1 / 6	1 / 3	3 / 7	1 / 2	3 / 79	1 / 1	1 / 3	--	11 / 101
Tetraodon lineatus	--	--	--	--	2 / 3	--	--	--	2 / 3
TOTAL IDENTIFIED [NISP]	44	16	23	3	410	8	29	0	533
TOTAL INDETERMINATE	30	2	18	2	158	0	25	0	235
# OF TAXA PRESENT	5	4	4	2	13	7	4	0	14
TOTAL FISH: {#TAXA} #FRAGS	{5} 74	{4} 18	{4} 51	{2} 5	{13} 568	{7} 8	{4} 54	0	{14} 768

APPENDIX 2

ADDITIONAL HUMAN REMAINS FROM AKUMBU (MALI)

Rachel Hutton MacDonald and Kevin C. MacDonald
Department of Archaeology
Cambridge University

During the analysis of the faunal remains from Akumbu, two more human burials were identified (in addition to that of AK3 levels 20 and 21, analysed *in situ* by K.C. MacDonald.

The first of these is only attested to by a single fragmentary adult left second metatarsal from AK3 level 14. It is conceivable that this could have derived from a burial only partially within the confines of the unit. The breakage is recent – the result of a blow from a digging tool.

The second burial, from AK3 level 28, is more substantial. It is represented by the following elements:

- 3 fragments of the Occipital (unfused)
- 5 fragments of the Parietal and/or Frontal
- 1 fragment of the mandible – inferior-anterior portion with diagrastic fossae
- 22 teeth (deciduous and unerupted permanent, mandibular and maxillary), see chart below which illustrates presence/absence of teeth in dental charts for the deciduous dentition and then permanent dentition.
- 1 fragment of the Axis Vertebra (unfused)
- 2 Cervical Vertebrae (fused)
- 1 fragment of the proximal epiphysis of the tibia (unfused)

Deciduous Dentition Present (nomenclature after Gladfelter 1975)

A B X X E | X X H X X
T X R X X | O X M L K

Permanent Dentition Present (nomenclature after Gladfelter 1975)

X X 3 X X X X 8 | 9 X 11 X X X X X
X X 30 X X X 26 25 | 24 X 22 21 X 19 X X

All permanent dentition was unerupted and in various stages of apical formation. All teeth were from a single individual, aged about 4 years (± 6 months), after Ubelaker & Grant (1989). This age assignment is in agreement with the fusion states of the other bones present (Krogman & Iscan 1986). Sex is only determinable osteologically with great difficulty for individuals of this age and the elements present are not sufficient for this to be attempted. Thus it may only be stated that the human remains from AK3 level 28 were from a single individual of indeterminate sex aged 4 years ± 6 months.

Bibliography

Gladfelter, I.A. 1975. Dental Evidence. Springfield, IL: Thomas.
Krogman, W.M. & Iscan, M.Y. 1986. The Human Skeleton in Forensic Medicine 2nd edition. Springfield, IL, Thomas.
Ubelaker, D.H. & Grant, L.G. 1989. Human Skeletal Remains: Excavation, Analysis, Interpretation. 2nd edition. Washington, D.C. Taraxacum.

APPENDIX 3: SURVEY DATA

Cer.= Ceramics
GS = Groundstone

Code	Site name	Chronol.	Size	Landform	Features	Surf. Art.	Funct.
1043-1	Goudourou A	Early	3 ha	Bras de Namp.	Burnt clay str. 1 looters' hole w/ human bones	Ceramic GS, slag	
1043-2	Goudourou B	Middle	14 ha	Bras de Namp.	Burnt clay str. slag	Cer., GS	
1043-3	Goudourou C	Middle	0.3 ha	Bras de Namp.		Cer. GS. Slag	
1043-4	Goudourou D	Middle	5 ha	Bras de Namp.	Burnt clay str.	Cer. GS Slag	
1043-5	Goudourou Furnaces	Uncert.	0.1 ha	Bras de Namp.	Furnace remains associated w/ slag heaps	Cer., Slag Broken	Iron smelting
1117-1		Uncert.	Scatter	Longitudinal dunes		Cer. GS.	
1117-2		Uncert.	Scatter	Longitudinal dunes		Cer. GS	
1117-3		Uncert.	Scatter	Longitudinal dunes		Cer. GS	
1117-4		Uncert.	scatter	Longitudinal dunes		Cer. GS	
1043-6	Barkerou A	LSA	0.1 ha	Degr. dunes/ Bras de Namp.		Cer. GS Stone rings	
1043-7	Barkerou A	LSA	0.1 ha	Degr. dunes/ Bras de Namp.		Cer. GS stone rings	
1043-8	T. Famé A	Late	3 ha	Longit. dunes Modern well	Modern hut GS. Frag.	Cer. Slag. of tobacco pipes	
1043-9	T. Famé B	Late		Longit. dunes.	GS. Frag.	Cer. Slag. of tobacco pipes	
1117-5	Hiré Wid.	Late	0.1 ha	Longit. dunes	Remains of rectang. mud structures.	Cer. Slag GS. Frag. of tobacco pipes	
921-1	Toulé South	LSA?		Degraded dunes	Recent sand deposits	Cer. GS	
921-2	Toulé A	Middle	5 ha	Degraded dunes		Cer. GS Slag	
921-3	Toulé B	Middle	6 ha	Degraded dunes	1 urn eroding from ravine	Cer. GS Slag	
921-4	Toulé C	Early		degraded dunes	Burnt clay str. Probable architectural remains. Numerous pot hunting holes	Cer. GS Slag Fired bricks	
921-5	Toulé D	Middle	4 ha	Degraded dunes		Cer. GS. Slag	
921-6	Toulé E	Middle	12 ha	Dgraded dunes		Cer. GS Slag	
872-1		Uncert.	Scatter	Degraded dunes		Cer. GS Slag.	
872-2	Akumbu A	Middle	21 ha	Degraded dunes/ Niakéné Maoudo	Burnt clay str.	Cer. GS Sandstones slabs Fired bricks Slag. Copper	

Appendix III: Survey Data

872-3	Akumbu B	Middle	7 ha	Degraded dune/ Niakéné Maoudo	1 pot hunting hole w/ apparent child burial	Cer. GS Slag	
872-4	Akumbu C	Middle	3 ha	Degraded dunes/ Niakéné Maoudo	Few urns eroding from pot hunting holes and ravine. Sandstone and laterite slabs	Cer. GS Slag	
872-5	Akum. LSA-1	LSA	0.1 ha	Degraded dunes/ Niakéné Maoudo		Cer. GS	
872-5	Akum. LSA-2	LSA	0.4 ha	Degraded dunes/ Niakéné Maoudo		Cer. GS	
872-7	Akumbu D	Middle	0.2 ha	Degraded dunes/ Niakéné Maoudo		Cer. GS Slag	
872-8	Akumbu Furnace #1	Uncert.		Degraded dunes/ Niakéné Maoudo	Furnace remains	Slag Broken tuyeres.	Iron Smelting
872-9	Akumbu jarfield #1	Middle		Degraded dunes/ Niakéné Maoudo eroding from	Numerous urn remains pot hunting holes	Cer. Slag	Probable cemetery
872-12	Akumbu jarfield #2	Middle		Degraded dunes/ Niakéné Maoudo	Numerous urn remains. Site used as cattle kraal. Very damaged	Cer. Slag	Probable cemetery
872-10	Akumbu Furnace # 2	Uncert.		Degraded dunes/ Niakénee Maoudo	Furnace remains	Slag Broken tuyeres.	Iron smelting
872-11		Early	3 ha	Niakéné Maoudo		Cer. GS Sag	
1041-1	Ndondi T.	LSA		Bras de Nampala		GS. Lithic Cer.	
1119-1	Ndondi T. A	LSA	0.4	Bras de Nampala		Cer. Lithic GS.	
1119-2	Ndondi T. B	LSA		Bras de Nampala		Cer. Lithic GS.	
1119-3	Ndondi T. C	LSA	1 ha	Bras de Nampala	Numerous small mounded areas consisting of bone concentrations	Cer. Lithic GS	
1119-4	Ndondi T. D	LSA	1 ha	Bras de Nampala	Mini midden mounds similar to the ones in Ndondi T. C	Cer. Lithic GS	
1119-5	Ndondi T. E	LSA		Bras de Nampala		Cer. Lithic GS	
1119-6	Ndondi T. F	LSA	1 ha	Bras de Nampala		Cer. Lithic GS	
1041-2	Ndondi T. G	LSA		Bras de Nampala		Cer. Lithic GS	
1119-7	Amakobé	Late	0.4 ha	Bras de Nampala		Cer. GS Slag. Fragmt of tobacco pipes	
1041-3	Niak. Nd. A	Late	1.5 ha	Bras de Nampala		Cer. GS Slag. Fragmt of tobacco pipes	
1041-4	Niak. Nd. B	Early	1 ha	Bras de Nampala		Cer. GS Slag	
1041-5	Niak. Nd. C	Early	1 ha	Bras de Nampala		Cer. GS Slag	
1041-6	Niak. Nd. D	Early	0.2 ha	Bras de Nampala		Cer. GS Slag	
1041-7	Niak. Nd.E	Early	0.1 ha	Bras de Nampala	Burnt clay structures	Cer. GS Slag	

ID	Site	Period	Size	Location	Features	Finds	Notes
1041-8 Furnace	Niak. Nd.	Uncert.		Bras de Nampala	Furnace remains Tuyeres Slag conc.	Slag.	Iron smelting
1041-9	Ndoupa	Middle	14 ha	Degraded dunes/ Bras de Nampala	Burnt clay structures 1 modern	Cer. GS Slag. Some iron objects. flint	
1041-10	Ndoupa Furnace	Uncert.		Degraded dunes/ Bras de Nampala	Furnace remains Slag conc.	Slag. Cer.	
1919-1	Boundou Sekou	Middle	17 ha	Degraded dunes	Burnt clay structures	Cer. GS. Slag. Some 1 iron ring	
874-1		Early	3 ha	Iron pan peneplain	Leterite pebbles	Cer. GS Slag. Sandstone and laterite slabs.	
874-2		Early	1 ha	Iron pan peneplain	laterite pebbles	Cer. GS Slag. Sandstone and laterite slabs.	
1119-8	Kobadi	LSA	2 ha	Bras de Nampala	Bone Concentrations Several burials	Cer. GS Lithic	
1119-9	Bourgou Silatigui A	Middle	15 ha	Bras de Nampala	Burnt clay structures	Cer. GS Slag.	
1119-10	Bourgou Silatigui B	Early	0.2 ha	Bras de Nampala		Cer. GS Slag.	
1119-11	Bourgou Silatigui C	Early	0.4 ha	Bras de Nampala		Cer. GS Slag.	
1119-12	Bourgou Silatigui D	Early	0.2 ha	Bras de Nampala		Cer. GS Slag.	
1119-13	Bourgou Silatigui E	Early	0.4 ha	Bras de Nampala		Cer. GS Slag.	
1119-14		Early		Bras de Nampala	Furnace remains slag conc.	Cer. Slag.	Iron smelting
1119-15		LSA		Bras de Nampala		Cer. GS Lithic	
1119-16		Late	0.2 ha	Bras de Nampala		Cer. GS Slag.	
1119-17	Bourgou Silatigui F	Early	3 ha	Bras de Nampala		Cer. GS Slag.	
1253-1		Late		Longitudinal dunes		Cer. Gs Slag	
874-3		Uncert.		Iron pan peneplain/ Niakéné Maoudo		Grindstones	
874-4	Boundou Boubou south A	Early	2 ha	Iron pan peneplain/ Niakéné Maoudo	Burnt clay Structures Slag. Laterite pebbles	Cer. GS Sandstone and laterite slabs	
874-5	Boundou Boubou south B	Middle	5 ha	Iron pan peneplain/ Niakéné Maoudo	Burnt clay Structures Slag. Laterite pebbles	Cer. GS Sandstone and laterite slabs	
874-6	Boundou Boubou south C	Early	0.1 ha	Iron pan peneplain/ Niakéné Maoudo	Slag.	Cer. GS	
874-7	Boundou Boubou south D	Early	1 ha	Iron pan peneplain/ concentrations Niakéné Maoudo	Laterite pebble Slag.	Cer. GS Sandstone	
874-8	Boundou Boubou south E	Early	0.1 ha	Iron pan peneplain/ Niakéné Maoudo	Laterite pebble concentrations Slag.	Cer. GS	

Appendix III: Survey Data

874- 9 Boubou	Boundou south F	Early	0.2 ha peneplain/	Iron pan concentrations Niakéné Maoudo	Laterite pebble Slag.	Cer. GS Sandstone slabs
874- 10 Boubou	Boundou south G	Early	1 ha peneplain/	Iron pan Niakéné Maoudo	Laterite pebbles Slag.	Cer. GS Sandstone slabs
874- 11 Boubou	Boundou south H	Early	1 ha peneplain/	Iron pan Niakéné Maoudo	Laterite pebbles Slag.	Cer. GS
874- 12 Boubou	Boundou south I	Early	0.3 ha peneplain/	Iron pan Niakéné Maoudo	Laterite pebbles Slag.	Cer. GS
874- 13 Boubou	Boundou south J	Early	0.1 ha peneplain/	Iron pan Possible Niakéné Maoudo	Laterite pebbles Slag. architecture	Cer. GS
874- 14 Boubou	Boundou north A	Middle	12 ha peneplain/	Iron pan Burnt clay Niakéné Maoudo	Laterite pebbles Slag. structures	Cer. GS Sandstone slabs
874-15 Boubou	Boundou north B	Early	0.1 ha peneplain/	Iron pan Niakéné Maoudo	Laterite pebbles Slag.	Cer. GS
874- 16 Boubou	Boundou north C	Early	1 ha peneplain/	Iron pan Niakéné Maoudo	Laterite pebbles Slag.	Cer. GS Sandstone slabs
874-17 Boubou	Boundou north D	Early	1 ha peneplain/	Iron pan Burnt clay Niakéné Maoudo	Laterite pebbles Slag. structures	Cer. GS Sandstone slabs
874-18 Boubou	Boundou north E	Early	0.2 ha peneplain/	Iron pan Niakéné Maoudo	Slag.	Cer. GS
874-19 Boubou	Boundou north F	Early	0.1 ha peneplain/	Iron pan Niakéné Maoudo	Slag.	Cer. GS
874-20 Boubou	Boundou north G	Early	2 ha peneplain/	Iron pan Niakéné Maoudo	Laterite pebbles Slag.	Cer. GS
874- 21 Boubou	Boundou north H	Early	1 ha peneplain/	Iron pan Niakéné Maoudo	Laterite pebbles Slag.	Cer. GS Sandstone slabs
874- 22 Boubou	Boundou north I	Early	0.3 ha peneplain/	Iron pan Niakéné Maoudo	Laterite pebbles Slag.	Cer. GS Sandstone slabs
874-23 Boubou	Boundou north J	Early	0.3 ha peneplain/	Iron pan Niakéné Maoudo	Laterite pebbles Slag.	Cer. GS Sandstone slabs
874-24 Boubou	Boundou north K	Early	2 ha peneplain/	Iron pan Urns eroding Niakéné Maoudo	Laterite pebbles Slag. from ravines	Cer. GS Sandstone slabs
874-25 Boubou	Boundou north L	Early	1 ha peneplain/	Iron pan Niakéné Maoudo	Laterite pebbles Slag.	Cer. GS Sandstone slabs
874- 26 Boubou	Boundou north M	Early	1 ha peneplain/	Iron pan Burnt clay Niakéné Maoudo	Laterite pebbles Slag. structures	Cer. GS Sandstone slabs
874-27 Boubou	Boundou north N	Early	0.2 ha peneplain/	Iron pan Niakéné Maoudo	Laterite pebbles Slag.	Cer. GS Sandstone slabs
874-28 Boubou	Boundou north O	Early	1 ha peneplain/	Iron pan Niakéné Maoudo	Laterite pebbles Slag.	Cer. GS

ID	Site	Period	Size	Location	Features	Finds	Notes
874-32	Boundou north P	Early	0.1 ha	Iron pan peneplain/ Niakéné Maoudo	Laterite pebbles Slag.	Cer. GS	
874-29		Uncert.	0.1 ha	Iron pan remains peneplain/ Niakéné Maoudo	Furnace Slag. Slag concentrations	Cer.	Iron smelting
874-30		Uncert.	0.1 ha	Iron pan remaims peneplain/ Niakéné Maoudo	Furnace Slag concentrations	Cer.	Iron smelting site
874-31		Uncert.	1 ha	Iron pan remains peneplain/ Niakéné Maoudo	Furnace Slag concentrations of slag occurring in boulders	Cer.	Iron smelting site
874-33	Boundou north Q	Early	0.1 ha	Iron pan peneplain/ Niakéné Maoudo	Laterite pebbles Slag.	Cer. GS	
1167-1	Sabéré Faita	LSA	6 ha	Laterite butte/ North channel		Cer. Lithic GS	
1167-2				North channel Slag conc.	Furnace remains	Slag. Tuyeres	
1167-3	Faita West	LSA	0.5 ha	North channel		Cer. Lithic GS	
1167-4		Late		North channel/ Degraded dunes		Cer. Slag GS. Fragmt of tobacco pipes	
1121-1	Bérétouma A	Middle	13 ha	Bras de Nampala	Burnt clay structures 1 rounded house foundation	Cer. GS Slag. 1 copper ring Petrified wood	
1121-2	Bérétouma B	Middle	10 ha	Bras de Nampala	Burnt clay structures. Crude mud brick walls	Cer. GS 1 fgmt of terra cota figurine 1 Iron object	
1121-3	Bérétouma LSA # 1	LSA	2 ha	Bras de Nampala	Numeroous burials	Cer. Lithic GS	
1121-4	Bérétouma LSA # 2	LSA	0.2 ha	Bras de Nampala		Cer. Lithic GS	
1121-5	Bérétouma LSA # 3	LSA	4 ha	Bras de Nmapala		Cer. Lithic GS	
1121-6	Bérétouma C	Middle	0.2	Bas de Nampala		Cer. Slag GS.	
917-1		Early	1 ha	Niakéné Maoudo/ iron pan peneplain	Laterite pebbles	Cer. GS Slag	
917-2	Niessouma A	Early	3 ha	Niakéné Maoudo	Laterite pebbles Rounded house foundations	Cer. Slag GS.	
917-3	Niéssouma B	Eraly	1 ha	Niakéné Maoudo	Laterite pebbles rounded house foundations	Cer. Slag GS	
917-4	Niessouma C	Early	0.5 ha	Niakéné Maoudo	Laterite pebbles	Cer. Slag GS	
917-5	Niessouma d	Early	1 ha	Niakéné Maoudo	Laterite pebbles	Cer. Slag GS. Fired bricks	
917-6	Niessouma E	Early	2 ha	Niakéné Maoudo	Laterite pebbles Rounded house foundations	Cer, Slag GS Sandstone and laterite slabs	
917-7	Niessouma F	Early	0.5 ha	Niakéné Maoudo	Laterite pebbles	Cer, Slag GS	

Appendix III: Survey Data

ID	Name	Period	Size	Location	Features	Finds	Notes
917-8	Niessouma G	Early	1 ha	Niakéné Maoudo	Laterite pebbles Burnt clay structrures	Cer. Slag GS	
917-9	Niessouma A	Early	0.1 ha	Niakéné Maoudo	Laterite pebbles	Cer. Slag GS	
1167-5		Uncert.		North channel	Furnace Slag concentrations	Slag Cer.	Iron smelting
1167-6	Tissilit	Middle	2 ha	North channel	Burnt clay structures	Cer. GS Slag 1 iron objects	
1251-1		LSA	8 ha	Bras de Namap. Backswamp	Bone Numerous burials concentrations	Lithic. GS	
1251-2		LSA	0.4 ha	Bras de Namap. Backswamp	Numerous burials Bone concentrations	Lithic. Cer. Lithic GS	
1121-7	Kolima A	Middle	11 ha	Bras de Namapa	Burnt clay Structures	Cer. GS Slag 1 spindle whorl	
1121-8	Kolima B	Middle	6 ha	Bras de Namapa	Burnt clay Structures	Cer. GS Slag	
1121-9	Kolima C	Early	0.6 ha	Bras de Namapa		Cer. GS Slag	
1121-10	Kolima sud	LSA	14 ha	Bras de Namapa	Bone concentrations Numerous burials	Cer. GS	
1121-11		Uncert.	0.3 ha	Bras de Namapa	Furnace remains Slag concentrations	Cer. Slag Broken tuyeres	Iron smelting
1121-11		Uncert.	0.2 ha	Bras de Namapa	Furnace remains Slag concentrations	Cer. Slag Broken tuyeres	Iron smelting
998-1	Toladié A	Miiddle	76 ha	Bras de Nampala/ degaded dunes	Burnt clay structures	Cer. GS Some iron objects Slag.	
998-2	Toladié B	Middle	8 ha	Bras de Nampala/ degaded dunes	Burnt clay structures	Cer. GS Slag	
998-3	Toladié C	Miiddle	17 ha	Bras de Nampala/ degaded dunes		Cer. GS Slag	
998-4	Toladié D	Middle	14 ha	Bras de Nampala/ Degraded dunes		Cer. GS Slag	
998-5	Toladié E	Middle	6 ha	Bras de Nampala/ Degraded dunes		Cer. GS Slag	
915-1		LSA	Scatter	Iron pan peneplain	Cer. GS	Lihic	
1037-1	Dianguina	LSA	0.1 ha	Degraded dunes/ backswamp	1 burial	GS. Cer. Lithic	
878-1	Péhé	Middle	30 ha	Fala de Molodo	Urns Burnt clay Structures Rounded house foundations	Cer. GS Slag	
878-2		Middle	6 ha	Fala de Molodo	Burnt clay Structures	Cer. GS Slag	
978-3		uncert.		Fala de Molodo	Furnace remains Slag heaps	Cer. Slag	Iron smelting
913-1	Boulel Funace #1	Uncert.	7 ha	Iron pan peneplain/ Fala de molodo	Numerous Furnaces. Slag heaps	Cer. Slag	Iron smelting

913-2	Boulel Furnce #2	Uncert.	0.5	Iron pan peneplain/ Fala de Molodo	Furncaes slag concentrations	Cer. slag	Iron smelting
880-1	Tiabel Goudiodié	LSA	5 ha	Fala de Molodo	Bone/shell concentrations	Cer. GS Lithic	
1043-10	Nampala	LSA	0.1 ha	Bras de Nampala		GS. Cer lithic.	

CAMBRIDGE MONOGRAPHS IN AFRICAN ARCHAEOLOGY

No 1   BAR S75, 1980   **The Niger Delta** *Aspects of its Prehistoric Economy and Culture* by Nwanna Nzewunwa. ISBN 0 86054 083 9

No 2   BAR S89, 1980   **Prehistoric Investigations in the Region of Jenne, Mali** *A Study in the Development of Urbanism in the Sahel* by Susan Keech McIntosh and Roderick J. McIntosh ISBN 0 86054 103 7

No 3   BAR S97, 1981   **Off-Site Archaeology and Human Adaptation in Eastern Africa** *An Analysis of Regional Artefact Density in the Amboseli, Southern Kenya* by Robert Foley.   ISBN 0 86054 114 2

No 4   BAR S114, 1981   **Later Pleistocene Cultural Adaptations in Sudanese Nubia** by Yousif Mukhtar el Amin. ISBN 0 86054 134 7

No 5   BAR S119, 1981   **Settlement Patterns in the Iron Age of Zululand** *An Ecological Interpretation* by Martin Hall. ISBN 0 86054 143 6

No 6   BAR S139, 1982   **The Neolithic Period in the Sudan, c. 6000-2500 B.C**. by Abbas S. Mohammed-Ali. ISBN 0 86054 170 3

No 7   BAR S195, 1984   **History and Ethnoarchaeology in Eastern Nigeria** *A Study of Igbo-Igala relations with special reference to the Anambra Valley* by Philip Adigwe Oguagha and Alex Ikechukwu Okpoko. ISBN 0 86054 249 1

No 8   BAR S197, 1984   **Meroitic Settlement in the Central Sudan** *An Analysis of Sites in the Nile Valley and the Western Butana* by Khidir Abdelkarim Ahmed. ISBN 0 86054 252 1

No 9   BAR S201, 1984   **Economy and Technology in the Late Stone Age of Southern Natal** by Charles Cable. ISBN 0 86054 258 0

No 10   BAR S207, 1984   **Frontiers** *Southern African Archaeology Today* edited by M. Hall, G. Avery, D.M. Avery, M.L. Wilson and A.J.B. Humphreys. ISBN 0 86054 268 8. £23.00.

No 11   BAR S215, 1984   **Archaeology and History in Southern Nigeria** *The ancient linear earthworks of Benin and Ishan* by P.J. Darling. ISBN 0 86054 275 0

No 12   BAR S213, 1984   **The Later Stone Age of Southernmost Africa** by Janette Deacon. ISBN 0 86054 276 9

No 13   BAR S254, 1985   **Fisher-Hunters and Neolithic Pastoralists in East Turkana, Kenya** by John Webster Barthelme. ISBN 0 86054 325 0

No 14   BAR S285, 1986   **The Archaeology of Central Darfur (Sudan) in the 1st Millennium A.D.** by Ibrahim Musa Mohammed. ISBN 0 86054 367 6.

No 15   BAR S293, 1986   **Stable Carbon Isotopes and Prehistoric Diets in the South-Western Cape Province, South Africa** by Judith Sealy. ISBN 0 86054 376 5.

No 16   BAR S318, 1986 **L'art rupestre préhistorique des massifs centraux sahariens** by Alfred Muzzolini.. ISBN 0 86054 406 0

No 17   BAR S321, 1987   **Spheriods and Battered Stones in the African Early and Middle Stone Age** by Pamela R. Willoughby. ISBN 0 86054 410 9

No 18   BAR S338, 1987 **The Royal Crowns of Kush** *A study in Middle Nile Valley regalia and iconography in the 1st millennia B.C. and A.D.* by Lázló Török.. ISBN 0 86054 432 X

No 19   BAR S339, 1987   **The Later Stone Age of the Drakensberg Range and its Foothills** by H. Opperman. ISBN 0 86054 437 0

No 20   BAR S350, 1987 **Socio-Economic Differentiation in the Neolithic Sudan** by Randi Haaland. ISBN 0 86054 453 2

No 21   BAR S351, 1987   **Later Stone Age Settlement Patterns in the Sandveld of the South-Western Cape Province, South Africa** by Anthony Manhire. ISBN 0 86054 454 0

No 22   BAR S365, 1987 **L'art rupestre du Fezzan septentrional (Libye) Widyan Zreda et Tarut (Wadi esh-Shati)** by Jean-Loïc Le Quellec. ISBN 0 86054 473 7

No 23   BAR S368, 1987 **Archaeology and Environment in the Libyan Sahara** *The excavations in the Tadrart Acacus*, 1978-1983 edited by Barbara E. Barich. ISBN 0 86054 474 5

No 24   BAR S378, 1987   **The Early Farmers of Transkei, Southern Africa Before A.D. 1870** by J.M. Feely. ISBN 0 86054 486 9

No 25   BAR S380, 1987   **Later Stone Age Hunters and Gatherers of the Southern Transvaal** *Social and ecological interpretation* by Lyn Wadley. ISBN 0 86054 492 3

No 26   BAR S405, 1988 **Prehistoric Cultures and Environments in the Late Quaternary of Africa** edited by John Bower and David Lubell. ISBN 0 86054 520 2

No 27   BAR S418, 1988 **Zooarchaeology in the Middle Nile Valley** *A Study of four Neolithic Sites near Khartoum* by Ali Tigani El Mahi. ISBN 0 86054 539 3

No 28   BAR S422, 1988   **L'Ancienne Métallurgie du Fer à Madagascar** by Chantal Radimilahy. ISBN 0 86054 544 X

No 29   BAR S424, 1988 **El Geili The History of a Middle Nile Environment, 7000 B.C.-A.D. 1500** edited by I. Caneva. ISBN 0 86054 548 2

No 30   BAR S445, 1988   **The Ethnoarchaeology of the Zaghawa of Darfur (Sudan) Settlement and Transcience** by Natalie Tobert. ISBN 0 86054 574 1

No 31   BAR S455, 1988   **Shellfish in Prehistoric Diet Elands Bay, S.W. Cape Coast, South Africa** by W.F. Buchanan. ISBN 0 86054 584 9

No 32   BAR S456, 1988   **Houlouf I** *Archéologie des sociétés protohistoriques du Nord-Cameroun* by Augustin Holl. ISBN 0 86054 586 5

No 33   BAR S469, 1989 **The Predynastic Lithic Industries of Upper Egypt** by Liane L. Holmes. ISBN   0 86054 601 2 (two volumes)

No 34   BAR S521, 1989   **Fishing Sites of North and East Africa in the Late Pleistocene and Holocene** *Environmental Change and Human Adaptation* by Kathlyn Moore Stewart. ISBN 0 86054 662 4

No 35   BAR S523, 1989   **Plant Domestication in the Middle Nile Basin** *An Archaeoethnobotanical Case Study* by Anwar Abdel-Magid. ISBN 0 86054 664 0

No 36   BAR S537, 1989 **Archaeology and Settlement in Upper Nubia in the 1st Millennium A.D.** by David N. Edwards. ISBN 0 86054 682 9

No 37	BAR S541, 1989	**Prehistoric Settlement and Subsistence in the Kaduna Valley, Nigeria** by Kolawole David Aiyedun and Thurstan Shaw. ISBN 0 86054 684 5
No 38	BAR S640, 1996	**The Archaeology of the Meroitic State** *New perspectives on its social and political organisation* by David N. Edwards. ISBN 0 86054 825 2
No 39	BAR S647, 1996	**Islam, Archaeology and History** *Gao Region (Mali) ca. AD 900 - 1250* by Timothy Insoll. ISBN 0 86054 832 5
No 40	BAR S651, 1996	**State Formation in Egypt**: *Chronology and society* by Toby A.H. Wilkinson. ISBN 0 86054 838 4
No 41	BAR S680, 1997	**Recherches archéologiques sur la capitale de l'empire de Ghana** *Etude d'un secteur d'habitat à Koumbi Saleh, Mauritanie. Campagnes II-III-IV-V (1975-1976)-(1980-1981)* by S. Berthier. ISBN 0 86054 868 6
No 42	BAR S689, 1998	**The Lower Palaeolithic of the Maghreb** *Excavations and analyses at Ain Hanech, Algeria* by Mohamed Sahnouni. ISBN0 86954 875 9
No 43	BAR S715, 1998	**The Waterberg Plateau in the Northern Province, Republic of South Africa, in the Later Stone Age** by Maria M. Van der Ryst. ISBN 0 86054 893 7
No 44	BAR S734, 1998	**Cultural Succession and Continuity in S.E. Nigeria** *Excavations in Afikpo* by V. Emenike Chikwendu. ISBN 0 86054 921 6
No 45	BAR S763, 1999	**The Emergence of Food Production in Ethiopia** by Tertia Barnett. ISBN 0 86054 971 2
No 46	BAR S768, 1999	**Sociétés préhistoriques et Mégalithes dans le Nord-Ouest de la République Centrafricaine** by Étienne Zangato. ISBN 0 86054 980 1
No 47	BAR S775, 1999	**Ethnohistoric Archaeology of the Mukogodo in North-Central Kenya** *Hunter-gatherer subsistence and the transition to pastoralism in secondary settings* by Kennedy K. Mutundu. ISBN 0 86054 990 9
No 48	BAR S782, 1999	**Échanges et contacts le long du Nil et de la Mer Rouge dans l'époque protohistorique (IIIe et IIe millénaires avant J.-C.)** *Une synthèse préliminaire* by Andrea Manzo. ISBN 1 84171 002 4
No 49	BAR S838, 2000	**Ethno-Archaeology in Jenné, Mali** *Craft and status among smiths, potters and masons* by Adria LaViolette. ISBN 1 84171 043 1
No 50	BAR S860, 2000	**Hunter-Gatherers and Farmers** *An enduring Frontier in the Caledon Valley, South Africa* by Carolyn R. Thorp. ISBN 1 84171 061 X
No 51	BAR S906, 2000	**The Kintampo Complex** *The Late Holocene on the Gambaga Escarpment, Northern Ghana* by Joanna Casey. ISBN 1 84171 202 7
No 52	BAR S964, 2000	**The Middle and Later Stone Ages in the Mukogodo Hills of Central Kenya** *A Comparative Analysis of Lithic Artefacts from Shurmai (GnJm1) and Kakwa Lelash (GnJm2) Rockshelters* by G-Young Gang. ISBN 1 84171 251 5
No 53	BAR S1006, 2001	**Darfur (Sudan) In the Age of Stone Architecture c. 1000 - 1750 AD** *Problems in historical reconstruction* by Andrew James McGregor. ISBN 1 84171 285 X
No 54	BAR S1037, 2002	**Holocene Foragers, Fishers and Herders of Western Kenya** by Karega-Mūnene. ISBN 1 84171 1037
No 55	BAR S1090, 2002	**Archaeology and History in Ìlàrè District (Central Yorubaland, Nigeria) 1200-1900 A.D.** by Akinwumi O. Ogundiran. ISBN 1 84171 468 2
No 56	BAR S1133, 2003	**Ethnoarchaeology in the Zinder Region, Republic of Niger: the site of Kufan Kanawa** by Anne Haour. ISBN 1 84171 506 9
No 57	BAR S1187, 2003	**Le Capsien typique et le Capsien supérieur** *Évolution ou contemporanéité. Les données technologiques* by Noura Rahmani. ISBN 1 84171 553 0
No 58	BAR S1216, 2004	**Fortifications et urbanisation en Afrique orientale** by Stéphane Pradines. ISBN 1 84171 576 X
No 59	BAR S1247, 2004	**Archaeology and Geoarchaeology of the Mukogodo Hills and Ewaso Ng'iro Plains, Central Kenya** by Frederic Pearl. ISBN 1 84171 607 3
No 60	BAR S1289, 2004	**Islamic Archaeology in the Sudan** by Intisar Soghayroun Elzein. ISBN 1 84171 639 1.
No 61	BAR S1308, 2004	**An Ethnoarchaeological Study of Iron-Smelting Practices among the Pangwa and Fipa in Tanzania** by Randi Barndon. ISBN 1 84171 657 X.
No 62	BAR S1398, 2005	**Archaeology and History in North-Western Benin** by Lucas Pieter Petit. ISBN 1 84171 837 8.
No 63	BAR S1407, 2005	**Traditions céramiques, Identités et Peuplement en Sénégambie** *Ethnographie comparée et essai de reconstitution historique* by Moustapha Sall. ISBN 1 84171 850 5
No 64	BAR S1446, 2005	**Changing Settlement Patterns in the Aksum-Yeha Region of Ethiopia: 700 BC – AD 850** by Joseph W. Michels. ISBN 1 84171 882 3.
No 65	BAR S1454, 2006	**Safeguarding Africa's Archaeological Past** *Selected papers from a workshop held at the School of Oriental and African Studies, University of London, 2001* edited by Niall Finneran. ISBN 1841718920
No 66	BAR -S1537, 2006	**Excavations at Kasteelberg, and the Origins of the Khoekhoen in the Western Cape, South Africa** by Andrew B. Smith. ISBN 1 84171 969 2.
No 67	BAR –S1549, 2006	**Archéologie du Diamaré au Cameroun Septentrional** *Milieux et peuplements entre Mandara, Logone, Bénoué et Tchad pendant les deux derniers millénaires* by Alain Marliac ISBN 1 84171 978 1.
No 68	BAR –S1602, 2007	**Chasse et élevage dans la Corne de l'Afrique entre le Néolithique et les temps historiques** by Joséphine Lesur. ISBN 978 1 4073 0019 1.
No 69	BAR –S1617, 2007	**The Emergence of Social and Political Complexity in the Shashi-Limpopo Valley of Southern Africa, AD 900 to 1300** *Ethnicity, class, and polity* by John Anthony Calabrese ISBN 978 1 4073 0029 0.
No 70	BAR –S1658, 2007	**Archaeofaunal remains from the past 4000 years in Sahelian West Africa** *Domestic livestock, subsistence strategies and environmental changes* by Veerle Linseele ISBN 978 1 4073 0094 8.
No 71	BAR –S1667, 2007	**Il Sahara centro-orientale Dalla Preistoria ai tempi dei nomadi Tubu / The Central-Oriental Sahara. From Prehistory to the times of the nomadic Tubus** by Vanni Beltrami con le fotografie e i riassunti in inglese di Harry Proto / with English summaries and photographs by Harry Proto. ISBN 978 1 4073 0102 0.
No 72	BAR –S1679, 2007	**Memory and the Mountain: Environmental Relations of the Wachagga of Kilimanjaro and Implications for Landscape Archaeology** by Timothy A. R. Clack. ISBN 978 1 4073 0117 4.

www.ingramcontent.com/pod-product-compliance
Lightning Source LLC
Chambersburg PA
CBHW041705290426
44108CB00027B/2859